THE
GIRL
BEFORE
ME

BOOKS BY LAURA WOLFE

Two Widows

She Lies Alone

Her Best Friend's Lie

We Live Next Door

THE
GIRL
BEFORE
ME

Laura Wolfe

bookouture

Published by Bookouture in 2022

An imprint of Storyfire Ltd.
Carmelite House
50 Victoria Embankment
London EC4Y 0DZ

www.bookouture.com

Paperback ISBN: 978-1-80314-271-5
eBook ISBN: 978-1-80314-270-8

For Mom and Dad.

PROLOGUE

Annie shouldn't have gone back for another look. Her search had been reckless in the first place, but it had been impossible to ignore the ugly thing she'd glimpsed. She thought she'd been careful—stealthy even—when she'd slipped out into the hallway in the dead of night to confirm her suspicions. What she'd found on her return trip was more chilling than she'd imagined. Now back inside her fourth-floor apartment, she'd barely had time to catch her breath when a knock sounded at her door. Terror surged through her as she pressed her eye to the peephole, her arm pinning the stolen box to her side. A familiar face stared from the hallway, distorted and angry. She'd been found out. A key clicked into the door, rotating the deadbolt.

Frantic, she grabbed a steak knife from the kitchen and fled to the bathroom, securing the flimsy button lock inside and shoving the box into the cabinet. The tiles were cold against her legs as she crouched on the floor. She hid beside the toilet and gripped the makeshift weapon in her hand. Footsteps crept closer through the living room. She eyed the tiny lock on the knob, thankful for at least a temporary layer of protection. In hindsight, she should have raced for the phone instead of the knife. But the sight of the face in the hallway had unhinged her. There hadn't been time to think. Her only means of calling for help sat out of reach, charging on the bedroom nightstand.

Annie pressed her back against the wall and squeezed the base of the knife, her heartbeat thrumming in her ears as shards of memories pierced her thoughts. She'd been so happy when she arrived in Chicago and moved into this apartment. But she'd made bad decisions. Now, her recklessness had caught up with her, and her American dream felt more like a nightmare. She should have stuck to her original plan and fled to the airport, unseen. Two large suitcases waited on the other side of the door, packed and ready to go. She imagined the Uber driver she'd summoned idling in his car outside of the building, debating whether to linger for a couple of more minutes. But there'd been that one thing she couldn't forget.

"Help!" She angled her face toward the ceiling. "Someone, please help me!" Her sleeping neighbors didn't stir. The knob rattled. The person on the other side of the door stepped back, responding.

"Annie, there's no reason to be scared. Open the door. Let's talk."

The voice sounded hollow, insincere. Still, it occurred to Annie that maybe she *could* explain her way out of the situation. Back in Australia, people had always praised her for her magnetic personality, her power of persuasion. Spinning an innocent tale about what she'd been doing was her best chance to escape to the airport and catch a flight. She could alert the authorities later. She forced herself up from the floor, lowering the knife and inhaling a breath of courage as she unlocked the bathroom door.

ONE

Three weeks later

Lily's hand was hot in mine as the Lyft driver pulled to the curb. "This is it." The man threw on the flashers. "420 Roslyn Place." The city paraded around us, a proud show of rumbling motors, colorful storefronts, and eager people striding toward their destinations.

"Thank you." I turned toward my daughter. "Can you believe we're moving to the big city, Lily?" She stared back at me, her six-year-old eyes shining with a mixture of fear and excitement. We'd arrived at our new apartment building, a ten-story brick mid-rise in Chicago's upscale Lincoln Park neighborhood. Traffic zoomed past us along the narrow residential street, with cars parked bumper to bumper along either side. We'd beaten the moving truck here.

Lily clutched her blanket, her forearm strangling her favorite stuffed animal, a blue elephant with tattered, floppy ears named Daisy. Competing threads of excitement and doubt pulled through me, and I hoped I wasn't making a mistake, taking too big of a risk by abandoning our dead-end life in the suburbs for the glamour and opportunities of the city. My mom had tried to convince me to stay in Addison "for Lily's sake." And, of course, my ex-husband, Keith, was furious about the move—more proof that I was an idiot.

"C'mon. We'll get out on the sidewalk side. Then we'll take a look at our new apartment."

"Where's the zoo?" Lily followed me out of the car and craned her neck toward the lake.

"It's just a few blocks away. We can walk over there tomorrow. Okay?"

My daughter nodded again. She'd been sullen about moving from the suburbs and the only house she'd ever known, a two-bedroom starter home I'd purchased with Keith when she was a baby. But I'd gotten Lily excited about our new life in the city with promises of her fancy school, regular trips to the free Lincoln Park Zoo, and the beach, all of which sat just a few city blocks from our apartment. A breeze whipped past my cheeks as I exited the car and crossed the sidewalk. It was unseasonably warm for a Saturday in mid-April, and people were outside, enjoying the weather.

A truck honked. Someone yelled at a passing driver as he sped down our one-way street. Two women who looked like fashion models brushed past me, speaking in a language I didn't recognize, maybe Italian. Their perfume swirled with the scents emanating from the café around the corner—chocolate and espresso beans. Across the street, a man stared, his eyes looking me up and down as a grin pulled at his lips. It took a second to realize he was checking me out, and something stirred inside me. I glanced away and he moved on. It had been so long since I'd thought of myself as a single woman; even longer since I'd felt attractive. Though sometimes friends used to tell me how they were jealous of my high cheekbones, shiny hair, or slender build, Keith had always made me feel ugly.

I turned back to Lily and a sudden shot of adrenaline pumped through me as if the city itself was plugged into my core, supplying my power. I stood on my tiptoes and tried to glimpse a slice of Lake Michigan's waters churning beyond the traffic on Lake Shore Drive.

I wasn't up high enough to see the lake, so I turned back to 420 Roslyn Place. Our new building cast a long shadow over me in the morning sun, and I looked up, scanning the facade of the 1920s building. It brimmed with character and charm. Intricate details of inlaid brick demarcated each floor, and carved limestone framed the windows and roofline. It was architecture so different from our generic, 1980s vinyl-sided ranch house in Addison, which was virtually identical to every other place on the street.

I snapped back to Lily and led her safely toward the entryway. "This is our building. Isn't it cool?"

Her brown eyes lit with wonder. "Wow."

"It's pretty tall, isn't it?" I said, taking in all ten stories.

"Yeah. But not as tall as that one." Lily pointed to a glassy high-rise across the street.

"That's right. But ours is just the perfect height. Shall we go inside?"

"Yeah." Lily hopped up and down, still clutching her blanket and elephant. I gripped her clammy hand and led her through the heavy glass doors at the front entrance. Beyond a sitting area featuring sleek leather chairs and oversized potted plants, a doorman with thick glasses waited behind a counter, smiling as we approached. He was dapper in his crisp, blue button-down shirt; his thinning gray hair combed into neat lines. He looked to be about the same age as Mom—early sixties —but with a more cheerful demeanor.

"Good morning, ladies. How can I help you?"

"Hi. I'm Rachel Gleason." I patted Lily's head. "And this is Lily. We're moving into 4B."

"Ah, yes. Welcome to the building." He tapped a notepad in front of him. "I'm Henry, one of the doormen. There's another guy named Robbie who works some nights and weekends, but he's not as handsome as me."

Lily and I giggled. The man had a warm way about him, which was just what I needed to put Lily at ease.

"I've got your keys right here. Mr. Daniels dropped them off yesterday." Oliver Daniels was the owner of the condo, the one who my realtor, Penelope, had emailed before we toured the apartment and signed the lease. Penelope had explained that most of the people living in the building owned their condos. But Oliver and a handful of other owners had gotten permission from the board to rent their units. Henry extended a keyring toward me, dropping the bundle of keys in my hand. "There's the front door key, the laundry room key, one for your storage locker in the basement, a mailbox key, and two copies of your apartment key." He eyed Lily through his lenses, a sparkle in his watery blue eyes. "We don't get many kids living here. You're going to be a celebrity, young lady." He winked.

A wide, gap-toothed smile spread across Lily's face.

I gave Lily a nudge. "We're excited to move in."

"It's a nice unit. You face the front, toward Roslyn, so you'll get lots of light just like I do here."

Morning light poured into the lobby through the front windows, and I could see he was right. "That's great."

"The freight elevator is reserved for you until noon. It's just beyond the regular elevator and across from the mailroom." He thumbed toward a glass wall and door that sat behind the doorman's station, providing a barrier to entry to the elevator and mailroom. The extra security was one of the many things that had attracted me to the building. "I'll buzz you through this door whenever I see you, or you can always let yourself past the lobby by scanning your card on the sensor." He pointed to a white piece of plastic with a barcode that dangled from the keyring. "Your moving truck can park in the alley on the east side of the building."

"Thanks. We don't have too much." That was the truth. Apartment 4B had come partially furnished, which was a rare find and also a blessing. I'd surrendered most of the furniture in the divorce agreement. It had been eight months since we'd separated, but only six weeks since Keith and I finalized the sale of our house and split the meager proceeds. While I'd searched for affordable housing in the city, Mom had reluctantly allowed Lily and me to move into her basement back in Addison; our belongings pared down to about five pieces of furniture, twenty cardboard boxes, and a couple of suitcases. "We might go up and take a look while we're waiting for the movers to get here."

The doorman waved toward the elevators. "Go on through."

Lily smiled over her shoulder at Henry as we made our way toward the elevator. I let her push the call button. After a second, the doors groaned and lurched open. We stepped inside, finding the enclosed space well-worn and smelling faintly of perfume. I told Lily to press number four and watched as her pudgy finger hit the button. The doors heaved and moaned.

"Hold it, please," a voice yelled from a few feet away.

I held the doors as a ponytailed brunette woman wearing athletic leggings and a Nike T-shirt slipped inside and smiled, her breathing labored. Sweat slicked her forehead. "Thank you."

"It's a nice day for a run."

She nodded as Lily pressed the button for our floor again, and the other woman pressed the button for the fifth floor.

The woman removed an earbud. "Are you visiting?"

"No. We're moving into 4B today." I touched my chest. "I'm Rachel. This is Lily."

"Oh. Welcome to the building!" Her heart-shaped face brightened. "I'm Bridget. Where are you moving from?"

"The western suburbs. Addison."

Bridget nodded. "I've heard of it. I'm from Michigan originally, but I've lived here since I graduated from law school. I live in 5B, right above you."

"Oh, that's great. It's nice to meet you."

She looked from Lily to me. "Is it just the two of you?"

"Yes."

"Cool. I'm single too." She smiled. "No kids yet, though."

I nodded.

"Can't beat this location."

"No kidding."

Bridget and I looked to be about the same age, although she could have been a few years younger. I hoped I'd just met a new friend, despite the different paths we'd traveled to get here. From what she'd said, it seemed that Bridget was a single attorney following her dreams in the city, while I was a divorced, single mom barely making ends meet by working from home in a dead-end insurance job. Not quite as glamorous. Yet, somehow, we'd both landed in this building.

She leaned down. "And how old are you, Lily?"

"Six."

"Cool. I have a niece about your age. We always have a blast together whenever she visits."

The doors opened on the fourth floor with the same dramatic lurch as before. Bridget shoved her elbow against the open frame. "I should get your number before you go, Rachel. We can grab a coffee after you get settled, and then I can answer any questions about the area for you—the best pizza and where to get your hair cut—whatever you need."

"Sure. That's so nice." I dug into my purse for my phone.

"I don't mean to be too forward. It's just nice to come across someone..." she paused, biting her lip, "more like me."

I offered a reassuring nod, happy Bridget had lumped me into her category, whatever that was. "No need to apologize. I'm so excited you live right upstairs." I told her my name and number, and she texted me back immediately. *Bridget Morrison 5B.*

"Take care," she said as we stepped out of the elevator, doors closing behind us. Mom had always told me that people in the city were rude and abrasive, but she'd been wrong. Bridget had already been friendlier than half the women on my street in the suburbs.

Our hallway was long and narrow, lined with doors to six apartments and dim lights affixed to the wall every ten feet or so. Lily hopped along the diamond-patterned carpeting until we spotted 4B two doors down on the right.

"Here we go," I said to Lily as she tugged at the end of her braid. The key slipped easily into the lock, and I turned to open the door to our new home. My poor girl had been through so much in the last year. I hoped our moving day would be a fun and positive experience for her. She stepped through the threshold first, releasing a joyful squeal. I'd seen the apartment the week before with my realtor. Before we'd located 420 Roslyn, Penelope had searched for weeks as I took pass after pass on the two-bedroom options in the vicinity of Lily's new school. The staggering Lincoln Park rental rates had pushed our prospects further and further north and west, making the commute to Lily's school longer and longer.

Desperate for another way, I'd called the school and asked if they knew of any affordable housing options nearby. The woman on the other end said not really, but that one of her co-workers who lived a few blocks away had broken her lease. She gave me the address and suggested I call the building, that maybe the owner would give me a break just to get the space filled. I passed the address on to Penelope, who'd tracked down the condo's owner, Oliver Daniels, the same day. As it turned out, the previous tenant had left him in a lurch, having moved out suddenly with no notice. Oliver wanted to get someone responsible lined up as quickly as possible before he lost any additional months of rent. I signed a year lease for the partially furnished, two-bedroom apartment for the price of a one-bedroom, and it was just blocks from Lily's new school. It was a dream come true.

Lily hopped across the hardwood floors, head pivoting around the living room and open kitchen. "Wow. Cool!" She raced to the expansive window on the far wall of the living room, where we had a view of the bustling street. "We're high up!"

"Yeah. Look at that. Those cars look small from up here, don't they?"

Lily pressed her face against the glass. I tapped her shoulder and pointed toward a door. "Why don't you go look at your new bedroom?"

She ran across the living room and through the door. Both bedrooms were small, but I couldn't complain, considering the deal we'd gotten. I'd designated the room with the pale yellow walls for her, although it didn't have a window. Lily paced around the room, staring in wonder at the nooks and crannies, the white dresser, the closet, and the crown molding with its ornate detailing, snaking around the edge of the walls. The owner had removed the beds that had been there last week just as I'd requested. Our beds were on the truck, some of the few pieces of furniture I'd kept.

"Pretty nice, huh?"

"Yeah. I love it." By the force with which she wrapped her skinny arms around me and squeezed, I could tell she was just as relieved as me to get out of Mom's basement.

"And my bedroom is right next door, so you can simply knock on the wall if you need me."

Lily rapped her knuckles on the drywall, then ran into my room, her face dropping at the sight of the plain walls.

"We have one bathroom to share." I waved Lily ahead of me

into the compact bathroom, featuring a tiled floor, a vanity with a single sink, a newer-looking toilet, and a tub with a shower-head above it.

Lily wrinkled her nose. "What's that smell?" The chemical smell of bleach lingered throughout the apartment, but it was more potent in the bathroom, stinging my nostrils as we stepped toward the sink. The odor had been just as powerful when I'd toured the apartment last week. I was happy, at least, that the owner had hired someone to do a thorough job cleaning between tenants.

"Someone did a deep clean. No germs left for us, so that's a good thing."

Lily ran back into the living room, and I followed.

"What do you say we go back down to the lobby and see if our movers are here yet?"

"Okay."

We filed into the hallway, and I secured the lock. A door cracked open further down the corridor, releasing the sound of thumping bass that reverberated through my chest. A young man who appeared barely older than a teenager popped his head out. A mop of black hair hung around his pale, gaunt face. He wore a black trench coat, despite the sunny weather. The inky, black legs of a spider tattoo stretched across his right cheek, and silver rings pierced through his eyebrows and nostril. His lifeless stare sent a cold wind blowing through me.

"Hi." I smiled, even though he gave me the creeps. I taught Lily not to judge people based on their appearances, so I tried to lead by example.

The man didn't respond, didn't offer so much as a blink. The dazed expression never left his face as he retreated into the blaring music and closed the door.

"Is that our neighbor?" Lily asked.

"Looks like it. I guess we spooked him." I squeezed her shoulder, happy we didn't share a wall with him.

"Yeah." She giggled, and we continued toward the elevator.

Once back in the lobby, a text from the moving company appeared on my phone: *Our ETA is in ten minutes.*

Another text buzzed through from Penelope: *Did you get into the apartment okay?*

I wrote back: *Yes, thank you :)*

Tension built in my shoulders. I rolled them back and wandered toward the wall of tiny metal mailboxes, finding the one labeled 4B. I'd submitted the new address to the post office several days earlier and wondered if they'd forwarded any mail yet. The smallest key slipped into the lock, opening the compartment. A few flyers from local restaurants filled the tiny space, but one light pink envelope was wedged into the side. I retrieved it, holding it close to my face, noticing the excessive postage and the neat writing.

The sender was a Julia Turner, and she had addressed the envelope to Annie Turner in Unit 4B. Annie must have been the tenant before me, the young woman who'd left without notice. The letter had originated in Australia. I remembered how Oliver had complained about not knowing how to contact the previous tenant after she'd broken the lease, about how she was from Australia, and how challenging it would be to collect his money from an ocean away. It seemed the sender and Annie were possibly related as they shared a last name, and I wondered if something inside this envelope might offer a clue to Annie's whereabouts.

I tossed the flyers into the garbage, but pinched the envelope between my fingers. Lily followed me out through the glass doors, across the lobby, and over to the sitting area. Behind us, Henry bantered with residents and guests as they entered and left the building. I sat on one of the chairs as Lily watched people pass outside. The edge of the envelope poked my skin. It was illegal to open someone else's mail; a federal crime, actually. But something about the card in my hand felt important. I supposed taking it to the post office was the responsible thing to do, but the chances of the envelope making its way back to Australia seemed slim. Annie hadn't left a forwarding address when she'd disappeared. The alternative was throwing away the letter with the carefully printed address, which felt wrong. My eyes followed the curve of the lettering. A tiny tear along the seam taunted me, my curiosity boiling over. I glanced over my shoulder to make sure no one was paying attention to me. Then I slid my finger into a gap in the seal and ripped it open, finding a piece of cardstock with a handwritten note inside:

Annie,

I'm so worried. Why aren't you responding to my texts and emails? You aren't safe in that apartment! Please get out and contact me as soon as you can.

Jules xx

My eyes traveled over the words again, registering the ominous message. A coldness trickled through me as I stuffed the note back into the envelope and shoved the whole thing in my purse. My gaze flickered toward Lily, who hopped between the potted plants. *You aren't safe in that apartment!* The previous tenant had left suddenly, disappearing without a trace. Why hadn't Annie been safe in my apartment? Just as I asked myself the question, the moving truck pulled up outside.

TWO

The taller of the two movers unloaded the last box onto the kitchen floor. "That's it." He wiped his brow and stood near the door, clearly waiting for payment.

I wandered in a circle, still flustered by the message in the mailbox and the whirlwind of movers and boxes surrounding me since the discovery. "Thank you." I located my purse in the corner of the kitchen and removed the wad of cash, feeling slightly nauseous at the thought of parting with five-hundred dollars right off the bat. Hiring movers had been an extravagance, but it was a one-time expense, and the beds and boxes would have been way too heavy for me to transport by myself. I'd make up the money some other way, by buying second-hand clothes or eating ramen two nights a week. The cost of living in the city would be more expensive than in the suburbs, but with my paycheck plus the underwhelming child support Keith paid me every month, I'd make it work. Plus, I'd made some extra money from selling my car, which I no longer needed. No one changed the course of their life for free.

The man thanked me for the tip I'd added. Then he left, leaving Lily and me alone in our new home. I gazed around at the apartment, noticing a few imperfections I hadn't seen before —the worn wooden floors, a broken seal on the window, a slightly off-kilter blade on the ceiling fan, and a few smudges on the walls. I stepped toward the crown molding, noticing a wire camouflaged with the same white paint running along the bottom edge toward the front door. I followed the thin line, finding where it abruptly came to an end above the door. Someone had cut the cord, painted over it. It didn't seem the right place to run a wire for a landline phone or cable television, both of which had fixtures in the wall on the far side of the living room.

The 1920s building had a long history. I embraced the flaws. They embodied the character that my sterile, suburban house had sorely lacked. I wondered how many others had moved into this space—excited and hopeful—just like me. What dreams were they chasing? Why hadn't they stayed? The message in the envelope circled through my mind again, marring the perfect day I'd imagined. *You're not safe in that apartment!* Why hadn't Annie been safe here? Whatever had made her feel that way was most likely the reason she'd broken her lease and vanished. I looked at the wire again, unable to form an explanation. I wished the walls could tell me the true story.

"Mommy, where are my clothes?" Lily's voice snapped me from my troubling thoughts.

"Over here." I waved Lily toward her bedroom, opening a few of the boxes so that she could see her things. I pointed to a box filled with toys and another one with books, and I encouraged her to arrange them how she liked on the bookshelf in her bedroom. Lily knelt next to the box and got to work. I'd make up her bed as soon as I located the sheets, but first, I was anxious to inspect the card from the mailbox again.

I returned to the kitchen and pulled the envelope from my purse, removing the letter to ensure I hadn't misread it or missed anything. *I'm so worried... please get out.* The message was just as ominous as the first time I'd read it. My gaze moved from the writing, scanning across the apartment walls and searching for anything unsafe. The windows were locked. The electrical outlets appeared new enough. A green light glowed from a smoke detector clinging to the ceiling between the kitchen and living room. Nothing seemed worrisome or hazardous within the apartment itself, which was somewhat reassuring.

The woman who lived here before me was most likely having some sort of personal issue. I turned the envelope over in my hand and studied it again, finding the postmark was dated three weeks earlier. A lot could have happened in three weeks' time. Perhaps the previous tenant had merely lost her cell phone or forgotten to pay her phone bill, explaining why she hadn't been in touch with Julia, the sender of the letter. She would have eventually replaced it and reached out to Julia while the letter was in transit. I tucked the notecard back into the envelope and slipped it into an empty drawer in my desk. Whatever had happened between the owner of this condo and his delinquent renter wasn't my concern. I should have been thankful that Annie Turner broke her lease, leaving me with an affordable place to live in a prime location. Otherwise, I'd be moving into some dingy apartment fifteen or twenty blocks northwest of here, struggling to figure out how to transport Lily to and from her new school. A random letter addressed to someone else wouldn't tarnish my shiny fresh start. By now, Annie was probably back in Australia, sipping coffee at a café with Julia sitting across from her. The mysterious note had caused me to worry over absolutely nothing.

A few hours later, I clapped my hands together. "How about we order some pizza? We'll bring it back and have a little pizza party?"

"Yeah!" Lily nodded, running toward the door. We'd been unpacking and setting things up all afternoon, and only a couple of boxes remained full. A stack of flattened cardboard sat in a pile next to the wall. I'd have to ask Bridget or Henry where to put the recycling.

"Hold on. Let's call the order in first. Then we'll walk over and pick it up."

"Because we don't have our car?" Lily stared at me, but her fingers were busy picking at her cuticles.

"Right. And now we live in a place where we can walk to almost everything we need, or take a quick ride on the bus or train. Isn't that cool?"

"Yeah." Lily continued plucking at the skin around her thumb; it seemed she wasn't quite convinced by our lack of independent transportation.

I used my phone to locate a nearby restaurant specializing in stuffed pizza, and placed an order. It was just after 5 p.m. and still bright outside. Tomorrow, I'd buy some groceries and stock the fridge, but tonight would be for celebrating. I'd never wandered too far off the beaten path, and I was proud of myself for taking a risk at this stage of my life by committing to move to the city. The universe must have taken note, and was already offering some dividends, first with Lily's scholarship at Shorewood Academy and now with this apartment.

Mom had always encouraged me to take the path of least resistance, the safest route to nowhere. Since my dad left us over twenty-five years ago, she'd been leery of anyone with too many aspirations. She'd buried her dreams so deeply I doubt she even remembered what they'd been. *The higher they climb, the harder they fall.* She loved reciting that line, smirking and shaking her head at celebrities and politicians on TV after they'd been caught in high-profile scandals and lost all they'd earned. In her mind, it was safer to have never had anything at all.

I'd briefly escaped Mom's demoralizing way of thinking when I'd gone off to college. A career in the arts had called to me, although I hadn't been able to pinpoint what that was, precisely, maybe being a docent at an art museum, or an architect, or a graphic designer. My mind had been open to learning a little about each profession before committing to any single path. My high school counselor helped me apply to Northern Illinois University. NIU was a school she was confident would accept me, despite my lackluster ACT score. Even more appealing, the school sat an hour away from Addison, which meant I'd have to live on campus.

Mom didn't stop me from accepting NIU's offer of enrollment when it arrived via email a couple of months later, although she did not encourage me either. She took pleasure in mocking my wanderlust and my determination to improve my life, making sarcastic comments about my fancy college degree and the price tag attached to it. I didn't understand her behavior. A degree from NIU had never felt very fancy to me, and the student loan was my burden, not hers. But then my career plans came to a screeching halt when I met Keith the summer between my junior and senior years of college and moved back to Addison. I'd been married by the age of twenty-three and pregnant by twenty-five. I'd thrown myself into supporting Keith's landscaping business and raising our daughter. My own dreams had crumbled slowly, like loose bricks falling off the sides of a building before it collapsed.

"Should I wear a coat?" Lily asked, reminding me of our mission to pick up pizza.

"Zip on your hoodie. Then we can go." I followed Lily as she plucked her sweatshirt from a hook in our entryway and stepped into the hallway. The mess of keys on the keyring felt heavy and unfamiliar in my hand, but I located the key for 4B and turned the lock, jiggling the handle to make sure it was secure. As we moved to catch the elevator, the door to the apartment next to us opened. A man wearing dark jeans and a Cubs T-shirt emerged, carrying a bulky garbage bag tied at the top. He towered over me, his sandy brown hair cut close to his head. A surprised look stretched over his face when he noticed us standing outside his door, but he quickly masked his shock with a smile.

"Hi. You must be my new neighbors." His eyes were soothing and blue, and when they connected with mine, I felt a little stunned, like I'd fallen into a lake. He placed the trash bag against the wall behind him and extended his free hand. "I'm Alex. I live in 4A." His voice was deep. A five o'clock shadow accentuated his strong jawline. Unlike the beer gut that hung over Keith's belt, this man was trim and fit. I gripped his hand, unable to deny the electricity his touch sent through me. He motioned toward a shiny metal door about halfway down the hall. "I'm just making a run to the garbage chute."

I offered a demure smile and smoothed back my hair. I'd been breaking down boxes and rearranging furniture all day. I was sure I looked a mess. "Hi. I'm Rachel. Nice to meet you." I stretched my shoulders back, reminding myself we'd moved to the city for Lily's sake, not so I could flirt with attractive men. I'd promised myself no relationships for a year. I'd take some time for my personal growth. Besides, although this man's ring finger lacked a wedding band, that didn't mean he was single.

Alex rested a hand on his hip, looking at Lily. "And where will you be going to school?"

"Shorewood Academy."

He tilted his head. "No kidding. Well, you're not going to believe this, but I'm a teacher at Shorewood."

I couldn't help gasping at the coincidence. "Really?"

"Yeah." He flashed a questioning glance at Lily. "Wait. You're not in eighth grade, are you?"

Lily giggled as she hugged my leg. She seemed as entranced by our new neighbor as I was. "No. Kindergarten."

A smile tugged at Alex's lips. "Shoot. Then I won't be your teacher. But if I ever see you in the hallway, I'm definitely going to wave."

"Okay." Lily hopped up and down, and I could tell that she was pleased.

"That's great that you're a teacher there," I said. "Have you been at the school long?"

"Almost two years. I was at a different school for a few years before that. I teach seventh- and eighth-grade social studies." He shoved his hand in his pocket. "It's late in the year to be starting, but they'll show you the ropes."

"Lily got the Bright Paths scholarship." I bit my lip, immediately wishing I hadn't shared so much. I didn't want Alex to think we were destitute or had escaped from a family of serial killers. Our story wasn't quite that dramatic. I'd gone to Shorewood's website on a whim, based only on a handful of Facebook photos posted by Liz Meyer-Barnes, a woman from my high school class who I'd barely known. I remembered Liz as someone confident and put-together. She'd been popular, easily navigating a variety of social circles and fitting into the in-crowd, which included hanging out with people in older grades. She and Keith had even been an item for a few months during my junior year, although I'd run with a much less social crew back then, and my memory of the two of them together was vague. Keith had gone through at least seven or eight girlfriends during his high school heyday, so I'd never felt jealous of his brief teenage fling with Liz. Through Facebook, I'd watched Liz graduate from DePaul and marry a heart surgeon, moving downtown to a fancy Gold Coast high-rise. Her stepson, Davis, was several years older than Lily and attended Shorewood. I'd been enthralled by Liz's Facebook photos, as if I'd stolen a glimpse into some secret society—the manicured grounds, wrought-iron gates, and confident kids standing in neat rows, waiting for their God-given right to enter the sprawling limestone school.

I returned to the posts several times, especially during the separation. A mix of envy and anger had simmered beneath my skin because I yearned for the same opportunities for Lily. Somehow, Liz Meyer-Barnes had escaped Addison for a privileged life, while I had gotten stuck marrying her high school sweetheart, Keith. It wasn't fair that my poor decisions influenced my daughter's future. I'd scoured the Shorewood Academy website, finding no tuition listed as if to imply: *If you have to ask, you can't afford it.* Eventually, I located information on three different scholarships the school awarded every year. Lily qualified for the Bright Paths scholarship, created for kids who had suffered hardship in their personal lives and whose parents didn't have the means to pay tuition. I filled out an online application, explaining how I'd escaped an emotionally and physically abusive marriage, and had recently been through a nasty divorce, all of which had taken a toll on our daughter. I was a single mom making less than forty-thousand dollars a year in a job with no upward mobility. I wanted something better for Lily, who was only in kindergarten and had her whole future ahead of her. Moving to the city and receiving an education from Shorewood would give Lily opportunities I could only dream of and would surely change the course of her life.

The following week, an office assistant had contacted me to set up a fifteen-minute video call with the school's principal. I'd been nervous during the call, terrified, really. I tried to smile a lot while repeating the same information I'd written on the form. A month later, the school informed me that they'd awarded Lily the only Bright Paths scholarship available that year. As long as she continued meeting the school's behavioral and academic standards, she would receive free education through twelfth grade at one of the state's finest schools. I'd been so happy, I couldn't speak. Truth be told, I was a bit shocked at the news. I assumed there would have been more deserving candidates in the mix. My job with the insurance company wasn't the greatest, but it paid the bills most of the time. Then again, the application link had been difficult to locate, practically buried under the last tab of the website. Maybe not many people had applied because they didn't know about it. Either way, I wasn't about to argue with the school's decision as there was no way I could ever afford the yearly tuition, which—it turned out—cost more than I made in a year.

Alex slid the garbage bag further away, then turned toward us. "Well, Shorewood has a great reputation, especially when it comes time to apply for college. I hope Lily will be happy there."

"I'm sure she will be."

A door further down the hallway opened with a creak. The strange man I'd seen earlier stepped into the middle of the carpeting, his dark trench coat skimming the tops of his combat boots. He leered at me as he paced toward us with his thin lips pulled back into a snarl. His eyes were rimmed with black eyeliner, accentuating his face tattoo.

I sucked in a breath. "Hi." My voice squeaked like a mouse as he passed. Without responding, he turned short of the elevator and disappeared into the stairwell.

"Now you've met Drake." Alex had lowered his voice to a loud whisper. "He's an enigma. A wannabe rocker and trust-fund baby. Drake's dad was a drummer in some semi-famous rock band in the eighties. Avoid him wherever possible." Alex must have seen the fear flash across my face. He raised his chin. "The guy is harmless, though. All bark and no bite, as far as I can tell."

"He looked like a magician," Lily said.

I couldn't help chuckling at my daughter's observation.

Alex almost doubled over with laughter. "Maybe I'll suggest that he learn some card tricks and submerge himself in a tank of water if the morbid, heavy metal rocker thing doesn't work out." Alex peered at the stairwell into which Drake had vanished. He stepped toward his abandoned garbage bag. "I'll let you go, but I'm sure I'll see you around. Moving day is always exhausting."

I stepped to the side, blocking his path. "I actually just have one question, if you don't mind me asking?"

"Sure thing."

"Did you know the woman who lived here before us? Annie?"

A shadow passed across Alex's face, his lips pulling down. I couldn't tell whether he was angry or merely annoyed by the mention of her name.

"Yeah. I knew her, but not well." He placed a hand on his hip. "She was from Australia. Real outgoing. She wanted to experience life in America for a year, or something like that. I also helped her get an administrative position at Shorewood. The school only hired her because I put in a good word for her, but then she skipped town." He huffed and shook his head. "I mean, it was only two more months until the end of the school year."

"How did she afford to live here?"

Alex shrugged. "She seemed to have plenty of money. I think she only wanted the job because she was bored and wanted to meet people."

"Did you see her leave?"

"No. I barely ever saw her at all, unless I happened to run into her in the elevator or the school office." Alex rubbed his chin, studying me. "Why do you ask?"

"Oh. It's probably nothing. There was a note from one of her relatives in my mailbox." I bit my tongue, feeling a sharp twinge of conscience. I couldn't reveal that I'd broken federal law by opening the letter. "It was mailed several weeks ago. I'm sure everything's fine by now."

"I wouldn't worry about it. Annie seemed very capable."

"Can we go get the pizza?" Lily tugged at my sleeve.

I raised my hand in the air. "So nice to meet you, Alex. We'll let you throw away your garbage now."

"Enjoy your night."

Our first evening in the new apartment was fun. Lily and I huddled around our coffee table, sipping lemonade and twirling strings of cheese around our forks as we cut into our stuffed pizza. We played several of Lily's favorite games, including Sorry! and Uno. We talked about the new school, where she'd start on Monday. By 8:30 p.m., Lily's eyelids were sagging, and her hand couldn't stop the barrage of yawns that followed. I helped her change into her pajamas and walked her into the bathroom, where she wearily brushed her teeth. The bleach smell still hung in the air, giving the tiled room a clinical feel. I spritzed some air freshener toward the ceiling, hoping the odor would fade quickly.

Lily smiled and told me she loved me as I tucked her into bed with her ladybug nightlight casting tiny stars across the ceiling of her new bedroom. I dropped a kiss on her forehead and told her she was brave and that I loved her too. By the time I'd crossed the bedroom and closed the door, I got the feeling Lily was well on her way to being fast asleep.

Now I sat on the couch, browsing through a *City Guide* magazine I'd snagged from a table in the lobby's waiting area. As I scanned through the restaurant ads and upcoming festivals, footsteps stomped above my head. I closed the magazine, imagining Bridget pacing above me, cleaning her living room or getting ready for bed. She coughed twice, and it sounded as if she'd been standing next to me. I looked over my shoulder, confirming she wasn't there. A vent in the corner of the living room ceiling drew my eye toward it. Now a laundry detergent commercial with a well-known jingle played from upstairs, the noise traveling directly through the metal grate. My jaw tightened as I worried about setting up my home office in my living room. I listened to my neighbor's show for a minute until exhaustion got the better of me. Tomorrow, I'd climb up on a chair and close the slats.

I hoisted myself from the couch and moved into the bathroom and then my bedroom, getting ready for bed and turning off the lights. My legs slid under the covers, the fresh sheets tight around my ankles. I'd cracked my window open earlier. Now a cool breeze seeped through, along with more strange noises. A siren screamed from somewhere outside, growing louder before it faded. Men's voices bantered from the sidewalk, followed by booming laughter. A pipe hissed and creaked from somewhere in the apartment. I closed my eyes, annoyed. This was a piece of city living I hadn't prepared for. Then again, maybe it was reassuring to know I wasn't alone. I rolled onto my back but couldn't get comfortable.

Another sound kept my eyes from closing. It was Alex's voice coming from behind my bedroom wall, echoing through the vent directly above my head. He mumbled a sentence of two I couldn't decipher. "Stop!" he yelled. "Just stop it already!"

Bam! An object collided with the wall, causing me to sit up in bed. Memories of Keith's violence rushed through me, quickening my pulse. I forced myself to focus on my breathing, to ground myself in the present. I was here, safe in my new apartment, many miles away from Keith.

Had my neighbor thrown something against the wall? Or punched it? I hoped Lily had slept through the commotion. The action seemed out of character with the friendly, down-to-earth teacher I'd met in the hallway. I hoped Alex wasn't in trouble.

More than that, I worried I'd pegged him wrong. My instincts about men had been off in the past.

I waited for a minute, even considering going next door and checking to see what had transpired, if only to prove to myself that Alex wasn't anything like Keith. But I quickly decided against it. There were no further noises from the apartment next door other than the faint clang of a few pots and pans. I couldn't leave Lily alone, and people in the city minded their own business. I'd barely met Alex and I didn't want him to think I was nosy.

I stared up at the ceiling through the darkness, unable to stop the worries from swirling through my mind. I'd been determined to forget about that note in the mailbox, but the message stained my thoughts, refusing to disappear. *You're not safe in that apartment.* Now Mom's smug, gravelly voice echoed in my head, too: *Moving to the city is the biggest mistake you'll ever make, Rachel.*

I pulled my sheets up to my neck and squeezed my eyelids closed. Cars honked at each other outside.

What if Mom was right?

Doubts nagged at my dreams as I drifted in and out of sleep, strange noises whispering and creaking from behind the walls. At 3 a.m., I awoke with a start to the thump of a cupboard closing—or maybe a drawer? I raised my head from the pillow, staring into the darkness and listening. A floorboard creaked somewhere beyond my bedroom door, a light shifting beneath the crack. I told myself it was only a passing headlight, somehow reflected upward through my fourth-floor window, but my gut contracted, unconvinced. I tightened my fingers around the edge of my sheets, my breath suddenly ragged. Another creak. Another click. It sounded like someone was inside my apartment, creeping through the living room. I hoped it was only Lily who'd awakened to retrieve a glass of water. But Lily had never been light-footed. Her feet landed like bricks as she plodded along. These footsteps were quiet, almost imperceptible.

I held my breath, ears alert for a tapping along the floorboards. I wished I'd thrown the piece of mail away, unopened, because the suggestion that our apartment was somehow unsafe had burrowed into my conscience. Slowly, I lowered one leg to the floor, then the other, crouching low as I tiptoed toward my door, gripping the cold knob in my fingers and turning. I peered through the crack, met by a dim living room, an even darker kitchen beyond. I threw on the bedroom light, casting a glow across the apartment. No one was there.

The sight of the vacant rooms seemed to poke a hole in me, releasing all my air. I crept to Lily's room and peeked inside, finding her asleep, chest rising and falling. I closed the door and checked the bathroom. Also empty. I chuckled at my overactive imagination and headed back toward my bedroom. But the locks on my front door caught my eye. I thought I'd locked both top and bottom locks after putting Lily to bed, but only the bottom one sat horizontally now. Had I misremembered my movements? Maybe I'd only thought about locking both but had gotten distracted before securing the top lock. Now I wasn't sure.

I shifted my feet, head foggy with exhaustion. My fingers pinched the metal dial and turned it toward the frame until it clicked.

THREE

Sunday morning light filtered through the kitchen window. I sipped my coffee a little too fast, the hot liquid burning my throat. Lily and I had gone out to grab drinks and muffins from the café around the corner. It wasn't the caffeine that jolted me from my sleepy state but the sky-high price of a plain cup of coffee. I'd have to pick up some groceries later to minimize our expenses.

Before Lily had awoken this morning, I'd made a quick check of the apartment, remembering the noises I'd imagined from the night before. I couldn't find anything out of place, nothing missing. The quiet creaks and thumps must have been coming from another apartment, either upstairs or downstairs.

Lily sat at the kitchen table, picking apart her muffin and rubbing the sleep from her eyes. She'd dressed herself in pink leggings and a yellow shirt with a glittering rainbow heart.

"We'll go to the zoo at ten. Okay?"

Her head bobbed up and down. "Yeah!"

I'd promised her we'd walk through the Lincoln Park Zoo. I'd been there once when I was a girl with my third-grade class. The attraction had seemed like a dream to me then, with acres of meandering paths, grassy knolls, and leafy trees dropped into the middle of an urban setting. Exotic animals roamed their enclosures as Lake Michigan sparkled in the distance.

A noise drew Lily's gaze upward. Her widened eyes followed the sound of footsteps plodding across the floor upstairs. "Is that the lady from the elevator who lives above us?"

"Yes. That must be Bridget." I swirled my coffee as all the strange noises from the night before whispered in my ears. "We can hear our neighbors a lot more than in the suburbs, can't we?"

Lily nodded. She leaned closer to me, lowering her voice. "I heard Bridget crying last night. She kept me awake for a long time."

I removed the cardboard cup from my lips, too stunned to take another sip. "Really?" My eyes crept across the ceiling toward the open vent. In the hour or two after Lily had gone to bed, I'd been on the couch, flipping through the *City Guide*. I'd only heard the TV jingles and some coughing emanating from Bridget's apartment.

"Is she okay?" Lily cocked her head, lower lip protruding as if she might start crying herself.

"I'm sure she's fine, honey. People sometimes cry when they're sad." My upstairs neighbor had been brimming with positive energy when we'd met in the elevator. I wondered if Lily had gotten it wrong.

Lily lowered her chin, not speaking. She crumpled the muffin wrapper in her hand and carried it toward the garbage bin. There was probably another vent in Lily's bedroom. I'd locate it later and close the metal slats to mute the noise. I had a white noise machine packed away somewhere. I'd find it and set it on Lily's nightstand too.

"Hey," I said, eager to change the subject. "I'm going to take a box down to our storage locker in the basement. Want to help carry some things?"

My daughter's face brightened. "Yeah. I want to see the basement."

"Great. You can carry this." I located a light bag filled with my linen tablecloth and napkins and handed it to her. "And I'll carry this box." I hoisted a heavier box containing a Crockpot and a double boiler, both of which I seldom used and couldn't fit into the limited kitchen storage space.

I locked the door behind us as we heaved our belongings out into the hallway toward the elevator. After a minute, the metal doors opened with a groan. An older couple stood inside, stepping to the side to make room for us. They looked like two pieces of the same puzzle with blue sweaters and khaki pants stretched over their stout frames. The woman touched the bifocals hanging from a cord around her neck and smiled.

"Going down?"

"Yes." I flashed a polite smile and ushered Lily in front of me. "Lower level, please."

The man pushed the button for the level below the lobby, his watery eyes appraising us as the elevator lurched downward. "And how old are you, young lady?"

"Six." Lily clutched the bag in front of her and stared straight ahead.

The woman clasped her hands together. "Aren't you darling? What's your name?"

"Lily."

The woman studied the box in my arms. "You must be new to the building. I would have remembered you."

I nodded. "Yes. We moved in yesterday."

She fixed her eyes on Lily. "How wonderful to have a child in the building. I think you're the only one."

Maybe it was the enclosed space, but the way the couple stared—as if we were rare specimens examined under a microscope—made me uncomfortable. The woman had spoken warmly, but I felt a familiar pang of regret, like maybe I'd made a mistake by bringing my daughter here. Lily was the only child in the building. A few people had mentioned that now. It wasn't lost on me that I was doing things out of order, that most parents fled to the suburbs before their babies were out of diapers, drawn in by the easy parking and grassy yards. But my marriage hadn't gone the way I'd planned. Now I'd chosen a different path for myself and my child because we were chasing down the future we wanted. I'd convinced myself it was better to stand out from the crowd, that the biggest risks led to the most gratifying rewards.

"Which unit have you moved into?" the man asked as his wife continued to stare at Lily.

"We're in 4B."

The woman's smile faded as she swung her head toward her husband. "4B? Isn't that where Annie lives?"

He angled his bushy eyebrows together. "Who's Annie?"

"That nice girl from Australia. You remember. I watered her plants for her a couple of months ago when she went to New York City for a week."

"Oh. Yeah." The man's thick hands rubbed the stubble on his chin. "Well, she must have moved."

"But she was supposed to join my book club. Why didn't she say goodbye?"

I told the couple what I'd heard about Annie breaking her lease and leaving without notice. They stared at each other for a moment.

"That's odd."

The man shrugged. "Everyone's always in a hurry these days. People can't seem to stay in one place."

The elevator door opened into the lobby. The man held his arm against the door, preventing it from closing. "I'm Stan Levy," he said, sticking out his other hand, which I shook. "My wife, Judith, and I have lived in apartment 10A for fourteen years."

"It's really 10ABC," Judith said. "We bought three units and combined them by knocking out the walls."

"Wow." I could only imagine the spacious layout and spectacular views from their penthouse condo. I told them my name was Rachel and that it was nice to meet them.

Judith puffed out her chest. "We know everything about this building, so don't be shy if you have any questions or problems."

"That's nice of you. Thank you."

At last, the Levys waved goodbye and continued through the lobby toward the front door.

The doors closed, and the elevator plunged one floor lower. Lily tossed me a nervous glance as we came to an abrupt stop, the doors struggling to open. We stepped out into a dingy corridor, where sparse lighting fixtures adorned the ceiling. A few bulbs had either burned out or were flickering, giving the area a cavernous feel. We followed the hallway past a brightly lit laundry room lined with ten or twelve washers and dryers. A man transferred his clothes from a washer to a dryer, looking over his shoulder and giving us a nod as we passed. I waved and turned into the maze of storage lockers on the opposite side of the hall.

"Cool!" Lily looked around in wonderment as we entered the room. The air was cooler down here, damp against my skin. Metal cages stretched from floor to ceiling, each one numbered and locked. People had stuffed most of the storage areas with suitcases, cardboard boxes, holiday decorations, fake plants, and extra furniture. But a few barely held anything. We wandered through the aisles until we found the lockers belonging to residents of the fourth floor. A cage labeled "4B" sat empty.

"Here's ours!" Lily pulled at the lock, but it was secure. I took out the keyring and opened the door. As Lily wandered inside, I noticed the locker for unit 4A bordering mine. *Alex's locker*. He'd organized it neatly—just some luggage and a few boxes, all marked with labels like "Kitchen," "bedding," and "holiday stuff." He'd wedged a bike into a narrow space at the side. Across the way, another locker was overflowing with a drum set, guitars, a synthesizer, and other sound equipment. I presumed it belonged to Drake.

"Wow. We can put a lot of stuff down here." Lily set the bag in the corner of our empty locker.

I heaved the box onto the floor next to her. "That's for sure. Maybe I can get that little Christmas tree and the plastic jack-o'-lantern we left at Grandma's house. I didn't think we'd have room."

"Yeah. And my bike."

"Yep." I wiped my palms against my pants, wondering where it would be safe for Lily to ride her bike in the city. I locked the cage and turned back toward the elevator. But Lily giggled and ran in the opposite direction, disappearing behind the far row of lockers.

"Try to find me, Mommy!"

"Lily." I bit back my annoyance at her antics, reminding myself that I was currently the only playmate she had available. I inhaled a breath, playing along. "Okay. Ready or not, here I come!"

My daughter's giggles could have led me right to her, but I wanted to make it fun. I went the other way, moving further from her voice. "Hmm. I wonder where Lily went. I bet she's over here."

Her giggle echoed through the room again, reverberating off the metal cages.

I continued in the wrong direction down the narrow path, turning around the far aisle of lockers. This side of the room was even more poorly lit. I squinted through the shadows, spotting a row of doors on the far wall. I inched toward them, making out the writing on each entryway. One was marked UTILITIES – Do NOT ENTER! A pipe hissed and rattled from somewhere behind the door. A second door was propped open with a bucket, revealing mops, a vacuum cleaner, and cleaning supplies inside. It was a janitor's closet. A sign above the third door read STAFF ONLY. I wondered what staff the building kept, other than the doormen and a couple of janitors who I imagined cleaned the lobby and vacuumed the hallways. I supposed they needed somewhere to take a break, although I couldn't imagine choosing to relax in this gloomy setting instead of sitting outside, at least when the weather was nice.

"You'll never find me."

Lily's voice pulled my attention from the doors. I tiptoed down the narrow, dark corridor and spied around the corner, spotting her crouched against a storage locker. Leaping out, I threw up my hands. "Boo!"

Lily screamed.

"I got you!" I scooped her into my arms and kissed her head.

She poked a finger into my chest. "Now, you hide."

I glanced across the low ceiling, a sense of unease rising in me. The room was so dreary, possessing all the warmth of a 1960s psychiatric ward. Maybe it was the rows and rows of locked cages or that the lack of windows reminded me too much of living in Mom's basement. Or perhaps it was precisely that there were so many hiding spaces available among the shadowy, cramped corridors. Someone could be down here watching us, and we wouldn't even know it. A thickness in the air made me feel like we weren't the only ones here.

"Sorry, hon. I think we should go back upstairs now."

Lily dropped her head. "Okay."

We wandered between the cages until I found the hallway leading to the elevator. I pushed the button several times; two long minutes passed before the doors opened. It wasn't until we'd closed ourselves safely inside, wobbling and lurching back above street level, that I felt like I could breathe again.

FOUR

The buttery scent of popcorn wafted past my nose as I placed my hand on Lily's shoulder. It was a perfect day for the zoo—sixty degrees with the sun warming our cheeks. We'd secured a spot for ourselves in front of the birds of prey exhibit, watching a red-tailed hawk blink its eyes and a bald eagle stretch its enormous wings. A plaque explained how the zoo had rescued the birds in the enclosure after they'd been injured. We'd already watched the zebras grazing in their enclosure and smiled at the penguins, who had waddled in single-file lines before plopping into the water, torpedoing away. Then we'd toured the Bird House, where the air was hot and stuffy. Lily's eyes were wide as she took in the sights. I pointed south toward the downtown skyline, where the spires of skyscrapers pierced through hazy clouds.

"Look. We can see all the buildings downtown."

"Wow."

I leaned toward her ear. "Are you having fun?"

"Yes. I love it here."

Her words warmed my heart. I so wanted the city to be fun for her, a step up, not down, in her six-year-old mind. After my night of spotty sleep and the uneasy sensation that had crawled through me in the basement earlier, this fun morning outside with my daughter was the perfect remedy.

Lily shot me a pleading look. "Maybe Natalie can come here with me."

"Maybe." I nodded but knew it wasn't likely. Natalie was Lily's friend who lived down the street from our old house. They'd started kindergarten together. But Natalie's parents had sided with Keith during the divorce. Everything was complicated now. Lily needed to start her new school and make new friends.

I pointed down the pathway. "Let's go see the monkeys next. And maybe you can take a ride on the endangered species carousel."

"And then what?"

"I'm not sure. We don't have to see the whole zoo today. We can come back anytime."

"Because it's free?"

"Well, yes. That's part of it. But it's also so close to our new home."

My phone buzzed inside my pocket, and I pulled it out, my positivity deflating at the sight of the message: *I want to see my daughter.* It was from Keith, and I knew him well enough to know that he meant to intimidate me, to ruin our fresh start. Lily had been an afterthought to him for the last six years, a child who was there to entertain him when it was convenient—and it had rarely been convenient. Regardless, we had a court order that said he got to spend one weekend day a month with her. He'd lost his custody rights the moment he'd hit me, the moment he'd shoved Lily down the back steps, injuring her wrist. His timeline for monthly visits started once he completed a three-part domestic violence awareness and anger management class.

With tense fingers, I typed my reply: *Leave us alone. Your day with Lily is May 31st.*

I gripped the phone in my palm, feeling it buzz again but not wanting to give Keith the power to ruin my afternoon with Lily. We had six weeks to enjoy life without Keith.

"Who was that, Mommy?"

"No one. It's nothing." I reset my face, forcing a smile.

"Is it Daddy?" Lily asked, grabbing at my arm.

I pulled the phone out of reach, but found it impossible to lie to my little girl. "Yes."

"Can I see him?"

"He wants to see you. And the good news is that we already have a date set up for May 31st, so that's when you'll see him."

Lily kicked at a crack in the cement walkway. "But that's still a long time."

"Only a little over a month." I looked away, wondering if Lily had forgotten how Keith had ignored her cries for attention, had shoved her down the back steps. Lily clung to positive memories about her dad—a behavior I found heartbreaking. There was probably a healthier way for me to navigate this situation, but I didn't know what it was. I tucked the phone into my pocket. "How about we head over to the Primate House?"

A few minutes later, we peered through the glass, watching a group of monkeys crouching down and eating bananas and apples that a worker must have placed inside their habitat. Another monkey swung among the branches of a fake tree to the gasps and squeals of the human onlookers. But I didn't feel the same excitement because I couldn't stop looking at the monkey's human-like eyes. There was something glassy and deadened in them, as if the creature knew it was living in a cage, and that it would never get out. And even though I knew the zoo was doing important work for conservation and education, I felt sorry for the monkey. I also knew what it felt like to be trapped, to lose hope. That's how I'd felt with Keith.

Lily squeezed my hand. "Let's go to the carousel, Mommy."

Another hour passed before we trekked west on Fullerton Avenue pathway, watching the people picnicking and playing soccer in the parks and the cars lurching past as they made their way to Lake Shore Drive. I spotted our building as we approached from the Lakeview sidewalk. It was easy to identify as the second tallest one on our block of Roslyn Place. Lily dragged her feet. She wasn't used to this much walking, and neither was I. The soles of my feet ached.

I pulled open the building's heavy front door, and we entered the lobby, where it was cooler inside. Henry welcomed us back with his usual boisterous greeting. "There's our little lady. How's your big city adventure going?"

"Good. We went to the zoo." Lily walked over to his counter, and I followed.

"Ah. That's wonderful. My daughter used to love animals when she was your age." He stared out the window, a gleam of nostalgia in his eyes. "She still does, I guess. Now she's all grown up."

I grinned. "I didn't know you had a daughter, Henry."

"Let me see..." Henry smiled as he opened a drawer beneath the counter and rummaged around. "I have a favorite photo of her when she was younger. Here it is. That's my Lisa." He lifted a small, framed picture and turned it toward us. A freckle-faced girl of about ten years old smiled back at us. She leaned against a tree with her brown hair pulled back into a messy ponytail. Henry's gaze flickered between Lily and me. "The years go by fast. That's the truth. You have to enjoy every moment."

I pulled the photo closer, studying it. "Oh, she was a cutie. I bet your daughter is beautiful now."

"Yes. And she's smart too. She was always at the top of her

class." He shook his head. "She didn't get that drive from me, that's for sure."

I handed the frame back to him. "Do you get to see her much?"

"Not as often as I'd like. She lives out in California and likes to do her own thing, I guess." He glanced away, lips tightening. "I wasn't always there for her when she was growing up. It's my biggest regret."

There was a heaviness to his voice. I sensed the pain behind Henry's story, aware that I was picking around the edges of an open wound.

Henry straightened his shoulders. A switch seemed to flip as he focused on my daughter, his cheerful demeanor returning. "But having Lily here... She is going to really brighten my day. Other people in the building have noticed her too. A lot of us have kids that are all grown up now. Seeing this little girl skip through the lobby takes us back to happier times. Your daughter is like a breath of fresh air."

"I'm glad she's making you happy. We're both very thankful to live here." I patted Lily's head, and she looked up at me with rosy cheeks.

Henry tapped his fingers on the counter. "Well, it's been a pleasure talking with you, but I don't want to hold you up any longer. Enjoy the rest of your day. And if you need anything, you know where to find me." He winked.

Lily and I said goodbye. Henry buzzed us past the lobby, and we rode the elevator up to the fourth floor. A man and a woman who looked about my age walked a dog toward us from down the hallway, black with four white paws. "Doggie!" Lily inched toward it, the spring suddenly returning to her step.

I introduced myself and Lily as the new occupants of 4B. They were Marie and Sheldon Reed with their black lab mix, Bingo. They lived next door to us in 4C. They spoke with

British accents. I thought again how wonderful it was to have people from all over the world as our neighbors.

"You can pet him," Marie said.

Sheldon watched Lily pet the dog. "Dogs over fifty pounds aren't allowed in the building. Bingo weighs forty-nine, so we take him on lots of walks. Don't want Judith Levy to kick us out." He made a face, pausing for dramatic effect.

Marie sighed as if she'd heard the joke several times before. "Sheldon and I are website designers. We work from home most of the time unless we're traveling."

"Oh, that's good to know. I work from home too." I paused, adding vaguely, "Insurance." I hoped they wouldn't ask for further details about my job, but I didn't have to worry. The word "insurance" generally produced an automatic cooling effect, causing people to yawn and their eyes to glaze over. We chatted for a few more minutes before the couple and their dog continued on their way.

Lily and I entered our apartment, where I fixed us glasses of ice water as Lily plopped on the couch. I thought about the neighbors we'd just met and how nice they'd been. I wondered if they'd been friends with Annie or if they knew anything about why she'd left so suddenly, anything that could explain the unsettling note I'd discovered in my mailbox. I'd promised myself not to think about the previous tenant's mysterious departure anymore, but my curiosity tugged at me every time I glanced toward the desk drawer where I'd stashed the envelope.

A man coughed in the hallway outside, then cleared his throat. I stood from the couch and crept close to my door, peering through the peephole; I worried that I might find Drake's probing eyes staring right back at me. Instead, Alex drifted past with his hands raised over his head. He wore running shorts and a bright green-and-yellow athletic T-shirt with patches of sweat seeping through. The stubble on his skin had grown darker since yesterday. He strode past again, fingers laced in the air, muscles working under his skin. I couldn't deny the excitement that bristled through me at the sight of him. But I remembered the noises I'd heard coming from his apartment last night: the mumbling, the yelling that had kept me awake. He'd been upset enough that he'd thrown something at the wall or punched the drywall. I wasn't sure which.

I turned the knob and opened the door, stepping out into the hallway so that Alex nearly ran into me as he paced back in my direction.

"Hi. Sorry." I smiled and tried not to stare at the sweat glistening across his biceps.

"Hey, Rachel." Alex lowered his arms. "Are you and Lily settling in okay?"

"Yes. Thank you."

He glanced down at his clothes. "I just got back from a run. I'm training for the Chicago Marathon."

"Wow. That's impressive."

"My running group meets every Tuesday night and Sunday morning. This is where I cool down. I hope you don't mind." He continued pacing, so I walked next to him.

"Not at all."

He released another long breath. "Is everything okay with the apartment?"

"Yeah. Just a couple of boxes left to unpack. Nothing major." I swallowed, fiddling with my fingers.

"Do you need help moving furniture or anything?" he asked, probably sensing my hesitation.

"Oh, no. It's just that... well... to be honest, I didn't sleep that great last night. The walls are pretty thin."

Alex stopped walking and faced me. "Oh. I'm sorry."

"I heard a loud bang."

Alex dropped his gaze to the floor, fingers touching his forehead. "Ah, crap. I'm so sorry. I wasn't even thinking about the paper-thin walls. And on your first night too."

"No. It's fine." I paused, deciding to probe a little further. "You sounded pretty upset, and I just wanted to make sure everything was okay."

"Yes. I'm fine. That's nice of you to ask."

"Are you sure? I know it's none of my business, but it didn't sound like it."

He closed his eyes and opened them again, looking over his shoulder. An empty hallway stretched out on either side. "Okay, not really. The truth is that my ex-girlfriend called me last night."

"Your ex-girlfriend?"

"Yeah. Things ended badly between us. Our relationship has been over for weeks, but she won't let it go." He made a face and shook his head. "She's just so frustrating. I mean, she was the one who broke up with me."

A puff of hope expanded in my chest, but I exhaled it. Although Alex was attractive—and apparently single—I remembered the bang against the wall and reminded myself that I didn't know him at all.

Alex rested his hands on his hips. "I'm sorry. That's probably way more information than you wanted."

"No. It's fine."

He shook his head. "I feel terrible you had to hear that last night. Sarah brings out the worst in me. I got so frustrated after I hung up with her that I snapped and punched the wall. I can only imagine what you think. I'm not a violent person. Not even in the slightest."

I smoothed down my shirt. "Oh, it's okay. I'm sorry you're going through that. My ex-husband is a piece of work too." *And he is a violent person,* I thought to myself.

Alex gasped, glancing toward my door. "Lily didn't hear me, did she?"

"No. She was fast asleep."

"Oh, thank God." He rubbed the edge of his jaw and pivoted away from me.

"Well, I've got to get going. I still have to pick up groceries at Jewel and get Lily ready for her first day tomorrow."

"Why don't you text me when you're done shopping, and I'll help you carry your groceries home? It's the least I can do."

I waved him off. "I don't want you to go to that much trouble."

"It's no trouble."

I looked at my hands, unsure if he was just being polite. "I'm starting to realize my car came in handy for certain things."

"I don't have a car either. Haven't driven in years." He tilted his head. "You'll get used to walking and carrying lots of bags."

"Really, I don't want to mess up your afternoon."

A smile flickered at his lips. "I want to help. You can buy more groceries that way. I insist." He stepped so near to me that I could feel the heat radiating from his body. The overwhelming urge to touch him overtook me, but I stopped myself.

"Okay. Thank you." I pulled out my phone as Alex gave me his number. But as I entered the information, the text I'd ignored earlier caught my eye. Keith had replied to my message, the one suggesting he leave Lily and me alone and wait for his appointed date. My fingers tightened around the phone as I read the words: *No one can stop me from seeing my daughter.*

FIVE

"Smile for the camera!" I snapped Lily's photo in front of the engraved stone sign for Shorewood Academy, the school's limestone facade rising behind her. It was Lily's first day at her new school, and she looked adorable in her colorful outfit of a pink skirt, striped shirt, and sneakers I'd picked up from a children's resale shop. Through my virtual interviews, I'd learned this was the kind of private school that cringed at uniforms. Shorewood believed children expressed themselves through their choice of clothes, and the school refused to interfere with an individual's self-expression, except in the rare cases where it was vulgar or offensive to others.

I snapped two more photos to capture the moment as parents, nannies, and kids streamed past us, everyone waving to friends and seeming to know where they were going. Although the gated entrance was now open to the sidewalk, a stone wall kept the school separated from the city street. A few teachers, who were easily identifiable by their upright postures and perma-smiles, were posted around two entrances. I spied Alex by a far door, standing tall in his khaki pants and a blue button-down shirt. He greeted each student who passed him. He must have felt the weight of my stare because his eyes snapped toward me, a fresh smile forming on his lips as our eyes locked. I waved, no longer trying to fight the attraction that pulsed through me. He'd been so kind to help us with our groceries yesterday, arriving within five minutes of when I texted him, carrying four reusable grocery bags filled to the brim as if they'd weighed nothing at all. We'd chatted all the way home as he pointed out various stores and restaurants, offering tips about which ones to frequent or avoid. Surely, his helpfulness had been a sign that he might be attracted to me too. But I didn't want to seem overeager, didn't want to rush things. I'd made that mistake with Keith.

I pulled my eyes from him and refocused on the school, which covered nearly an entire city block. The manicured grounds were like something out of a movie—a grassy lawn spanning brick walkways and raised flower beds. A fountain shot up in the middle, two pathways arching around it and meeting up again before the front door. A well-groomed soccer field stretched across the far side of the school. We walked closer to one of the flower gardens, reading a sign marked BUTTERFLY GARDEN.

I nudged Lily, who was staring around in wonder. "This is a pretty nice place, isn't it?"

Her mouth opened as she nodded. "It doesn't look like my other school."

I bit back my smile as I watched her mind working, taking in the stately surroundings. "It's a lot fancier, isn't it? Let's go find your classroom. You don't want to be late on your first day."

I held her hand as we made our way up the brick pathway. Principal Brickman stepped through the front door. His features lifted beneath his salt-and-pepper hair as he strode toward us. "Welcome, Rachel and Lily. It's so nice to see you again." The principal had the presence of an aging football quarterback with the kind of booming voice and towering stature that could command a room. We'd never met in person before, but I was impressed he recognized us from the video call.

"Hello. Nice to see you." I reached out my hand to meet his.

He kept his hand on mine a moment longer than I expected, gently squeezing my fingers. "Ms. Lisle is anxious to meet you, Lily. I'll walk you to her classroom if you'd like."

"That's great. Thank you." We followed the principal into the school and down a wide hallway, where painted murals of city scenes adorned the walls. He explained how the eighth-grade students had painted the murals and how the older kids attended most of their classes in the south wing. We were in the north wing, set up for the elementary-age kids. The principal pointed out a few things as we walked—the location of the art room, a student lounge complete with a skylight, oversized bean bags, shelves of games, and a series of cubbies where students could stash their coats and lunches. It was all so different from Lily's previous school, which was so bare bones that it had reminded me vaguely of a prison. The biggest extravagance there had been a new climbing wall some parents had installed on the dusty playground. Shorewood would provide Lily with plenty of opportunities to grow and learn and meet all kinds of people. Moving to the city wasn't a mistake. Mom and Keith were wrong, too bitter about their own failures to wish success on others. Getting Lily into this school was proof I'd done the right thing for my daughter.

"Here we are," Principal Brickman boomed, drawing all eyes in the sun-drenched classroom toward us. A rainbow-colored banner hung across the far wall: WELCOME TO SHORE-WOOD, LILY! Each of Shorewood's eighteen kindergarten students had printed their name somewhere on the banner.

The principal cleared his throat. "Ms. Lisle, this is Lily Gleason and her mom, Rachel."

The middle-aged teacher clasped her hands together and

leaned down to meet Lily at eye level. She had pink lips and kind eyes, and she wore her wiry-blonde hair clipped back from her face. Strings of wooden beads clinked around her wrists. "We've been waiting for you to arrive. We're excited to get to know you. I bet you're feeling a little nervous, and that's okay."

Lily nodded, entranced by the woman who spoke to her as if she were an adult. Principal Brickman nodded and edged out of the room.

"We are all friends in this classroom, but I have an extra special buddy lined up for you." Ms. Lisle motioned toward a girl with shiny, black hair and a corduroy skirt. "Marnie, come here and say hi to Lily."

The other girl bounded over and waved. "Hi. I'm Marnie. Your seat is next to mine. I'll show you." The girl tapped Lily's arm and pointed to a table near the window. I watched as Lily followed after the other girl. Marnie whispered something in Lily's ear, and a smile played at my daughter's lips.

Ms. Lisle beamed at me. "Rachel, you're welcome to stay in the classroom as long as you'd like."

"Oh. Thank you. I think it's best if I leave. I have to get to work."

She nodded. "I understand."

I walked over to Lily and planted a kiss on her head. "Mommy's leaving now. Have a great day, and I'll be waiting outside for you at 4 o'clock."

Lily gazed at me, her eyes churning with worry. "Okay."

"It looks like you already have a new friend here." I leaned next to her ear and whispered, "I love you, brave girl."

"I love you too," she whispered back.

A wave of emotion rushed through me as I hurried out of the classroom and into the hallway, thankful Lily couldn't see my face. I blinked back my tears, realizing they weren't sad tears but proud ones.

"Are we doing okay, Mom?" Principal Brickman's voice startled me from behind. I hadn't realized he'd been waiting outside the door.

I whisked the tears away with my fingers and forced a smile. "Yes. It's just taken a lot to get to this point. We're very grateful to be here."

The bell rang, and the last of the straggling students hurried into their classrooms, leaving the principal and me alone in the hallway.

"Well, I, for one, am happy you found your way here." He flashed a million-dollar smile, his teeth white and straight, his eyes shining.

I felt something on the small of my back and realized it was Principal Brickman's hand, his thumb stroking up and down. I calmed my face, trying to hide my shock at the unexpected touch.

"Thank you." I stepped away and headed in the direction of the front door. The principal walked next to me, chatting about a summer vacation he and his wife had planned in Italy. I realized I must have misinterpreted his gesture. Some people were more affectionate than others. Placing a hand of support on my back must have been the man's natural reaction when he'd seen me crying. He'd only been trying to comfort me. I had probably been overly sensitive to other people's touch ever since Keith had backhanded me into the wall.

I managed a rushed goodbye and hurried out the door, around the gushing fountain, and toward the gate, which now sat closed. As I stood in front of it, a platinum-blonde woman in a tailored suit and glossy sunglasses headed toward me with a teenage boy by her side. She pulled out a keycard and scanned the barcode, causing the gate to unlock. She opened it to let me out.

"Wait." The woman paused, hand on hip, staring. "Don't I know you?"

I looked up. It took me a second to realize the connection.

My acquaintance from high school, Liz Meyer-Barnes, was facing me as she propped her black shades on her head. Her hair was blonder now and cut into an angled bob—the kind of designer haircut that probably cost a fortune. But I recognized the slope of her nose, her pronounced cheekbones, the intensity in her blue-green eyes. She was the woman whose photos I'd seen on Facebook, the one whose charmed life had led me to this school.

"Hi. Yes." I touched my chest. "I'm Rachel Gleason. From Addison."

"Oh my gosh. That's it!" She tipped her face toward the sky. "It's been a long time." She pointed to herself. "Liz Meyer-Barnes."

"Yes. I remember." My eyes flickered to the side, and I hoped she'd never find out how many times I'd visited her Facebook profile, studying the photos of her fairy-tale life.

"Someone told me you married Keith Belden. Is that right?"

I nodded. "Yes."

Her eyes lit up. "Wow. I used to have such a thing for him." Liz shook her head. "I just thought about Keith for the first time in forever. It's so crazy that I'd run into you."

"Keith and I recently got divorced," I said, my jaw tightening.

"That's too bad." She cocked her head. "Although, I always wondered how you and Keith ended up together. No offense." She flashed a fake smile as her eyes traveled from my scuffed shoes to the black pants and floral blouse I'd picked up at TJ Maxx two years earlier.

I could feel the heat gathering in my neck. It was clear Liz remembered an idealized version of Keith—the popular, charming, easygoing football player. It was the same view held by so many women my age who'd grown up in Addison. I hardened my voice. "I live in the city with my daughter now. We're getting a fresh start."

"How wonderful."

I fiddled with my bracelet. "And I think I saw on Facebook that you married a surgeon?"

"Yes."

"I'm happy things turned out so well for you."

Liz smirked. "Well, don't believe everything you see on social media."

"I'm late." The boy next to her kicked at the ground, annoyed.

The other woman threw him a stern look. "Just wait a minute." She motioned toward the boy, softening her voice. "This is my stepson, Davis. He had an orthodontist appointment this morning." She faced me, eyelids lowering. "What brings you to the school, Rachel?"

"My daughter, Lily, just started kindergarten today."

"Really?" Liz's lips parted slightly, and I could see the confusion swimming through her eyes. And a flash of something else, sharp and bright. *Disdain?* Liz was surely wondering how someone with my lackluster pedigree, who'd grown up as the shy, awkward daughter of a broke single mother, and who'd barely graduated from NIU, had not only married the star football player from her high school but also had a child at the same exclusive school as her stepson. "Aw. That's sweet," she added, covering her initial reaction. "And, what is it you do again?"

"Insurance." I aimed my eyes toward my feet, waiting out the awkward silence. When Liz didn't speak, I filled in the blanks. "Lily was awarded the Bright Paths scholarship."

"Oh. That's wonderful." Liz gave a trite smile, but the hollowness in her voice conveyed something else.

I turned my head toward the fountain, immediately wishing I hadn't been so forthcoming. I watched the forceful way the water shot up into the air and crashed back down into soothing ripples. Maybe if I paid fifty-thousand dollars a year for my kid to attend a private school, I'd have the same reaction as Liz—

annoyed that someone else was getting it for free. I stepped toward the gate, eager to get away from her judgmental stare. "I'll let you go. It was nice to see you."

"Yes. You too."

I clutched my purse to my side and hurried north on Clark Street as the sun slipped behind a cloud. From a half-block away, I peered over my shoulder. The school building appeared different in the altered light—gray and drab, not quite as idyllic. It seemed Shorewood Academy wasn't without pitfalls. There was an order to the school, unspoken rules with which I wasn't familiar. For Lily to succeed in this competitive environment, I'd have to tread carefully. I'd have to watch my back.

SIX

With my new modem installed and activated by the cable company, my home office was up and running. I pulled the wooden chair closer to the desk and clicked the next entry on my screen, wondering what Lily was doing in Ms. Lisle's classroom several blocks away. For the last two hours, I'd been clicking and reviewing forms filled out and submitted by Chicago Metro Insurance Company's adjusters in the field, making sure all the "i"s were dotted and the "t"s crossed, that there were no obvious indicators of fraud. Usually, my rote responsibilities left me feeling numb and underutilized, but today I was thankful not to think too hard. Fueled by nervous energy, I clicked, read, and approved a little faster, sailing through the entries. I hoped Lily's first day was going well.

I thought back to the morning drop off, wondering what I could have done differently. A couple of awkward moments had left an unsettling sensation buzzing through my veins. It had been a few hours, but I still hadn't fully regained my footing. Surely, Principal Brickman knew it was inappropriate to place his hand on my back, massaging the thin fabric of my blouse with his thumb. Or was I making too much of the gesture? He'd caught me crying, after all. He'd talked about his wife immediately afterward. So maybe it was nothing. Even more awkward was my run-in with Liz. I assumed I'd cross paths with her at some point, but I didn't think it would happen so soon. Her interest in Keith had been surprising. And it hadn't occurred to me that some of the parents might not be as excited about the tuition-free route Lily had taken into the school. I pinched the side of my cheek between my molars as I stared at the ceiling.

I dug my heels into the area rug I'd unrolled under my workspace. A faint conversation between Marie and Sheldon emanated through the wall. Bingo barked at something, followed by the command, "Quiet!" My head felt heavy as I leaned back in the chair, eyes traveling around the crown molding, landing on the cord again, painted the same color as the trim. It didn't appear to be the same kind of wire used for cable TV or internet. Maybe a previous tenant had installed a hard-wired doorbell or a security camera. A doorbell made the most sense. I didn't want to dwell on the other option. Even if it had been a camera, there was no way to know who had placed it there. I glanced at the drawer in front of me, envisioning the letter inside. Annie was likely back in Australia by now, just as Alex had said. She'd given me a gift by leaving so suddenly. There was nothing more to it.

I released a breath, eager for a few minutes' break. I paced into my bedroom and flopped on my bed, staring at the wall between my apartment and Alex's. His handsome face appeared in my mind—solemn eyes, dark stubble, and a slightly crooked smile that made my insides flutter. Unlike Keith, Alex was intelligent and honorable—a teacher at the city's top school. He was a determined athlete, fighting through his exhaustion to complete marathons. Finding a new man to share my life with hadn't been on my radar. Not even close. But I couldn't control the timing of when I met the right person. Before I could stop myself, I imagined Alex's sturdy arms wrapped around me, supporting my dreams and keeping me safe. He'd been such a gentleman yesterday. There'd been a special kind of heat surging between us, a bristle of electricity when his arm accidentally brushed against mine to lift the grocery bags. I wanted to get to know him better.

A text buzzed through my phone. I held up the screen, finding a message from Bridget: *Hi Rachel! Want to come up for a coffee or a glass of wine later? I work from home on Mondays.*

I sat up and lowered the phone, thinking about my schedule before typing a message back to her: *I pick up Lily at 4, but I can come at 3 if that works for you? I should probably stick to coffee :)*

Bridget's reply flashed up on my screen: *Sounds great. I'll be here!*

I tucked my phone away and returned to my desk. The thought of coffee with someone I hoped could be a new friend lifted my shoulders as I got back to work. Moving was always stressful. It would take time to settle into this new apartment, meet friends and neighbors, and adjust to Lily's school, but I was on the right track.

A few hours later, with my hair smoothed down and a fresh coat of lip gloss applied, I climbed the stairwell to the fifth floor. The hallway was an exact replica of the fourth floor, so I quickly located apartment 5B, rapping my knuckles lightly against the wooden door.

Bridget opened the door and greeted me with a warm smile. "Hey, come on in."

"Thanks for the invitation." I stepped inside, breathing in the smoky, herby scent of a burning candle, lemongrass maybe. The floorplan was laid out the same as mine, but the space looked different, homier. She had painted the walls a neutral shade of beige, but pops of color burst from unexpected places—

a framed painting of vibrant wildflowers hung from the wall, a striped area rug reached across the living room floor, and cozy throw pillows scattered across a light denim couch. "I love your place. I haven't had a chance to decorate ours yet."

"Well, you only moved in two days ago. It's taken me two years to get this far." She motioned toward the couch. "Sit down. How do you like your coffee?"

"With sugar, please."

Bridget headed toward the kitchen, and I studied a few framed photos resting on a side table. In a larger frame, Bridget beamed, looping her arm around another young woman who shared the same heart-shaped face and hazel eyes. A second photo captured Bridget posing next to an unsmiling, thick-necked, and tattooed man. She returned a minute later, carrying two mugs and a small bowl of sugar.

"Is that your sister?" I asked, pointing to the first picture.

"Yes. How did you guess?" Bridget smiled. "Amanda is four years older than me. She lives in the Detroit suburbs. She has a daughter a couple of years younger than Lily. That's the niece I mentioned."

"Cool. And is this your brother?" I asked, pointing to the other photo, although the man in that photo bore no resemblance to her.

"No. That's Leo. I met him during law school when I started volunteering for the Windy City Justice Project."

"What's that?"

"It's a group of law students and attorneys who volunteer their time to defend people who lack resources or who've been wrongly accused of crimes. They also help with rehabilitation and job placement. Unfortunately, justice isn't always done for people who can't afford decent representation."

I nodded. "Yeah. I don't doubt it."

Bridget stared at the photo, releasing a breath. "Leo's had a rough life. He did some time for attempted robbery, then got falsely identified in a lineup in a murder case. We got him out of that mess, but it's so sad. He's only twenty-two and has no positive role models." The corners of Bridget's mouth tugged down as she stared at the image. "He lives on the South Side. But at least he works some odd jobs now, thanks to some training and volunteers from the project. I make a point of spending time with him every few weeks. I just want to encourage him to make good decisions, to see there are other paths he can take in life."

"Wow. That's really cool of you. Are you a criminal defense attorney?"

"Nah. Probate. Boring wills and trusts. Not nearly as rewarding, but nice to work from home on Mondays. And I still volunteer with the project when I can." She took a sip and set down her mug. "Are you and Lily settling in okay?"

"Yes. We don't have too many things and most of the furniture was already there. I got my home office set up."

"What do you do?"

"I review claims for an insurance company. I'd really like to do something more creative, but I guess we've got to pay the bills."

Bridget offered an understanding nod. "That's reality."

"Yeah." I picked at the loose stitching near my pocket. "I'm more focused on getting back on my feet after my divorce and making sure Lily is happy. It's her first day at Shorewood Academy, so I've been a nervous wreck all day."

Bridget's eyebrows raised. "That's a nice school. She's lucky to have gotten a place there."

I recounted the details of the morning's drop off, my encounter with Liz Meyer-Barnes, and how I worried the other parents might be annoyed that Lily was getting a free education.

Bridget made a face like she'd smelled rotting garbage. "That's ridiculous. The school shouldn't offer scholarships if they're going to make people feel bad about using them."

"Yeah. That's what I think too." I raised my chin, already feeling better about having someone else in my corner.

Bridget was so warm and friendly. Hanging out with her was easy. She asked me a couple of questions about my recent divorce and how I was faring as a single woman, which I answered vaguely and quickly to avoid reliving memories of Keith's violent outbursts.

"You've probably discovered that your next-door neighbor, Alex, is a teacher at Shorewood." She nudged me with her elbow, flashing a sly grin. "I saw him helping you with your groceries yesterday when I was walking back from the drugstore."

Heat prickled up my neck and into my cheeks at the mention of Alex's name. "Yes. He was so nice to do that."

"Alex is probably the best-looking guy in the building." She blinked her eyelids. "I mean, objectively speaking. I'm not interested in him."

I couldn't help laughing. "I noticed him right away too. He seems smart and kind too."

She scooted to the edge of her seat with a sparkle in her eyes. "Okay, just between you and me, I used to have a huge crush on Alex. He and I moved into the building around the same time. I even took up running and tried out his running club so we'd have something in common." She shook her head and fluttered her eyelids. "My plan didn't work, of course. He had a girlfriend and didn't give me a second glance." She pulled away from me, her face changing. "Promise not to tell him I said that, though. I'd be so embarrassed, and I'm completely over it. I'm dating someone else now. His name is Marco, and he works in the same building as me."

I was a little surprised by her forthrightness but relieved to know nothing had transpired between her and Alex. "Your secret is safe with me. I'm glad you met someone." I thought about the noises I'd heard the other night, the hand slamming against the wall. "Although Alex told me he just broke up with his girlfriend. I heard him yelling at her the other night to leave him alone."

"Jeez. Well, that timing works out well for you. Doesn't it?"

"Apparently, she dumped him."

"No kidding." Bridget touched her chin. "I thought it would have been the other way around."

"What do you mean?"

"There was a woman who lived in 4B before you. Annie something or another. A couple of times I noticed Alex standing a little too close to her in the elevator, if you catch my drift."

"Oh. Alex told me he and Annie barely knew each other."

Bridget waved her fingers in the air. "Could be. I probably misread the situation. I really didn't know her at all, other than a few hellos in the lobby."

"Do you know why she left so suddenly?"

"No idea. I didn't even know she was gone until you moved in." Bridget crossed her arms and tilted her head as if considering something. "You and Alex would make a much better couple, in my opinion. And if things work out, you can bust out the wall between your apartments and live in a palace, like the Levys."

I smiled at the thought.

"Have you met the Levys?"

I nodded. "Yeah. Just in the elevator. They seemed nice enough."

"They are. But Judith is the head of the condo board and she's a ball-buster. And if I'm ever with the same person so long that we start wearing matching outfits, please shoot me." Bridget grinned. She had a blunt and unapologetic edge to her that I found refreshing.

"Will do." We sat for a moment, sipping our coffee. I took in the cozy room, my eyes pausing at the vent cover on her floor. I remembered what Lily had told me the other night, that she'd heard Bridget crying, and I set down my mug. "Is everything okay with you?"

Bridget cocked her head, surprised by the question. "Yeah. Why wouldn't it be?"

"Oh. It's just that... I guess Lily and I aren't used to sharing walls with people. It seems like we hear every cough and sneeze from our neighbors. Lily thought you might have been upset about something."

"Oh my gosh." Bridget covered her face with her hands, clearly embarrassed. "I was pretty torn up the other night, actually. I'm sorry if you heard me blubbering."

I placed my hands on my knees. "Don't apologize. If it's too personal, we can drop it."

Bridget sucked in a breath, waving me off. "No. It's okay. Lily was right. Marco broke up with me. It came out of nowhere."

"I'm so sorry. I thought you just said you were dating him."

"Yeah. I did say that." Bridget pinned her lips together. "We're on and off. Hot and cold. It's become a little bit of a pattern. But it's okay." She looked down and then raised her eyes from the floor. "There's plenty of fish in the sea, or so I'm told."

"Well, I'm glad you're doing okay." I paused, waiting for Bridget to say more, but she didn't. "Let me know if you ever want to talk about it or anything."

"Thanks." She stared at her mug of coffee, then swiveled toward me. "And if you ever need help with Lily on the weekends or at night, I'm happy to watch her for a few hours here or there. Kids usually like me." She winked. "And I don't charge anything."

"That would be really great. Thank you." I checked my phone, finding it was already 3:30 p.m. "Wow. That went by fast. I have to start walking to Shorewood, so I'm not late for pick up on the first day." I stood and set my empty mug on the counter. "Thanks so much for inviting me over."

"Of course." Bridget followed me to the doorway, watching me leave. "We'll have to do it again soon."

I waved over my shoulder, taking the steps down a floor to grab my jacket before heading back to Shorewood. As I pushed through the door to the fourth-floor hallway, something in the air shifted. A dark figure jerked up a few feet ahead, directly in front of the door to 4A. For a split second, I thought it was Alex. But when the man's pasty, tattooed face swiveled toward me, I realized my mistake. Drake dropped his hands to his side and strode past me with a grunt. I got the sense I'd interrupted something—might have even glimpsed a hand on the doorknob, although I wasn't certain. Alex would be at school right now, and I wondered if Drake had been trying to break into his apartment. I turned back to question my peculiar neighbor, but he'd already vanished into the stairwell.

My heart raced as I ducked inside my apartment and locked the door. I found my jacket, remembering how Alex had said he didn't feel threatened by Drake. He'd said that Drake was strange but harmless. A trust-fund baby would have no need to burglarize a neighbor. Whatever I'd just seen was probably nothing more than the awkward movements of an odd man.

Before I ventured out again, I turned my thoughts to a happier subject: my pleasant visit to Bridget's apartment. I was thankful for how kind and welcoming she'd been. But like a relentless pigeon pecking at breadcrumbs, there was Mom's destructive voice in my head, edging its way into my mind. Whenever a kid had asked me to join them at the playground, a new neighbor stopped by to introduce themselves, or a cashier at the grocery store attempted to chat her up, she'd always told me the same thing: *"Never trust people who are a little too friendly. It means they want something from you."*

SEVEN

A week later, Lily and I had gotten into somewhat of a routine with school drop off and pick up, cooking dinner together, followed by evening strolls along the lakefront while she told me about her day and we imagined fun ways to decorate our sparse living quarters—an area rug in the living room, a colorful bedspread in Lily's room, or a framed painting behind the kitchen table. Lily occasionally asked about Keith, or her friend, Natalie, back in Addison. I always answered her inquiries honestly but promised nothing.

On Monday night, I prepared tacos, chopping tomatoes and lettuce while the ground beef simmered on the stovetop. When I checked the cupboard, I realized I'd forgotten to pick up the tortilla shells when we'd gone shopping the day before. Lily pouted as I dragged her back out into the hallway and into the elevator, explaining that we had to go back to the store if we wanted to eat tacos for dinner.

"I'm tired. I don't want to go." Lily stomped and whined all the way down to the lobby, where I attempted to pull her toward the building's front door. She squealed like an injured animal, digging in her heels, and then collapsing on the shiny tile floor. Her theatrics drew Henry's attention, as well as stares from the Levys who stood near the doorman's station, chatting.

"Lily, come on. Don't be silly." I tugged her arm, but she lay in a heap, sobbing and refusing to move. "Sorry," I said to the other adults in the lobby. I was exhausted too, and also didn't feel like going to the store, but Lily was making things much more difficult than they needed to be.

"What's wrong, young lady?" Henry stepped toward us, a grandfatherly smile twitching at his lips. The Levys wore the same look of bemusement. Clearly, they didn't remember what it was like to deal with their children's tantrums in a public place.

"I don't want to go to the store again." Tears streaked Lily's pink cheeks.

"Aw. Poor thing." Judith Levy crossed her arms in front of her ample bosom.

I rubbed my forehead. "We're making tacos for dinner and I forgot to buy the tortillas."

"Are you just running down the street to Jewel?" Judith asked.

"Yes. I only need the one item, and I explained to Lily that it will only take a minute. I don't know why she's making such a big deal."

"The poor girl is tired. You can leave Lily here in the lobby with us." Judith looked at her husband. "Stan, go get that checkers set from upstairs. We can sit right here and play a game with Lily while her mom runs out." She looked at Henry. "That's fine, isn't it?"

Henry nodded. "Of course. It's a shame people don't use that sitting area up front more often."

I waved them off. "Oh, I don't want to interrupt your evening."

"Interrupt? It would be our pleasure." It was Stan who

spoke now. "Judith never plays checkers with me. Do you like checkers, Lily?"

My daughter peered up from her position on the floor and nodded.

Judith patted my arm. "We don't have any grandkids. This will be fun for everyone."

I bent down toward Lily and asked if she felt comfortable playing checkers in the lobby with the Levys while I ran to the grocery store.

"Yes. I want to stay here," Lily said.

I looked at the Levys' hopeful faces. Henry would be here overseeing them too. Plus, a security camera was mounted in the corner of the ceiling, aimed toward the front door and sitting area. I'd be gone for less than fifteen minutes. Mom would never have allowed such an arrangement, but I didn't want to be like her. These people were my neighbors, and they were only being kind and helpful. "Okay. I'll be back in just a few minutes. Thank you."

Judith clasped her hands together and smiled. "Wonderful."

"I'll go get the game." Stan was already heading back through the glass door and toward the elevators. Judith helped Lily off the floor and led her over to the leather chairs near the front window. The bounce had suddenly returned to Lily's step.

I edged over to Henry and whispered, "Can you do me a favor and make sure they all stay here, in the lobby? I'm sure the Levys are fine, but I just don't know them very well."

Henry tipped his head. "Will do. I'll make sure everyone remains in the sitting area until you return."

"Thank you." I scribbled my phone number on a scrap of paper and handed it to Judith, then waved goodbye to Lily, who now sucked on a lollipop and giggled at something Judith said to her. Turning down the sidewalk, I power-walked three blocks to the grocery store, where I quickly located a box of taco shells.

When I turned around, I jumped, nearly bumping into a tall figure standing behind me.

It was Alex. "Hi, Rachel." His teeth were straight and white when he smiled, and he held a bag of chocolate candies in his hand.

I stepped back, catching my breath. "Oh, hi."

"I haven't seen you much this past week. How's everything going with the apartment? And at Shorewood?"

"Great." I felt my cheeks flush. I noticed Alex had changed out of his work clothes and now wore jeans and a T-shirt. "We're getting settled and Lily loves her teacher, Ms. Lisle."

"Good. I'm sorry I haven't checked in sooner." He looked around. "Where is Lily, by the way?"

I chuckled. "Well, that's a long story. The short version is that I left her in the lobby of our building to play checkers with the Levys and Henry."

Alex made a face. "She's really making an impression on all the old folks, huh?"

"They seem enamored with her." I pushed a stray lock of hair behind my ear, aware of the way Alex stared at me. It was the same way I looked at him when he caught my eye across the grounds at Shorewood, like I wanted to memorize his features. I nodded toward the bag of candy in his hand. "I see you're stocking up on all the essentials."

He grinned. "Yeah. Believe it or not, I'm a healthy eater. The candy is for the kids at the Boys and Girls Club. I volunteer there a couple of times a month and I like to have prizes to give out." He glanced at the bag. "I usually play a trivia game with them. You know, try to teach them something."

"Wow. That's really cool that you do that." I shifted my weight, thinking again about how different this man was from Keith. My ex-husband had never done anything selfless in his life.

"Anyway, I was just about to check out, but I saw you here and thought I'd say hi."

"I'll go with you. I'm checking out too." As we made our way to the self-checkout lane, I told Alex how I'd forgotten the taco shells and about Lily's meltdown in the lobby.

After we'd paid for our items, he walked back to the building next to me, asking questions about my job and Lily's previous school. This time I wasn't so worried about rushing to my destination. After I'd answered his questions, I mentioned how I'd seen Drake outside Alex's apartment door several days earlier, and that I wasn't sure what our neighbor had been doing there. "It seemed like I caught him in the middle of something. Then he rushed away."

Alex huffed. "I'm sure it's nothing. That guy is weird but harmless. Thanks for letting me know, though." We walked a few steps, stopping at the corner to wait for the signal. "Where did you move from again?"

"Addison. It's about forty-five minutes west of here."

"Oh, yeah. I've heard of it."

"And where are you from?"

"I grew up in Morton Grove."

"I think I've heard of it."

"City living suits me much better. Small towns are so claustrophobic. Everybody knows everything about everybody."

"I know what you mean." I bit back my smile. That was exactly how I'd felt in Addison. Claustrophobic. It was refreshing to find someone who shared the same view.

Alex's hand brushed against mine, sending a warmth prickling up my arm. He didn't move his hand away, and I wondered, again, if he felt the attraction too. As we approached the building, I spied Lily through the glass, plucking a game piece from the checkerboard and jumping it over two other chips as Stan threw his arms in the air and made a pained face, followed by laughter.

Alex held the door open for me as I entered the lobby first.

"Hi, Mommy!" Lily yelled.

"Hi!"

Alex waved to Lily, then turned to me and winked. "See you soon."

Something in my chest fluttered. "Bye," I said as Henry buzzed him through.

I took a breath to steady myself and thanked the Levys for playing with Lily. I could see how happy everyone was, including my daughter. Letting her stay back with our neighbors had been the right decision, and had surely earned us some goodwill with the older residents of the building. We wished everyone well and waited as Henry buzzed us through the glass barrier. It had been an eventful thirty minutes and I should have been nothing but grateful for my good fortune: my helpful neighbors and the unexpected run-in with Alex at the store. Instead, a rush of panic speared through me as we stepped into the elevator. I squeezed Lily's fingers, searching for my breath. A few pulls of air into my lungs did the trick. Relief washed through me as the elevator lurched upward. Still, I got the strange and dire sensation I'd just escaped something, as if I'd narrowly missed being run over by a train.

EIGHT

The first two weeks at Shorewood Academy had gone better than I imagined. Lily loved her new teacher, Ms. Lisle, and had become fast friends with Marnie, the little girl who'd helped her on the first day. I'd avoided additional run-ins with Liz Meyer-Barnes and kept my distance from Principal Brickman, except to exchange a few breezy niceties. The man was a charmer and I'd overheard the other parents raving about him more than once. It was easy to see how he'd risen to his current position. The school year was winding down, with just six weeks to go, but allowing Lily to dip her toes into the Shorewood culture would make things easier for her in the fall. Each day at morning drop off, my eyes gravitated toward Alex as he stood at the far door, welcoming students. My next-door neighbor waved at me each time, his stare lingering a moment too long. He'd popped into my thoughts even more frequently since our run-in at the grocery store. But it seemed I wasn't the only one feeling whatever surged between us.

Now it was just after 5 o'clock on Friday. I hammered a nail into the wall next to the entryway, where I was hanging a framed photo of Lily, smiling in her striped jumper, Shorewood Academy's fountain spraying up behind her. I was determined to capture new memories, to make this apartment feel like home. Plus, I hoped to have Bridget over soon and wanted our place to look a little more settled.

The intercom buzzed, causing me to jump. The front desk had only called up once before to let me know a package had arrived and I still wasn't used to the loud burst of noise. I pushed the button next to the door to answer. "Hello."

"Hi, Rachel. This is Henry. There's a man in the lobby here to see you. Keith Belden."

My body went rigid as I wondered how Keith had gotten our new address. Had his attorney leaked the information? "Don't let him in."

"Sorry. What was that?"

"Please, don't let him in. That's my ex-husband. He isn't allowed contact with Lily, except on court-ordered dates."

"I understand." I could hear the jagged intake of Henry's breath. "Should I notify the police?"

"No. As long as he goes away, that won't be necessary."

"Okay. Stay put and I'll handle it."

"Thank you."

The hum of static cut out, leaving me standing in silence, heart pounding like a hunted animal. Lily sat on the couch, oblivious. Her giant headphones tilted back as she watched a cartoon. Keith's presence should have scared me, but hot anger simmered through me instead. *How had he found us here?* Mom's face flickered in my mind.

Thankfully, this building came with a couple of layers of security. No one who entered the lobby could access the elevator or stairs without scanning their keycard or getting buzzed through the glass wall behind the doorman.

My fingers fumbled across my phone, writing a text to Keith: *Stay away from us!*

Three bubbles appeared beneath. Then Keith's message popped through: *I was in the area. I miss Lily. I just wanted to see my daughter. I miss you too, Rachel.*

I leaned my weight against the wall, taking in the message. There was something desperate about it, and I almost felt bad for him. I felt a flash of Keith's humanity again and wondered if I'd been too harsh. But, as quickly as I'd softened toward him, painful memories of our violent past and the months Lily and I had lived in Mom's basement rushed through me. I'd attended the free weekly support group meetings for victims of domestic violence at a nearby church, where the other hollow-eyed women sat across from me with their shoulders slumped. A few of them had been lulled by compliments and guilt, returning to their abusers again and again, until they were beaten to within inches of their lives. That would not be me. I conjured more memories of Keith's true colors and stared them down—the aloofness, the cheating, the sting of his hand against my face. At the end of the day, my ex-husband was a manipulator, a mean bastard, and a horrible father. I reread his text: *I was in the area.* That wasn't likely.

Keith had rarely made the forty-five-minute drive into the city when we'd been together. He and his buddies had ventured downtown together for a Bears' game two years earlier. Afterward, Keith had done nothing but complain about how difficult it had been to park his pickup truck, how expensive it was. As far as I knew, he hadn't been back to the city since then. Now, he wanted me to believe he was suddenly in the area, on our street. And I knew for sure that a yearning to spend time with his daughter wasn't why he'd shown up here.

I crept toward the window and peered down toward the street, scanning for Keith's white pickup truck. The vehicle was easily identifiable by the words BELDEN LANDSCAPING printed in green across the sides. I spotted it a half-block down, double-parked with flashers on, sticking out like a sore thumb in this section of the city where compact, fuel-efficient cars dominated the landscape. Keith's surprise appearance at our new home was nothing more than a power play, a way for an insecure man to prove to himself that he was still in control. I wouldn't give that to him. I responded to his message: *Then you'll have to wait until May 31st.*

More bubbles percolated beneath my words. Then, Keith's response: *BURN IN HELL BITCH*

I turned off my phone and watched from my fourth-floor vantage point. A minute later, Keith stomped down the sidewalk in full tantrum mode, a toddler in man's clothes. He slammed the door of his truck and pulled into traffic.

The intercom buzzed again, and I answered.

"Hi, Ms. Gleason. I just wanted to let you know that he's gone."

"Thank you, Henry," I said, unable to calm the tremble in my voice. "Please let me know if you ever see him around the building."

"Will do. Take care now."

"And Henry?"

"Yes."

"Please call me Rachel."

The doorman chuckled. "Got it."

I returned to the entryway and hung the picture of Lily on the wall, my breath finally returning to normal. My fingers fumbled for Mom's number on my phone as I punched in a message: *Did you give Keith our address???*

A few seconds later, Mom responded: *Yes. A father deserves to know where his child lives. At the very least.*

I tipped my head back, swallowing my scream for Lily's sake. Mom still didn't get it. She believed a woman should stand by her man no matter what, that I must have done something to make Keith act the way he did, to berate and beat me and to push Lily down the steps. Mom had never recovered from my father leaving her when I was about Lily's age. Instead of taking control of her life once she was single, Mom had hidden away in a world of "if onlys" and "what ifs." She'd wasted twenty-five years imagining a better life in an alternate universe where her unloving husband had stayed by her side. I found her inability to take responsibility for anything in her life completely infuriating. In Mom's mind, leaving a spouse was the worst thing a person could do. Now *I* was that evil person because I'd left Keith.

I shut my eyelids, but the image of Keith stomping down the sidewalk looped through my mind. It was easy, in hindsight, to look back and chastise myself. To ask: *What were you thinking?* There'd been red flags along the way, of course, but Mom had set my expectations for life on the lowest rung. I hadn't been confident enough to heed the warning signs.

I remembered the night I'd met Keith. It was the July after my junior year at NIU. I'd found myself back in Addison for the summer. Mom had won eighty-grand on a scratch-off lotto ticket, causing her to become even lazier, even less motivated to achieve the simplest goals like cooking dinner or taking a shower. She'd quit her job as a nurse at the assisted living facility. I'd spent the summer escaping to the public park with library books and taking on extra hours waiting tables at the Olive Garden restaurant, earning money for the following semester and trying to spend as little time as possible at home.

During a Thursday night shift, I'd approached a booth filled with three boisterous men, setting down a basket of breadsticks and asking if they'd like to order drinks. I recognized Keith immediately as the jock from high school who I'd admired from afar, but I didn't think he'd notice me. He'd been two years ahead of me and had never given me the time of day. Keith had been the quarterback—popular, tall, and charismatic—a star athlete who always had a bubbly cheerleader by his side. But this night at the Olive Garden, his boyish eyes latched onto mine.

"Wait. I know you."

"You do?"

He snapped his fingers and smiled. "Yeah. You went to Trail View High, right?"

"Yes."

He jutted out his chin. "I played football."

"Dude. No one cares about that anymore." One of his friends punched his arm, causing the others to laugh.

He stuck his hand toward me. "Keith Belden." He nodded at my name tag. "And I see you're Rachel."

"Yes." My insides had fluttered as I shook his hand. His grip was strong and warm. My legs suddenly felt like jello as I took the drink orders. About an hour later, Keith surprised me by the kitchen doors and asked me out for dinner.

I'd been flattered by the attention from someone who I'd considered out of my league. We hung out for the rest of the summer, Keith telling me about the landscaping business he was building with his cousin, and me offering entertaining tidbits from college life. Mom caught wind of the romance, watching my comings and goings with suspicion, questioning my makeup and clothing choices.

The day I'd introduced her to Keith, she pulled me into her bedroom and leaned close to my ear, hissing at me in a loud whisper, "Marry him as soon as you can. Time will steal your beauty. Then no one will want you, and it will be too late." It was clear Mom approved of Keith, although her words left me stunned and scared. Despite Mom's warnings, I'd had the foresight to finish college before accepting Keith's proposal. I didn't realize until a year after the wedding that my husband didn't have much to offer beyond his good looks and outgoing demeanor. He had peaked in high school, and he must have realized his glory days were over too. Maybe that's what made him so mean.

By the time I was pregnant with Lily, my college friends had moved to the city to pursue their graduate degrees or careers. I'd settled into a nine-hundred-square-foot starter house in Addison with a man who'd dropped out of community college to start a landscaping business. His business struggled to get off the ground the first few years, so I'd gotten a work-from-home position with Chicago Metro Insurance Company, helping customers fill out claim forms as I tried to keep Lily from crying in the background. It was nothing like the career I'd imagined for myself. After Lily was born, Keith stopped complimenting me. He complained about everything I did—the way I dressed, the food I ate, the fancy words I used, the time it took me to get dinner on the table, the extra seven pounds of pregnancy weight I hadn't lost. His abuse wasn't obvious. It happened a tiny bit at a time, drip by drip, so slow I didn't even notice I was drowning. It wasn't until Lily was almost five that I knew for sure that Keith was cheating on me, that I was halfway down the path to becoming my mother. When I confronted him, he backhanded me into the wall.

It wasn't the first time Keith had struck me, but it was the first time Lily had witnessed the violence. She hovered in the doorway to our tiny backyard, screaming and crying, inconsolable. Keith told her to shut up, which made Lily cry louder. Before I knew what was happening, he'd shoved her down the four cement steps leading to our patio where she landed with a thud, clutching her wrist and shrieking in pain. That was the worst moment of my life. I immediately fled, taking Lily to the emergency room, then Mom's house, and filing for divorce two days later.

Now eight months had passed, negotiations between

lawyers, written court orders. Lily and I were finally moving on to better things. I didn't want to end up like Mom, hiding behind the tattered living room curtains and dreaming about what could have been as life passed me by. I refused to crack the door even a little bit beyond what was required. I would not let Keith worm his way back into our lives.

NINE

An hour after Keith's unwelcome appearance in the lobby, I rummaged through my cupboard, searching for dinner inspiration. It was Friday night, and it would have been easier to eat out. There were at least a dozen restaurant choices within one or two blocks of our new apartment, but I was being responsible and committed to ordering out only once a week. I gripped a box of elbow macaroni in my hand, debating whether to top it with marinara sauce or olive oil and parmesan. Three knocks cracked at our door.

Lily peered at me from her stool at the kitchen counter. "Who's that?"

"I don't know." A ripple of panic traveled through me as I wondered if Keith had returned, had somehow gotten past the doorman downstairs. I replaced the box of pasta on the shelf and skittered toward the front window, surveying the street below and finding no white pickup truck. I drew in a breath and headed toward the door, spying through the peephole.

Alex stood in the hallway, face and body distorted by my pinhole view. My fingers fumbled with the lock and opened the door. "Hi."

"Hi. I hope I'm not disturbing you." He looked handsome in a Patagonia T-shirt and dark jeans, hands shoved into his pockets.

I stepped back, smoothing back my hair. "No. Not at all. Come on in." I waved him inside, warmth prickling through me as he stepped closer.

"Hi, Lily." Alex waved at my smiling daughter. "How were your first couple of weeks at school?"

"Great! My teacher is nice."

"Awesome." Alex shifted his weight, glancing around the apartment. "It's looking good in here."

"Thanks. We still need lots of finishing touches, but we've been working on it."

Lily nodded.

Alex shifted his weight. "I was just wondering if the two of you wanted to come over to watch a movie tonight? I can order a pizza or Chinese food, whatever you like. And we could watch one of the classics like *Charlie and the Chocolate Factory* or *The Wizard of Oz*. Assuming you don't have other plans, of course."

"Chinese food!" Lily hopped from her stool. "Can we, Mom? I love *Charlie and the Chocolate Factory*."

I stared at Lily, pretending to think about it. Inside, my heart raced, palms tingling. Alex's invitation was more than I dared to hope for. He was a gentleman enough to invite Lily too, to think about movies that would appeal to her, to save me from fixing dinner after all. There was a chance Alex was merely being neighborly, but his movements were rigid, his speech quicker than usual. I got the feeling he was just as nervous as me.

"That would be wonderful." I locked eyes with him, something inside me warming at the sight of his smile. "Thank you so much."

"Great."

We both hesitated, appraising each other.

I snapped myself back to the conversation. "What time should we head over?"

"How about seven?"

"Sure. Can I bring anything?"

Alex waved me off. "Nah. I've got plenty of drinks, and I'll text you a couple of menus. You guys can tell me what you'd like, and I'll have it delivered."

I thanked him again and told him we'd see him soon. My feet practically floated across the apartment floor as I moved toward the kitchen. What were the odds that I'd land this apartment? Even more than the price and the location, the handsome and kind eligible bachelor next door was beyond anything I could have dreamed.

I looked at my phone. We had forty-five minutes until the big date. I sat on the couch to catch my breath, rereading a couple of friendly messages Bridget had sent in the days since she'd invited me over for tea. The most recent one said: *Has Alex asked you out on a date yet???* I hadn't responded to the question before, but now I was eager to share my news. I typed out a message back to her: *Alex invited Lily and me over for dinner and a movie tonight!*

A minute later, Bridget wrote back: *YES! I knew it. I want ALL the details tomorrow:)*

I gave her a thumbs up. I stood up, realizing I needed to find something more attractive to wear.

"Hey, Lily. I'm going to take a quick shower."

"Are you in love with him?"

Her little voice turned my head, halting my movement toward the bedroom.

"Oh." I shifted my feet, flustered by her astute observation and the directness of her question. For the first time in a long while, I felt the potential to be able to love someone like Alex someday, but I didn't want to confuse her. I barely knew him. "Alex is just a friend right now. He's nice. Don't you think?"

"Yeah."

"Why don't you get your blanket and pillow together. You can bring them next door to watch the movie."

"Okay."

I continued toward my bedroom, refusing to let my hopes soar too high. Alex had only recently broken up with his girl-friend. I needed to guard myself, to make sure I wasn't his rebound relationship, and to ensure I didn't repeat the same mistakes I'd made with Keith. No one would crash and burn here. At the same time, it seemed like the universe was finally repaying me for all the suffering I'd endured, that maybe things were coming together. Alex was the complete opposite of Keith. It might be worth it to put myself out there a little bit at a time and test the waters. No risk, no reward.

An hour later, I sat on Alex's couch, his leg hovering inches from my bare skin. I'd worn an above-the-knee skirt and a sleeveless blouse. Lily kneeled at the head of the coffee table with a spread of Chinese food laid out in front of us. Alex's apartment was smaller than ours, with only one bedroom and a different configuration. But his front window invited views of Roslyn Place, just like ours. He'd adorned his walls with framed black-and-white photos of iconic Chicago buildings—the Hancock Building, Willis Tower, the Merchandise Mart, Tribune Tower, the Wrigley Building, and Marina City. Lily had been drawn to the photos right away, and Alex had taken the time to tell Lily a few facts about each of the pictured build-ings. I could see why he made a good teacher.

"There's a super-cool observation deck on the 103rd floor of Willis Tower. You can walk out onto a glass floor and see the city below you. If it's okay with your mom, I'll take both of you there sometime."

Lily beamed toward me. "Can we?"

"Sure," I said, flashing a grateful glance toward Alex.

Now we spooned fried rice, vegetables, orange chicken, and egg rolls onto our plates. Alex had ordered way more than we'd suggested. He clicked through his oversized flat-screen TV and cued up the movie. I turned to adjust a cushion, a dent on the wall catching my eye. The indentation was about the size of a fist, the paint marred by the exposed white drywall. That must have been the spot he'd punched a couple of weeks earlier. My bedroom was just on the other side.

Alex caught me looking, his eyes following mine. "I'm going to fix that this weekend. I still can't believe I did that."

I nodded and smiled, but the sight of the dinged drywall reminded me of the mark my head had left when Keith smashed it into our bedroom wall. But this was a completely different set of circumstances. No one else had even been present when Alex took out his frustration on the drywall. I blinked away the painful memory of Keith's fist on my face, refusing to let my past interfere with my present.

Lily devoured her food, entranced by the movie. I felt comfortable sitting next to Alex, giggling at the blue-faced kid who hadn't followed Charlie's directions after winning the golden ticket to tour the candy factory. After we'd eaten, Alex cleared our dishes and put the food away, insisting we didn't need to pause the movie while he rinsed the plates. When he returned to the couch, he sat a little closer to me, his hand touching mine. I smiled and leaned into him, my head spinning with hopeful glimpses of what could be.

We sat like that for a while, Alex giving my hand a squeeze every time something funny happened. After another thirty minutes, Lily had fallen asleep on the floor, hugging her pillow.

"She's asleep," I whispered, nodding my head toward her.

"Thank you for coming over tonight. I've been wanting to get to know you better."

"Me too."

Alex leaned closer, and I got the feeling he might kiss me. But Lily rustled from her position on the floor. I pulled away, sitting tall.

I touched Alex's arm. "It's late. We should probably go."

Alex nodded, his eyes searching mine. "Okay. Maybe we can do this again sometime?"

"Yes. I'd like that."

Lily sat up, rubbing the sleep from her eyes as the final movie credits rolled. "I want to go to sleep."

It was after 10 p.m., well past her regular bedtime. We gathered her things and exited 4A to make the short walk back to our apartment. I stepped through Alex's door, hoping none of the neighbors would catch wind of our budding romance quite yet. Just as I had the thought, Drake's door opened further down the corridor. He peered out into the hallway, releasing a skunk-like smell from his apartment. His eyes were dazed and bloodshot, and it was obvious he'd been smoking pot. While his actions weren't a crime, it still wasn't something I wanted Lily exposed to.

"Hi, Drake," Alex said a little too loudly.

Our goth neighbor's eyes jerked up. He pulled his head behind the door and closed it. Alex waited, standing guard as I unlocked the door to our apartment.

"Have a good night."

"You too," I said as I closed my daughter and me safely inside. Soon, I tucked Lily into her bed and climbed between my own cool sheets, my insides dancing with the possibility of new love. I pictured Alex sleeping somewhere on the other side of the wall and couldn't help wishing he were next to me.

The next afternoon, I found myself weaving my fingers through Lily's and climbing onto a city bus, with Alex acting as our tour guide. He'd texted me first thing and invited us to visit the

Skydeck at Willis Tower with him, his treat. The Saturday crowd bustled around us as the vehicle lurched, halted, turned, and sputtered, slowly making its way south toward the business loop. The competing smells of body odor, vinyl, gasoline, and various perfumes overwhelmed my senses. Lily sat in a window seat, staring in wonder at the passing sights. Alex balanced in the aisle next to us, gripping the back of my seat and pointing out landmarks and attractions.

At last, we exited the bus and joined a line of tourists entering Willis Tower. After passing through security and showing our tickets, we packed into the elevator. Unlike the rickety and sluggish elevator in our building on Roslyn, this one rocketed upwards at an alarming pace, causing pressure to build and pop in our ears. We exited on the 103rd floor, gasping at breathtaking city views in every direction.

Alex motioned toward the wall of windows. "They say you can see four states from up here."

"Wow." Lily gasped, gazing out past several city blocks and toward the deep blue waters of Lake Michigan. "Cool!"

I hadn't seen so much joy on Lily's face in ages. It occurred to me that Alex had already planned more fun activities for Lily in two days than Keith had planned for his daughter in the entire previous year. I leaned close to his ear. "Thank you for bringing us here."

"You're welcome." He pecked me on the cheek as Lily's observant eyes darted between us. To my relief, she buried her face in her hands and giggled.

When it was our turn, we all held hands and edged out onto "The Ledge," a glass box protruding four feet from the side of the building.

"This is terrifying!" Lily and I clung to Alex, afraid to look down. We giggled and screamed, finally peering through the glass beneath our feet and down 1,353 feet to the street below.

Seconds later, our turn was over, and the next group ventured out onto the glass-floored box.

We spent some more time on the Skydeck. Alex told Lily he wanted to buy her a little souvenir to remind her of her bravery for walking out on The Ledge. We trailed her through the gift shop as she browsed the trinkets, eventually deciding on a blue keychain marked with "Willis Tower Skydeck."

We decided to take a different route home, riding the L train to the Fullerton stop. Lily gripped her new keychain the whole way as the wind whistled beneath the rattling train. We walked down from the platform, where Alex waved us a cab. He paid for everything, and I couldn't help wondering how much Shorewood paid their teachers.

A different doorman greeted us as we entered the building. He was younger than Henry, with a head of black curly hair propped on muscular shoulders. I'd seen the man the other day, but he'd more or less ignored me.

Alex raised his hand. "Hi, Robbie. Have you met Rachel and Lily? They moved into 4B a couple of weeks ago."

"Oh, yes." The man nodded at me. "I saw you coming in the other night." He buzzed us through without the usual small talk I got from Henry. The elevator doors opened, revealing Drake as his opaque eyes stared back at us. He looked down and moped toward the mailboxes, barely looking up. I pulled Lily past him into the elevator.

Alex stood next to us, shaking his head. "Drake. He's everywhere and nowhere, all at the same time."

"No kidding."

Once we reached the fourth floor, Lily and I thanked Alex for the fun afternoon.

Alex ran his fingers along his jawline. "I've got my running group early tomorrow morning, otherwise I'd ask if you could hang out tonight."

"Oh, that's okay. You probably need a break from us anyway."

"No chance of that." Crinkles formed around his eyes as he smiled. "I'll be in touch later tomorrow."

Lily waved. "Bye!"

I giggled like a lovestruck schoolgirl. "I'm sure we'll see each other soon."

Alex winked, thumbing toward his apartment. "I live next door. You can't get away from me."

TEN

"Now, do you love Alex?" Lily kicked off her shoes and bounded toward the couch, flopping back onto the cushions with a mischievous grin.

I followed Lily, sitting beside her and tickling her stomach as she squealed. "It's too soon for that, lovely. We're still getting to know each other."

Lily tugged at the ends of her hair, nodding. "I like him. He's nice and funny." She lowered her hand. "But when can I see Daddy?"

"On the dates set by the judge." I glanced away from her to hide my disdain for Keith. "Daddy is very excited to see you again."

"Will that lady be following us around again?" she asked, referring to the social worker assigned to their visits.

"Yes."

Lily nibbled her thumbnail, her child's mind trying to make sense of the complexities of adult relationships.

I patted her leg. "Hey, I have to run downstairs and get a load of laundry started."

Lily's lower lip protruded as she studied the keychain. "I want to stay here."

It had been a long day. I pictured her tantrum in the lobby from the week before and didn't have the energy to deal with a repeat performance. Taking the laundry downstairs wasn't much different than running down to the basement of a house. I wouldn't be gone more than five minutes and I could lock Lily inside the apartment.

Lily clutched her new keychain. "I'll stay in my room."

A minute later, I brought a bowl of pretzels and a juice box to her as she sat playing with her dollhouse next to her bed. With a laundry basket toppling with clothes, and a bottle of detergent balanced on top, I exited 4B and locked the door behind me.

I rode the elevator down to the lower level. The doors rattled open, exposing my face to the cool basement air. It was barely 4 p.m., but it could have been the dead of night in the windowless hallway. The basket handles pressed into my palms as I heaved the load into the corridor and turned left into the laundry room. Fluorescent lights flickered across the room's low ceiling. A couple of dryers spun with clothes, but the area was otherwise silent and empty. I chose the nearest washer, piled our darker-colored clothes inside, measured the detergent, and started the cycle.

A noise clanged from across the corridor, setting my senses on alert. I straightened my shoulders and angled my ear toward the clatter.

Bridget popped into the doorway, peeking in at me and holding a plastic storage container. "Hey, Rachel."

I released a breath. "Hi. I thought it would be a good time to get some laundry done."

"You're smart. There's always a big rush down here on Sundays." She tipped her head toward the container in her arms. "I'm grabbing my summer clothes now that the weather's getting warmer." She looked at me, eyes shining. "I can't wait to hear about your movie night with Alex."

"We also went to the Skydeck with him today."

Bridget's mouth opened. "Really? Two dates in two days? This is so great!"

"Do you want to come over for a glass of wine later? I'll fill you in."

"Sure. Thanks. I don't have anything going on." Her features sagged. "I was supposed to try to make up with Marco tonight, but he canceled."

"Oh, sorry." I watched the towels spinning in the dryer, wondering if Bridget and Marco were going to make amends again. The relationship she'd described to me had sounded tumultuous, and I hoped she would move on to someone who appreciated her. "Lily and I would love to have you visit. How about 8 o'clock?"

"Sounds great. I'll bring a bottle of white." She lifted her chin in a goodbye gesture and headed toward the elevator.

I returned to my task, loading our light-colored clothes into another washer as the other machine rumbled and whirred next to me. I hurried through the steps, anxious to return to Lily upstairs. But as I pressed the start button, an awareness descended on me, an animal instinct prickling up my neck and over my scalp. Something wasn't right. I turned toward the doorway, gasping and finding I was no longer alone in the room. Drake's black trench coat filled the doorframe, his face pinched and his dark eyes burrowing directly through me. The noise from the machines had prevented me from hearing his footsteps.

I tried to think of what to say, but something caught in my throat. My lips couldn't manage a simple hello.

He tilted his head, hands shoved deep into his pockets. The harsh light illuminated his chalky skin. "How did you get that apartment?"

"Huh?"

"The apartment. Unit 4B. How did you find it?"

His voice was flat, but I felt threatened. Maybe it was the spider legs tattooed across the left side of his face, his sudden appearance in this cave-like room, or the way he stood with a wide stance, blocking the doorway. He must have followed me down here.

"Oh." I waved my arm, attempting to lighten my voice. "I heard it was available through my daughter's school. I asked my realtor to contact the owner."

"I knew the person who used to live there. Annie. She disappeared in the middle of the night."

I swallowed against my scratchy throat, remembering the troubling letter I'd found in my mailbox. "Yes. I heard the previous tenant broke her lease. She must have been in a hurry to get back to Australia."

"That's the thing, though. She wasn't in a hurry to leave."

"How do you know?"

"Annie was my friend."

His statement tipped me off balance. I steadied my weight against the table, eyeing the strange man. "She was?"

"Yeah. She planned to live here for a year while she wrote a book. She was really into true crime, and we talked about unsolved cases sometimes. She was going to use one of them in her book, I think. I haven't heard from her since March 24th. That was over five weeks ago." He removed a bony hand from his pocket and touched the silver chain around his neck. "Someone did something to her." Drake's eyes fastened on me, smoldering like cigarettes.

She probably wanted to get away from you, I thought. Instead, I said, "Maybe she had a family emergency. Or couldn't pay her rent."

He continued talking as if I hadn't said anything. "I saw Alex leaving her apartment the day she vanished. He jumped when he saw me, like he'd been caught. Annie thought that guy was so charming." Drake's colorless lips pulled back. "I'm only giving you a warning because I know you have a kid. I've been watching your apartment. And his. I've seen you and Alex together. You look at him the same way Annie did."

My insides quivered as I stared at him. His eyes were an abyss, dark and murky. It was impossible to discern his true motives. I didn't want to believe him. I gave him a nod because I wasn't sure how else to respond.

Drake turned to leave, and I realized I'd been holding my breath. He stepped out of the room, and I decided to let him leave, to wait to ride the elevator back up alone. But just when I thought I was free of him, he paused, swinging his head back toward me, a sneer on his face.

"I'm only saying, Rachel, that I wouldn't want it to become a pattern."

After Drake left, I stood motionless, counting to one hundred and allowing the elevator time to deliver him someplace else before I jabbed the button, willing the doors to part. When they finally opened, the elevator was empty. It rattled me upward to the fourth floor, where I raced down the hallway, unlocking my door and finding Lily sitting safely and singing to herself just where I'd left her. *Of course she was!* But my heart still thrummed as I hugged her.

Now Drake's statements spun in my head. Had Alex and Annie been dating? I remembered the punch against the wall. Was it possible *Alex* had done something to the previous tenant as Drake had suggested? I retreated to the bathroom and splashed cold water on my face, banishing what I imagined would be Mom's gleeful refrain about Alex from my ears: *I told you so. He's too good to be true.*

"Stop it!" I scolded myself in the mirror. Mom's toxic way of thinking didn't control me anymore. I hadn't even heard Alex's side of the story yet. Surely, I would take his word over a weird, leering man who was high on drugs half of the time. It was ridiculous of me to even consider the possibility that Alex, a respected teacher and a man who I'd judged as trustworthy, caring, and down-to-earth, could have harmed Annie. I'd tell Alex about Drake's comments the next time I saw him, which I hoped would be tomorrow.

I continued about my afternoon and evening, eager to put the uncomfortable encounter in the basement behind me. I focused on my get-together with Bridget, checking off items on my to-do list: heating leftover Chinese food Alex had sent home with us, sweeping the floor, doing a quick clean of the bathroom, and rinsing two dusty wine glasses that I'd carried from house to house, but hadn't used in months. My next two trips down to the laundry room were quick and uneventful. My only run-in was with an older woman I'd never met before who sat next to a dryer, waiting for her clothes.

At just after 7 p.m., a text from Alex popped up on my phone: *I had so much fun today. Thank you and Lily for coming with me.*

I reread the message, my annoyance with Drake intensifying as I wondered why he'd attempted to taint my view of Alex. Even if Alex had been in this apartment the day Annie left, it didn't mean he'd harmed her. Annie was likely back in Australia, happy to have cut all ties with Drake. Drake's words hummed through me: *You look at him the same way Annie did.* Alex said he and Annie hadn't been romantically involved, but now I wondered if he'd stretched the truth a bit. Bridget had mentioned she'd sensed something going on between them too. Maybe Drake was merely jealous of Alex.

I shook away all thoughts of my strange neighbor down the hall and wrote back: *We had fun too. Thank you for being an amazing tour guide! Good luck on your run tomorrow.*

He gave my message a heart, which I couldn't help reading into.

I cracked the front window, letting in a brisk wind and the sound of a siren wailing in the distance. Freshly bathed and wearing her pink-and-white jammies, Lily rearranged a plate of cheese and crackers I'd set on the table. She was eager for Bridget's visit too.

"Does Bridget like to play Uno?"

"I don't know, but I bet she does."

A moment later, a few light raps sounded against the apartment door.

ELEVEN

I widened the door as Lily hopped up and down beside me. Bridget stood in the hallway, her berry-stained lips smiling toward us, and a bottle of Chardonnay gripped in her hand. Designer jeans hugged her legs, tapering down to trendy ankle boots. Her eyes popped beneath smokey eyeshadow, and silver bracelets clinked on her wrist. Bridget's fashionable appearance reminded me how much more time I'd had for myself once upon a time before Lily arrived and before I became a single mom. Maybe my upstairs neighbor could help me reclaim a piece of myself in that department, help me fit in with the women at Shorewood. I waved her inside.

Bridget stepped forward, surveying the living room and open kitchen. "Wow! You've really gotten settled. It looks great."

"We're trying." I eyed the new area rug we'd picked up at the thrift store the weekend before and the framed photos of Lily I'd added to the wall in the entryway.

I gave Bridget the five-cent tour, with Lily showing off every corner of her yellow bedroom. Bridget crouched down on Lily's rug, face beaming. "What a fun dollhouse! I had one just like that when I was your age."

Lily displayed the miniatures, one by one. I was happy she and Bridget had such a good rapport, and I left them to explore the dollhouse's rooms. I headed to the kitchen and poured two glasses of wine and a cup of lemonade for Lily. A minute or two later, we met back in the living room, where Lily and I told Bridget about our adventurous day downtown. I described the thrilling terror of standing on the glass ledge as people and cars buzzed like insects a hundred stories below us. Lily recounted her excitement over her first time riding the city bus and the L train.

Bridget listened, sipping her wine and seemingly enthralled by every word. "That sounds like a blast. I'm so glad you moved into the building. I bet Alex is happy about it too." She winked.

I gave her a bashful smile. "I'll tell you more about that later."

At Lily's insistence, we played a couple of rounds of Uno, which Bridget was more than happy to do. Then I set Lily up with a video in her bedroom so that Bridget and I could talk.

I slid to the edge of the cushion, lowering my voice. "Do you know Drake? The guy with the face tattoo that lives down the hall from me."

"Yeah. I know who he is, but I've never really talked to him. I caught him staring at me once when I was getting my mail. He weirds me out."

"He gives me the creeps too." I took a sip of wine, letting it slide down my throat as Bridget talked.

"Henry told me once that Drake's dad was a drummer for some rock band in the eighties. I can't remember the name of it, but it was something I'd never heard of. Anyway, Drake tries to act all badass, but at the end of the day he's a trust-fund baby."

"Yeah. I heard the same story from Alex."

Bridget pinched the stem of her wine glass, setting it back on the table. "Why do you ask?"

"I ran into Drake in the laundry room today, right after I saw you. I got the feeling he followed me down there."

Bridget's smokey eyelids widened. "Why do you think that?"

"He didn't have any laundry with him, for one thing." I detailed the brief and troubling conversation I'd had with Drake, including his implication that Alex had something to do with Annie's sudden disappearance from the building, and his eerie statement that I might somehow be next.

Bridget sat back in her chair, crossing her arms. "Hm. I don't know anything about where Annie went, but I suspect she left without a trace on purpose. Otherwise, the landlord would know how to find her and force her to pay the rent, at least for as long as this place sat empty." Bridget looked around.

"I can't stop wondering." I paused and bit my tongue. "What if something bad happened to her? What if that's why no one saw her leave?"

Bridget shook her head. "Think about it. If someone did something bad to Annie, wouldn't her belongings still have been in the apartment? From what you've told me, it sounds like she packed up her stuff and left. And Drake is full of crap. It wouldn't surprise me if he had a crush on Alex. He's probably just jealous of you and doesn't know how to handle his feelings."

I considered Bridget's theories, realizing she was likely correct about everything. As far as I knew, Annie hadn't left anything behind in the apartment. When I'd met Penelope at her office to sign the lease, Oliver had mentioned how the previous tenant took the time to clean before she disappeared, which was the only positive thing he could say about her. Annie's vanishing act was probably intentional to avoid paying for the remainder of her lease. It could even explain why Julia, the person who sent the letter, hadn't yet heard from Annie. I debated whether to show Bridget the letter, but she was an attorney. I didn't know if she'd have some lawyerly obligation to report my federal crime of opening someone else's mail. It was probably better to keep it to myself. Still, there was something else nagging at me.

I squared my shoulders at Bridget. "Drake said he thought Alex and Annie were dating. That's what you thought, too, right?"

Bridget waved me off. "I have no idea. They only seemed friendly in the elevator that one time. I was never close with either of them. You should just ask Alex about it. I'm sure he'll tell you the truth. I'd take his word over Drake's any day."

I nodded, staring at the splash of golden-clear liquid remaining in my glass. Of course, Bridget was right. Her advice was nothing more than common sense, but it was reassuring to have a level-headed friend in my corner, preventing my thoughts from spiraling.

Our conversation turned to Bridget's work at the law firm and the self-important partner who found flaws with almost everything she did. "It's way better than the last firm where I worked though." She paused, a shadow passing over her face. "The head partner was a sexist asshole. You wouldn't believe the things he said to me." She shook her head. "A week after I complained about him to a couple of the other partners, the firm fired me."

"Are you serious?"

"Yeah. You'd think a bunch of attorneys would know that you can't do that. Anyway, it gets crazier. A friend of mine from law school was helping me put together a case against the head partner, Roger, and the firm, for sexual harassment and wrongful termination. But a few days before his deposition, Roger killed himself."

"What? Over a lawsuit?"

"Yeah. He overdosed on pills." Bridget frowned. "I mean, I hated the guy, but I didn't want *that* to happen."

"I'm so sorry, Bridget." I studied her as she plucked at her bracelet. "You know that wasn't your fault, right?"

"Yeah. It took several sessions with my therapist, but I realized Roger must have had much bigger problems than me. Anyway, I only wanted my day in court so the truth would come out, but with Roger gone, there wasn't really any point. I ended up taking a meager settlement offer from the remaining partners and dropping the case. Thankfully, I landed the position at my current firm a couple of months later." Bridget looked at her hands, then back at me. "That was over a year ago already. Time flies, I guess."

I sucked in a breath, realizing Bridget's life hadn't been so shiny and perfect after all. "Well, good for you for overcoming that."

Bridget stayed silent for a minute, then changed the subject, announcing that she was officially over Marco. They'd attempted to get back together, but he'd been treating her like garbage the last few weeks, and she was relieved not to have to take it any longer. She asked about my interests outside of work and Lily, and I told her that I loved animals, especially dogs and horses. Bridget smiled along but confessed she was more of a cat person. I shared my dream of working at an art museum, recognizing that it was a long shot given my current job in the insurance industry.

Bridget's face brightened at my mention of art. "I'm obsessed with photography. I spend a lot of my weekends taking photos of the city landscape. Someday, I hope to sell my work at the Old Town Art Fair. Or maybe even set up an online store. I'll show you some of my prints sometime."

"I'll be the first to buy one." I glanced toward the window, black night looming outside. "The weather should be nice for tomorrow. Maybe you can get some photography in."

"I wish I could, but I'm going to hit the gym in the morning and spend the afternoon with Leo. His cousin was arrested yesterday. I want to make sure he knows I'm still there for him. I just hope this tragedy doesn't derail him."

My gaze hovered on Bridget. Despite her hardships, she was so driven, succeeding as a young attorney in the cutthroat world of the city, throwing herself head-first into everything she did. She could have spent her Sunday on a million things, but she chose to use her time to help a man from the wrong side of the tracks who'd been falsely accused of a crime and whose cousin had just been arrested.

I had very few female friends. Keith had kept me isolated whenever possible, making me feel guilty for any time I spent away from Lily. I'd lost touch with my old college roommates and didn't have much in common anymore with my high school acquaintances. But I was happy Bridget was so open and easy to hang out with. "I'm super impressed that you take such a personal interest in Leo. He's lucky to have crossed paths with you."

"That's nice of you to say. Leo helps me too, I guess." She paused, eyes glassy as she laced her fingers together and stared at the wall. I got the feeling she'd traveled somewhere else in her mind. "He helps me keep my problems in perspective."

"I wish I had time to do something meaningful like that." I recalled the tidbits Alex had shared about his volunteer work with the Boys and Girls Club and wondered if I was the only one not giving back. "I wouldn't know what to do with falsely accused people, of course, but maybe working with animals at the Humane Society."

"Well, I'm perpetually single and childless, so it's easier for me. You have a daughter who needs your time. But it is so important you find something you enjoy doing just for you."

Right on cue, Lily's door swung open, and she wandered back into the living room. "Is it bedtime yet?"

"Oh my gosh. I didn't realize how late it was." My phone showed the time as 10:26, over an hour past her 9 p.m. weekend bedtime.

Bridget stood up and smoothed down her shirt. "I think it's time to call it a night. Thanks so much for having me over. This was fun." She lowered her gaze toward Lily. "Let me know if you ever want to hang out again. Who knows? Maybe your mom wants to go off and do something on her own once in a while."

Lily nodded. "Yeah. We can play with my dollhouse."

"Sounds great."

"I might take you up on that," I said as I showed Bridget to the door and thanked her for coming.

I lay in bed, blinking into the darkness and listening to the street sounds infiltrate my cracked window. The car motors and loud conversations from passing people outside felt more familiar now. I closed my eyes, holding a breath in my lungs and letting it seep out slowly through my nose, grateful for the day's gifts. Alex was turning out to be more than I'd hoped for. He had gone out of his way to show us the sights and to get to know Lily. I'd met a new friend in Bridget. My eyelids weighed heavily, and my legs ached. It wouldn't take me long to fall asleep tonight.

I was about to drift off when the low din of Alex's voice murmured through the drywall. My head lifted off the pillow as I wondered if maybe he was talking to me. But last night, I'd noticed the vent on the wall behind his couch, the one that most likely connected my bedroom's ductwork. He'd closed the metal slats, likely in response to my confession of overhearing him. Now I realized Alex was talking to someone else. I only recognized an occasional word amid the murmuring. I wondered who was on the other end of the conversation, and I hoped it wasn't his ex-girlfriend calling again. I'd expected Alex to be asleep by now, especially given his early morning marathon training.

I rolled over, pulling the sheets tight around my shoulders and reminding myself it wasn't any of my business. Alex was certainly allowed to talk to other people at whatever time he liked. I listened to the hum of his voice, letting it comfort me and lure me to sleep. But just before I drifted off, a moment before my mind entered that foggy stage between wakefulness and sleep, two words spoken in Alex's voice jolted my eyes open. Maybe it was a trick of the mind, a materialization of all the unresolved worries swirling through my head. But I could have sworn I'd heard him say the name *Annie Turner*.

TWELVE

On Sunday morning, Lily and I returned to the Lincoln Park Zoo, admiring the animals we hadn't seen two weekends before. I'd suffered through a rough sleep last night. Now I yawned frequently; my awareness dulled at the edges. After forty minutes of following the pathway, peering between bars, behind rocks, and into caves to spot a variety of critters, we rested near the fence encircling "The Farm in the Zoo." Lily giggled at the antics of a fat, spotted pony who gobbled mouthfuls of hay, shaking its head up and down with each new bite. I studied the joy on her face, remembering how I'd yearned for a pony when I was her age. I'd gotten a free pony ride once at a friend's birthday party. I still remembered how the feel of the animal's breath, its legs walking beneath me, had been the coolest thing ever.

There'd been a girl in my sixth-grade class, Evelyn Pierce, who lived in the nicer section of town. Evelyn had a pony of her own and brought in photos from her horse show for show and tell. My classmate had looked so chic sitting tall in the saddle in a velvet helmet and crisp white shirt, both the girl and the horse braided and polished. After drooling over the photo, I'd made the mistake of mentioning my pony dream to Mom, who'd thrown her head back in laughter. "A pony? Do you think we're millionaires? Descendants of the Queen of England?"

I'd stared at my feet, feeling stupid.

"Ponies aren't for people like us, Rachel. Not since your father left. You might get a goldfish someday if you're lucky."

A pony hadn't been realistic then. Or now. But Mom had made me feel worthless in that moment. I never wanted Lily to feel that way. My daughter would never be afraid to dream.

I balanced against the fence, Lily's arm brushing my sleeve. The graceful lines of the horses in the paddock entranced me. There was something wise and patient in their eyes. I stretched my arm through the fence to try to pet the horses, but the elegant creatures remained at the center of the enclosure, well out of human reach. Still, being out in the cool morning air, near them and Lily, had a calming effect, washing away my worries from the night before. I'd been going over again and again what I thought I'd heard as I lay in bed last night. It sounded like Alex had said Annie's name from the other side of the wall, but his voice had been faint and blurry, practically inaudible. I'd been half-asleep. I must have gotten it wrong. Clearly, Drake's suggestion that Alex and Annie had been more than mere neighbors had wormed its way into my head.

It was still early when we left the zoo and wandered down to Fullerton Beach. Only a handful of people dotted the sand, spread out on blankets and wearing jackets. A chill in the air kept the swimmers and sunbathers away, but it wouldn't be long before the weather turned hot. In a matter of weeks, I imagined the area would be packed with people.

The lake was calm. Lily and I sat on a rocky ledge and gazed at the rippling water stretching into the horizon. Beneath us, a running path wound its way next to the water's edge, carrying runners, walkers, and bikers past in both directions. I'd timed our walk this way on purpose. Alex had mentioned he ran along this section of the path about this time of morning with his group, and I kept an eye out for him as Lily and I played one of our favorite games, where we assigned fictional names to the people who passed.

Lily stared at a power-walker. "She looks like an Alice."

"For sure." I angled my chin toward a lanky, older man with an awkward stride. "That guy is definitely named Ichabod."

Lily giggled.

I searched the path for my next guess, but my eyes snagged on a group of yellow-and-green shirts bounding toward us. I recognized the shirts as the same one Alex had been wearing during his hallway cool-down a couple of weeks earlier and wondered if this was his running group. There were about a dozen of them, slightly more men than women. They moved at an impressive clip, making the exercise look effortless. A few paces later, Alex's face became visible, sweat glistening on his skin and the wind tousling his hair. He had the body of a runner, long and lean, muscles bulging and shifting with each step. I sat up, pulse racing and palms sweating. Even the distant sight of him had that effect on me.

I nudged Lily and pointed. "Look who that is."

"Hi, Alex," she yelled, flagging him with her outstretched arms.

His eyes found us as he ran, a smile overtaking the determined look on his face. He gave a wave without breaking stride. "Hi, guys."

Alex put his head down and kept running. My eyes followed him down the path, the whole group gliding with ease like a herd of gazelles. I wondered how many miles he'd already covered. He said his group met at 8 a.m., which meant they must have been running for over three hours. Yet he looked like he wasn't out of breath, like he was enjoying himself. It was thrilling to see him in his element. I touched Lily's hair, realizing again how grateful I was for this chance at a fresh start.

Keith had made me gun-shy when it came to relationships. Still, I couldn't deny the attraction I felt toward Alex. While Drake's strange comments still niggled at the edge of my thoughts, I'd formed my own opinions of Alex. Drake's unsolicited opinions didn't hold much weight compared to what I'd witnessed first-hand. Admittedly, I didn't know my next-door neighbor that well, but he seemed like the kind of man I'd want in my life when the time was right. And in Lily's life too. Alex— the worldly teacher, the athlete, the volunteer—was so different from Lily's biological father, whose most significant goal was to see how many cans of beer he could drink in an hour. There were still another three weeks before Keith would have his scheduled visitation with Lily. I wouldn't let thoughts of him taint our peaceful morning.

A few hours later, Alex leaned back on my couch, freshly showered and clean-shaven with the faint smell of cloves and spices clinging to him. I sat next to him as his finger touched my thigh. I'd texted him after Lily and I returned from the lakefront, asking if he wanted to come over in the afternoon. He'd responded with a yes.

After talking about our morning's activities, Lily had migrated to her bedroom to play a game on her tablet. Now Alex and I were alone, and his hand gently touched my face. There was a hungry look in his eyes that couldn't be mistaken. I felt the same yearning but was also scared of another failed relationship. I silently renewed my commitment to take things slowly, especially as the unanswered questions from yesterday lurked in the dark corners of my mind.

"I've wanted to kiss you since the moment I first saw you." Alex spoke in a whisper, his lips merely inches from mine.

I smiled, lowering my eyes. He kissed me. Despite my worries, I let it happen, a thrill surging through me because I'd been dreaming of this moment too. But then I pulled away, doubts bombarding my thoughts as my eyes gravitated toward Lily's bedroom door. "Wait. Sorry. I have to ask you something."

Alex straightened his shoulders. "What is it?"

"Yesterday, I ran into Drake in the laundry room. Actually, I don't think it was accidental. It seemed like he followed me down there."

Alex sat forward, narrowing his eyes. "What did he want?"

I described my conversation with Drake, including his claims that he and Annie were friends and that he'd spotted Alex leaving this apartment the day Annie disappeared.

Alex shook his head, grunting and rubbing his forehead. "Drake is such a lying piece of crap. I doubt he and Annie were even friends. She was friendly with everyone."

I leaned into the cushion, waiting for more.

"Drake was right about me being inside this apartment that day, but it was because Annie asked me if I could help her with the window. She wanted to lock it and couldn't get it closed all the way. I was only being neighborly. I had no idea she was going to skip town later that night."

"Were her things packed up?"

"Not that I noticed. I was only in the living room, though."

I bit down on my lip, realizing Alex's explanations were more than plausible. I debated whether to ask him the next question. It was risky to address the subject, but I had to know. "Not that it's any of my business, but was there anything else going on between you and Annie? It won't make a difference to me either way. I just want to get everything out in the open."

Alex shook his head, face still. "No. Annie was a neighbor and nothing more. We chatted in the hallway and elevator sometimes. That's why I put in a good word for her for the office job at the school. Then she quit without giving two weeks' notice and moved out of the apartment without telling anyone. I was just as surprised as everyone else."

I watched Alex's face as he spoke. He seemed sincere, his words calm and collected.

He laid his palm on top of mine and squeezed, his rough callouses brushing my skin. "I swear, there was nothing romantic between us. I told you about my ex-girlfriend, Sarah, already. I don't have anything to hide." He cocked his head, smiling. "Now it's your turn to come clean with me. Was there anything going on between you and the UPS delivery guy back in Addison?" He winked, nudging me. "C'mon. Tell the truth."

I laughed, happy that Alex had kept his sense of humor. My question had been a bit invasive, and Alex was right. He'd been nothing but open and honest with me. Annie probably had a crush on Alex, her handsome next-door neighbor. Alex may not have even noticed, although it sounded like Annie's amorous feelings were obvious to others, including Bridget and Drake.

I cleared my throat, steering the conversation in a different direction. "Drake seemed concerned that he hadn't heard from Annie in over a month."

"Why would she contact him at all?" A pained sigh escaped Alex's lips. "Drake is a freak, a spoiled brat in goth clothes. I'm sure Annie was relieved to leave him behind."

I glanced toward the door, recalling how uncomfortable I'd felt in Drake's presence. "I was thinking the same thing."

Alex moved closer, tracing the back of my hand with his finger. I remained still, remembering the words I'd thought he'd mumbled from the other side of the wall. "Sorry to keep harping on about this, but did you hear anything strange that night? The night Annie left? The walls are kind of thin."

Alex pressed his lips into a line, glancing toward my bedroom door. "My bedroom is on the opposite side of my apartment. I usually sleep with a fan on to block out noises. I didn't hear anything."

I remembered Drake's words: *I wouldn't want it to become a pattern*, coupled with Bridget's theory that Drake was attracted to Alex. Now I wasn't sure if Drake had been warning me or threatening me.

"Do you think Drake could have done something to Annie?"

Alex smiled and touched my arm. "Rachel, I'm sorry that Drake freaked you out yesterday, but he's a total fraud. Besides that, Drake doesn't strike me as the sharpest knife in the drawer. He never could have pulled off a disappearance—or whatever—without being found out."

Alex's explanation made sense, but another memory tumbled through me and I couldn't let the subject drop just yet. I pointed to a spot on the wall where the drywall met the crown molding. "Do you see that wire?"

"Where?"

"The one that's painted the same color as the wall. I think it could have been for a doorbell. But maybe also for a hardwired security camera. Did Annie have a camera over her door?"

Alex leaned his shoulders back into the couch cushion, eyes following the wire. "Now that you mention it, I guess she did have a camera over her door in the hallway. Yeah. Someone must have complained to the board because she removed it a few days after putting it up. It's against the bylaws to hang anything like that in the common areas. It was probably one of the old-timers. They have nothing better to do than walk around and make sure everyone's obeying the rules."

"Why would she have a security camera?"

"I have no idea. I assumed it was because she was a single woman living by herself in an unfamiliar city."

"So, she wasn't scared of someone in the building?"

Alex's face stretched with disbelief. "No. Whatever you're imagining is much worse than reality. No one did anything to Annie. She left by her own free will."

My eyes darted toward the desk drawer as I thought about the troubling letter I'd hidden inside. I'd mentioned it to Alex, but he didn't know the details. "I have to show you something." I walked across the room, opening the drawer and retrieving the letter addressed to Annie Turner. My fingers shook as I slid the card from the envelope and opened the handwritten note, setting the paper on Alex's lap.

His face dropped as he read the lines. "Huh." He turned the paper over, finding no writing on the backside. Then he inspected the envelope. He narrowed his eyes at me. "Did you open this?"

"Yeah. I don't know why I did." I looked at my hands, wondering what he thought of me.

But Alex had already refocused on the envelope. "Julia Turner. I wonder if that's Annie's sister."

"Why would Julia write, 'You're not safe in that apartment'?" I peered at Alex, willing him to see that, between the security camera and the letter, I was on to something.

"I don't know. But this envelope was mailed five weeks ago. I'm sure she's gotten in touch with Annie by now."

"How can you be so sure?"

"Because the most logical explanation is usually correct. And..." Alex held up his hand, releasing a breath. "Louise, a woman who works in Shorewood's office, told me that the day Annie quit, Annie told her that she planned to travel to Europe for a few months before heading back to Australia. Supposedly, it was all very hush-hush and last-minute. Annie even instructed Louise not to tell anyone. I bet that's where she is."

I paused. "So, you think Annie's in Europe?"

"That's what I heard."

I turned the theory over in my mind. Maybe the sender—Julia—hadn't known Annie was going to Europe either. But why tell Annie she wasn't safe in the apartment? Something must have happened to make Annie install a camera, break her lease, and leave in the middle of the night.

"You know what?" Alex gave a contemplative look. "It's not

our concern where Annie went after she moved. To be completely honest, I'm glad she left so soon because I wouldn't have met you if she still lived here." His gaze was warm as he laid his eyes on me.

I squeezed his hand. "You're right. I'm happy she left too." I leaned back into the cushion, hoping Lily would remain in her room for at least several more minutes. The tense muscles in my body uncoiled as Alex wrapped his arm around me, his lips finding mine once more. Alex's weight pressed on me, his lips on my mouth, then my neck. I gave in to the moment, relishing the words he whispered in my ear, taking pleasure in his touch. The timing of my newfound romance wasn't ideal but matters of the heart couldn't always be planned. I deserved a good man in my life. Still, as I gazed upward, I couldn't stop my eyes from wandering to the painted cord running along the top of the wall, pausing at its frayed edge, and tracing the path that once led to a security camera.

THIRTEEN

The following Wednesday, I lingered near the fountain's edge, waiting for the school bell to ring. Clouds gathered in the sky, a mass of grays and purples forming like a bruise. Hopefully, Lily and I could make it home before the downpour. My eyes traveled across Shorewood's immaculate grounds, observing the approaching storm, the clusters of parents who stood around the pickup area, and the neatly trimmed forsythia bushes. I uncrossed my arms, acting approachable as thick air filled my lungs. I'd glimpsed Liz Meyer-Barnes idling in her SUV out front. We'd both pretended not to see each other. Inside the school's gates, the parents and nannies made small talk. Three women formed a circle several feet away, chatting. They looked like members of the same shiny-haired club: all wearing casual business clothes and a tasteful amount of makeup.

"No way!" one of them said as the other two threw their heads back, cackling with laughter.

I smiled toward them, but the women acted like they couldn't see me. A pang pierced my gut. I was an outsider here, standing alone. Lily had only been at the school for a few weeks, though. It hadn't been long enough to get to know anyone.

Maybe I could join a committee in the fall. I got the sense it would take some time to break into any of Shorewood's social circles, assuming I could do it at all.

The shrill ring of the bell cut through my thoughts. Thunder rumbled from somewhere off in the distance. Brakes squealed at the nearby intersection, followed by a car horn.

Alex appeared in the south doorway. The school released the higher grades first, and older kids streamed out of the building past him. It would take Lily another five minutes, at least, to gather her things together and come outside through the north entrance. I followed the pathway, swimming upstream against the tide of exiting preteens and teens.

Alex lifted his chin and smiled. "Fancy meeting you here."

My skin tingled at our proximity, the sound of his voice. "Did you have a good day?"

"Yeah. I spent most of it thinking about you." He waited for two students to pass, then stepped closer, his arm brushing against mine.

I savored the brief touch but leaned away in case anyone was watching. "I was thinking about you too. Maybe I'll see you later?"

"I'm staying late to do some grading, but I'll text you." He looked around, and I followed his gaze. Students scattered away from the school, no one paying attention to us. Alex reached over and grabbed my hand, giving it a squeeze.

His display of affection surprised me, but I couldn't wipe the smile from my face as I put my hand back to my side.

"Sorry." He shrugged. "I couldn't resist."

The little ones trickling out of the north entrance drew my eyes from him. "I'll see you. I have to get Lily."

He nodded as I stepped away. Lily traipsed through the far doorway wearing her pink backpack and carrying her lunch box. Marnie hopped along next to her.

I rushed to intercept my daughter, opening my arms wide. "Hi!"

"Hi, Mom." Lily hugged me, then looked at her friend. "Can I go over to Marnie's house one day soon? She said her mom doesn't mind."

"Um. I don't know." I shifted my weight, picturing the chatting groups of women who had no interest in introducing themselves. I wondered who Marnie's mom was and where they lived. Another boom of thunder sounded from the west, this time louder. The ominous sky crept closer.

Marnie peered up at me. "We live really close. I'm a walker, like Lily. We have a trampoline in our backyard."

"How fun!" I said, smiling down at her.

"Come on, Marnie. Let's go." A baby-faced woman with pink cropped hair and a denim jacket approached. She couldn't have been more than twenty.

Marnie motioned toward the young woman. "That's Amy. My nanny."

I said hello, and she nodded back.

Lily tugged my sleeve. "I wrote down your number for Marnie so her mom can text you."

"Okay." I'd made Lily memorize my phone number in case of emergency. But I could see the girls weren't leaving anything to chance, that they'd already taken the reins in arranging a playdate for themselves. My insecurities tunneled through me as I wondered if Marnie's mom would contact me, if she was friendly, if they lived in a mansion, and if I'd have to invite her into our smallish apartment for the second playdate. Regardless, Marnie seemed like a nice girl, and I was happy Lily had made a friend so quickly. I'd have to pack my social anxiety away in a box and suck it up for my daughter.

We said a brief goodbye to Marnie and her nanny and ventured around the fountain. The sky continued to darken, the storm threatening. I wished I'd thought to bring an umbrella.

Principal Brickman stood near the gate with a collapsed umbrella in his hand, chatting with students and parents as they left. He could have been a Hollywood actor with his booming voice, tailored suit, and glints of silver in his hair. I'd noticed the way the other moms treated him as if he were a celebrity. He spotted us, eyes creasing in the corners as he lifted his chin. "Rachel and Lily. Great to see you!"

"Hello."

"How's your third week going? Are you getting the hang of things?"

Lily nodded but didn't speak.

The principal tilted his head toward the south entrance, eyes shifting with something I couldn't identify. "I see you're getting to know Mr. Ballard."

I inhaled, looking over my shoulder to the spot where Alex had grabbed my hand. There was a clear view from this spot near the gate. *Had Principal Brickman seen us?* I could almost feel my stomach turning inside out. I tucked my hair behind my ear and rolled back my shoulders. "Yes. It turns out Alex lives right next door to us."

The principal glanced away, widening his stance. When he refocused on me, he wore a concerned expression. "Listen, Rachel. I know the transition to a new school, especially a school like Shorewood, can be tough. We're all a family here, which means we look out for one another." He paused, smoothing down his tie. "I'll introduce you to my wife, Whitney. And I'd like to treat you to a nice dinner out too. We can discuss Lily's future here, the school culture, and expectations. I'll help you fall in with the right people and you can ask me any questions you have."

"That's very kind of you. Thank you." I kept my voice steady and upbeat, although going out for dinner with the principal of Lily's new school was the last thing I felt like doing, and I didn't know what he meant about falling in with the right people. I hadn't been aware there were wrong people at Shorewood.

He thrust his umbrella toward me. "Here. Take my umbrella. You two better be on your way before this storm hits."

"That's okay. I should have brought my own."

He pushed the umbrella closer. "Please, Rachel. I insist. You have a long walk, and I only have to make it to the parking lot. We don't want Lily getting soaked and catching a cold." He winked at her.

I thanked him and took the umbrella.

A gust of wind blew the man's tie across his body. "I'll be in touch to find a good time for the dinner."

"Thank you." I nodded, keeping one eye on the angry sky, which looked like it was about to open up. "It's moving fast. We should go." I grabbed Lily's hand and double-timed it along the sidewalk, the wind chasing our backs. The principal didn't lack for people skills. He had a knack for small talk, maybe overly so. But something about his dinner invitation felt forced and awkward. *Why had he asked me to dinner and not to a meeting in his office during school hours? Was that the protocol at private schools?* I couldn't tell if the man was merely being helpful or if his intentions were somewhat more calculated, and I suddenly wondered if he'd just asked me out on a date. I remembered how Principal Brickman had touched my back on Lily's first day, and I felt sick.

"Is it going to rain on us?" Lily lagged a half-step behind, head tilted toward the sky.

"I hope not." I focused on my footsteps, leaping over a sewer grate and reframing the situation in my mind. Maybe the invitation to a welcome dinner was just that and nothing more. Thanks to Mom, I'd developed a habit of attributing the worst possible intentions to people. Ben Brickman was married. He'd just mentioned his wife again and had even told me about his summer travel plans with her. He'd selected Lily for the Bright

Paths scholarship, and I didn't want to appear ungrateful. A free private school education through twelfth grade wasn't something I'd risk Lily losing. The other afternoon, I'd overheard some parents heralding the principal as a top-notch educator who regularly got Shorewood's students into schools like Stanford and Harvard. An awkward dinner out with him and his wife was a small price to pay.

Lightning splintered overhead, followed by a boom of thunder. The sky opened, unleashing a torrent of rain. I opened the borrowed umbrella and grabbed Lily's hand. Then we ran.

FOURTEEN

At 4:15 p.m. on Friday, Amy, the nanny, led us to Marnie's house. I followed the young woman and the girls three city blocks past storefronts, restaurants, and cafés, until we turned south on Mohawk Street. This block was a residential, tree-lined street lined with massive homes, occasional apartments, and a few remaining smaller homes that sagged with age and sadness like they were waiting to be demolished and rebuilt. It had rained for nearly two days straight, and it was a relief to feel the sun on my face again, to blink against the light filtering through the budding trees.

"What a beautiful street," I said.

"Yeah." Amy dipped her chin, looking at her phone as she walked. Her habitual phone-checking bordered on rude.

I kept my eyes on Lily as we continued. I wasn't entirely sure what the playdate protocol was in the city, but I didn't feel comfortable sending Lily off to someone's house without meeting them first. "Will Marnie's mom be home?" I asked.

Amy glanced at me and nodded. "Yeah. Nicola will be there. I usually leave by 4:30. I watch Marnie's brother, Bryce, all day. He's two."

With the girls skipping in front of us, I followed the young woman's path for another half-block, no longer feeling like I was in the city but in a leafy suburban oasis.

"Here we are." Marnie paused in front of a double lot, opening a wrought-iron gate. My eyes traveled up the front walkway, landing on a sleek and modern mansion. Bold sections of natural wood accented the cement facade. Rectangular windows stretched tall, drawing my eye to the structure's clean lines. I got the feeling I was approaching a piece of art rather than a home of a six-year-old.

"Let's play in the backyard first." Marnie ran toward the side of the house.

Lily glanced over her shoulder at me, a smile on her face. I nodded for her to go ahead, and she raced after her friend.

"You can head back with them," Amy said, trudging up the front steps. "I'll let Nicola know you're here."

"Thanks." I edged along the narrow path, following the sound of the girls' squeals and giggles as I turned the corner. Past a row of evergreens that blocked the view from outside eyes, the walkway opened into an expansive backyard. Toddler toys were scattered across lush grass. A natural stone patio with a built-in outdoor kitchen stretched from the back of the house. The girls had already dropped their backpacks onto a lounge chair. Now they jumped up and down on a trampoline, their faces pink with laughter.

I hovered on the patio, finding satisfaction in their glee. I hoped the next two hours would pass quickly and Lily would have fun with her friend. Hopefully, introducing my daughter to this luxurious lifestyle wouldn't backfire. I didn't want her to wonder why her friend had this massive house, this fun yard, while she lived in a cramped two-bedroom apartment. If only I'd made different decisions.

I wiped my palms on my pants, scolding myself for thinking like Mom, knowing that kind of mindset wasn't productive. If

I'd made any different decisions, I wouldn't have Lily, and that was a dark alley I wasn't willing to navigate.

A sliding door opened. I turned to find a woman about my age smiling at me. She wore ripped jeans, and her shiny black ponytail hung through a hole in the back of her baseball cap. Her face was free of makeup, but she had a natural beauty about her. A pudgy toddler with the same inky hair wobbled next to her. The woman closed the door behind her and stepped toward me, reaching her slender arm forward. "Hi, Rachel. I'm Nicola. I'm so glad this playdate worked out."

"Hi. Yes. Me too." I shook her hand. "Thank you for the invitation."

"Marnie is so excited to have made a new friend."

"Lily, too. Marnie has made starting a new school so much easier for her."

Nicola directed her son to a Big Wheel as she asked me about myself – my job, our apartment, where we'd moved from, and how we liked the school so far. She nodded along, genuinely interested and asking occasional questions. She told me about her husband, who worked for the Board of Trade, and her position in fundraising for the Natural History Museum, and how she was lucky to work from home most days, but that balancing her career and two young kids was taking a toll. The conversation was easy. Nicola was down-to-earth and relatable, much more approachable than some of the other Shorewood moms I'd encountered.

Nicola peered at me from beneath the brim of her hat as she replaced the rock in Bryce's little hand with a toy car. "Is there a reason Lily has started at Shorewood so late in the year?"

"Yes." I swallowed, debating how much to share. Nicola had been so open and understanding. She didn't seem like the spiteful type, so I told her the truth. "My husband and I recently got divorced. Lily was awarded the Bright Paths scholarship. Principal Brickman said it might be easier if she got a taste of the school this year, so she'd be familiar when she starts first grade." I leaned back, waiting for Nicola's reaction.

"Lily got the Bright Paths scholarship?" Nicola cocked her head, face unreadable.

"Yeah."

The woman tipped her head back, clasping her hands together. "That's wonderful. I wish the school would award more of those. Lily must be a star."

"We're just so thankful for the opportunity."

"Have you looked into any day camps for Lily for this summer? Marnie is doing three weeks at the nature museum and another theater camp. They might still have some openings."

"Oh. I'm not sure." I wanted to schedule fun activities for Lily for the summer, but I worried about the cost of the camps. I had little left over after paying our rent and grocery bill. "I'll look into it."

"I'll send you the links. There are scholarships available, I'm sure."

I dipped my head, thankful for the information.

Marnie and Lily had left the trampoline and headed toward us. "Mommy, can we have a snack?" Marnie asked. "And can I show Lily my room?"

"Yes. Give me a minute." The other mom glanced at her phone then scooped Bryce into her arms, facing me. "It's been great talking to you, Rachel, but don't feel like you have to hang around. You can run an errand or go for a walk and come back in an hour. I mean, assuming you and Lily feel comfortable with that?"

Lily stood next to me, tapping my arm. "I'm fine with that."

A warm breeze brushed past my face and rustled the tree branches. Other than walking Lily to and from school, I'd been inside my apartment all day. It would be refreshing to take a walk, get some exercise, and enjoy the day.

"Are you sure?" I asked Nicola.

"Of course."

"I'd love to walk around for a bit. If you don't mind, I'll come back to pick up Lily in an hour."

"That's perfect. We'll see you then."

"Thank you so much." I exited along the narrow path and strolled down the sidewalk, admiring the historic homes interspersed with new builds. Even the condo buildings on this block featured inviting courtyards and attractive architectural features. On the opposite side of the street, a homeless man pushed a grocery cart rattling with a pile of aluminum cans. He was wearing too many layers of clothes for such a warm day, his face glistening with layers of sweat and dust. The contrast of the dirty, tattered man against the backdrop of the well-kept mansions disarmed me, and I had to look away.

I traveled to the end of the block, cutting five blocks to the west on Armitage, then north again, and back east along Dickens. I traveled past condos, parks, and storefronts, taking in the views, people-watching, and window shopping. I paused to admire a sleek dress displayed in the front window of a boutique and smiled at the writing on a woman's T-shirt as she entered a yoga studio— MINDFUL AS F*CK. I strolled past the Friday afternoon bustle, breathing in the sugary aroma of a cupcake shop and avoiding the steamy smells emanating from the sewer grates. The walk was awakening my senses.

But about twenty minutes into my stroll, a familiar object caught my eye. The sight of it caused me to freeze, and a jogger behind me narrowly missed running into my back. Someone had illegally parked a white pickup truck at the end of a row of parked cars. My feet refused to move, the cement seeming to harden around them. The truck was the same size and shape as Keith's vehicle.

I crept closer, hoping I was mistaken. But as I took a wider angle, the green words BELDEN LANDSCAPING leered at me.

My stomach convulsed. I scanned the surroundings as a terrorizing thought formed in my head. *What if Keith had followed Lily and me from the school to the playdate at Marnie's house?* Maybe he'd parked several blocks away so I wouldn't see his truck. I waited for traffic to clear and strode toward the vehicle, prepared to pound on the windows and scream at him. But the light shifted as I neared, and I could see that no one was inside.

I edged away, finding a nearby building and balancing my wobbling bones against the bricks. I checked my phone, hoping to find no distress cries from Nicola. There were no new messages. I wrote to Keith: *Why are you here? Stop following us!!! I will report you.*

I sent it, staring at the screen, heart pounding in my ears. There was no response for a minute or two as I supported my weight against the wall. Finally, a message popped up: *Jesus. Relax. I'm having a beer with an old friend. Maybe U R the one following me!*

I'd been holding a breath, but I let it go. *An old friend?* I tipped my head back, trying to come up with who that might be. Keith's small circle of friends all lived nearly an hour away in Addison. The only people he hung out with either worked in his landscaping business or were leftovers from high school who'd never ventured more than a few miles from home. In some cases, the two categories overlapped. There was no one in the city.

I drew in a few long breaths and re-entered the stream of people on the sidewalk. Curiosity got the better of me, and I approached a restaurant further up the block. A few outdoor tables lined the street with people sitting under red umbrellas and talking. Keith wasn't seated at any of them. I debated going inside but paused, rethinking my actions. This was exactly what he wanted, for me to seek him out, to get under my skin. I raised my chin and forced myself forward. I'd stick to my path by heading toward the lake and then looping back toward Nicola's gorgeous house to retrieve my daughter. Lily and I would follow a different route home to avoid any run-ins with Keith.

I continued on my way, covering another city block in record time. A different restaurant sat a few storefronts away. As I approached, the din of conversation and clinking glasses filtered through the air, competing with the rumbling motors of passing cars. An outdoor beer garden stretched from the side-walk back along the side of the restaurant. Potted plants and strings of white lights created an attractive and festive border around the space, and a melody from an acoustic guitar streamed through the speakers. I would have been delighted to stumble across the scene on any other day, imagining myself meeting a friend for a casual drink or taking Alex on a fun date. But now dread filled my mouth as the notes from the guitar thrummed in my ears. I couldn't stop myself from scanning the tables.

Keith sat three tables back and next to the wall. His back was to me, but I recognized him immediately. His square-shaped head, the cut of his hair, and his jerky movements were imprinted in my brain. Still, it wasn't my ex-husband sitting there in his green Belden Landscaping work shirt that caused me to lose my breath, to give me the sensation of falling down an elevator shaft. It was the combination of him and the woman leaning across from him: Liz Meyer-Barnes.

Her sunglasses shielded her eyes, but her blonde hair shimmered as she laughed, settling back into the severe angle of her chin-length cut. Her crimson lipstick popped against her silky white top as she spoke to him.

I held a gulp of air in my lungs as my mind reeled. *What was going on? What kind of trouble was Keith trying to cause?*

"Would you like to sit inside or out?" A teenage hostess stood next to me. I hadn't even noticed her approach.

My eyes flickered from the hostess back to Keith and Liz, and I forced myself to speak, "Oh, no. I'm meeting some friends." I nodded toward the table where Keith and Liz sat. "I see them over there."

She motioned toward the entry to the patio. "Go right ahead."

I could feel my jaw tightening as I strode toward them, anger simmering into a boil. Liz was the only person at Shorewood Academy with a direct connection to my past. I'd mentioned to Keith before we separated that Liz's stepson attended Shorewood. I was embarrassed now at the way I'd gushed over the photos on Liz's Facebook feed, believing the images were so authentic and perfect. Keith must have remembered what I'd shown him, or maybe Liz had contacted him after I told her about our divorce. The two had been an item in high school. Their lives had taken drastically different paths after Liz had escaped to college. But now they gazed at each other across the table and I recognized something reminiscent of that teenage, googly-eyed connection pulsing between them. Keith was either using Liz to sabotage our daughter's schooling or worm his way closer to Lily. Maybe both.

Liz finally noticed me when I was two paces away from their table. She straightened her shoulders and set down her glass as her smile disappeared.

"Rachel. I..." she stuttered, gesturing toward my ex-husband, "Keith told me he was in the area. We were just catching up."

The light and airy tone of her voice scraped at a raw nerve. But I ignored her, aiming my fiery stare at Keith as my hatred for the man intensified. "What are you doing?"

He shook his head like I was the dumbest person in the world. "She just told you. Catching up. Nice to see you too, Rachel."

"I don't know why you're really here." I spoke through clenched teeth. "But don't you dare do anything to make Lily's transition to her new school more difficult than it already is. She has a once-in-a-lifetime opportunity at Shorewood, and I'm not going to let you ruin it."

Keith held his palms in the air. "I'm not ruining anything. I'm trying to find out information about my daughter's life because you won't tell me anything. I contacted *my friend* because her stepson goes to Shorewood, and I only knew that because you cyberstalked her for so long."

Liz looked down at her unused silverware.

I ground my molars together, cheeks burning. "I didn't cyberstalk anyone."

When Liz looked up again, her face wore that same curious expression she'd given me when I first ran into her at Shorewood, like I was a circus freak she couldn't stop watching.

I jabbed my finger at Keith. "If I see you lurking anywhere around Lily or her school, I will call the police." I glared at Liz. "There's a court order in place, in case he didn't tell you."

Liz pursed her lips and shook her head. "Rachel, why don't you calm down? Keith wasn't bothering you. You texted him and showed up here. I've witnessed the whole thing."

I huffed out a breath of disbelief. The golden liquid in Keith's beer mug glistened, taunting me. I fought the urge to pick up the glass and splash the beer in his face. I bet my charming ex-husband hadn't told his old girlfriend that he was a wife beater, that he'd shoved his daughter down cement steps, spraining her wrist. It would feel so good to scream the truth to everyone sitting in the beer garden. But Liz couldn't be trusted with that kind of information. She was the kind of female who possessed that strange combination of entitlement and insecurity, a person who smiled and complimented another woman's shoes as she stabbed her in the back. Surely, Liz would blab a juicy piece of gossip about domestic violence to the other parents at Shorewood, where the story would spread like a virus from one household to another. Except Lily would be the only victim.

I closed my eyes and opened them again, grounding myself and feeling the weight of my body sink into my feet as I pulled in a breath and held it in my lungs. *Mindful as f*ck.* This time I fastened my eyes on Liz. "You shouldn't believe a word he says. Keith is a narcissist and a liar. Don't let him fool you."

Before she could respond, I turned and strode back through the patio and out to the sidewalk. My arms stayed close to my body, my feet moving in double-time toward Nicola's house as a singular goal hardened in my mind.

I needed to keep my daughter away from Keith and get her safely back inside our apartment.

FIFTEEN

I could feel the bones inside Lily's fingers and realized I was squeezing her hand too hard. She'd glanced at me a few times during our hurried walk along the lakeshore path, a sheen of confusion in her eyes, a series of questions flowing from her lips about the changed route, about whether I liked Marnie's mom, and Marnie's house. I made no mention of her father. I forced myself to stay engaged and positive and not dwell on the encounter with Keith and Liz. My fingers finally loosened their grip as we entered the lobby of 420 Roslyn Place.

Bridget stood in her athletic clothes talking to Henry but smiled when she spotted us. "Hi, guys. I'm heading out for a run. I'll catch up with you later."

"Sounds good," I said, as Bridget positioned her earbuds and scooted out the door.

Henry tipped his head. "Good evening, ladies. I'm glad to see you've been out enjoying the weather."

Lily pulled her hand away from me and did a little hop. "I was at my friend Marnie's house."

"Well, that sounds like fun." Henry's smile faltered as he

turned his attention from Lily to me, adjusting his glasses. "Rachel, may I talk to you in private. Just for a second."

"Sure." The serious tone of his voice gave me pause. I touched Lily's shoulder. "Can you go look out the window for a minute? See if you can spot any cute dogs."

Lily nodded and scooted over to the front window as I stepped closer to Henry's post behind the counter.

The doorman's gaze followed Lily, then returned to me. "I don't mean to alarm you, but I saw your ex-husband out in front of the building about two or three hours ago. I buzzed up to you, but you weren't home."

"Did he come inside the lobby?"

"No. He stayed inside his pickup truck. It said *Belden Landscaping* on the side. That's how I noticed him, at first. He stared at the front door for about fifteen or twenty minutes and then drove away. I'm sure it's nothing to worry about, but given what you told me the other day, I thought I should let you know."

"Yes. I appreciate that. Thank you for keeping such a close lookout." This new information confirmed my suspicion, igniting a fresh flame of anger inside me. Keith had been seeking us out before he met Liz in the beer garden.

Henry dipped his chin, revealing thinning white hair on top of his head and his shiny scalp beneath. "I've alerted Robbie and the other part-time doorman to the situation as well. And I've left another reminder here." He held up a piece of yellow paper with red writing.

Be on the lookout for a white pickup truck with Belden Landscaping on the side. Do not let Keith Belden into the building. Alert 4B (Rachel Gleason) if you encounter him.

I nodded at Henry, grateful. "Thank you. It's a relief to know Keith won't get through this lobby."

Henry lifted his chin. "Not if I have anything to say about it."

I called Lily over, and she told me about two dogs who had walked past with their owners. Henry buzzed us through to the elevator, wishing us a good evening. I glanced back at the doorman, thankful he took his job so seriously. But Henry was sixty-two. He'd told me so the other day. Although he appeared fit, his aging body was no match for Keith's brute strength. If Keith was determined to get past the barrier in the lobby, I doubted Henry could stop him.

Three hours later, Lily was freshly bathed, wearing her jammies, and listening to music on her headphones as she worked on an art project at the kitchen table. Alex sat next to me on the couch. We'd hung out for a few minutes on Monday night after Lily had gone to bed, but other than that, we hadn't seen each other much during the week because of Alex's work obligations, marathon training, and volunteer work. Now, with Lily absorbed in her music and art project in the next room, he pressed his leg into mine as we watched a documentary about a Canadian traveler who'd mysteriously vanished from a sordid hotel in Los Angeles. We gasped at the creepy elevator footage containing the last sighting of the young woman and took wild guesses as to what happened to her. I couldn't help thinking about Annie Turner and the way she'd also disappeared without anyone seeing her leave.

At 9 p.m., I paused the show and enforced Lily's weekend bedtime, reading her a book, turning on her white noise machine, and tucking her into bed. When I returned to Alex on the couch, the worries I'd been holding inside spilled out. I described the events I hadn't wanted Lily to overhear: the encounter with Keith and Liz at the beer garden, and Henry's sighting of Keith outside the building earlier in the day.

Alex tilted his head. "So, your ex and Liz Meyer-Barnes were friends in high school?"

"It's hard to believe now, but Keith used to be a bigshot on the football team. Liz was in the popular crowd. They were briefly a couple. I never thought too much about it." I bit down on my lip.

"Her stepson, Davis, was in my class last year. He was a good kid, but Liz was never my favorite. A couple of times, she stopped by my classroom unannounced to complain about the curriculum." He made a face like he'd stepped too close to a dumpster. "A little too self-important for my taste."

"Liz was never a close friend of mine." I pulled in a breath, memories from my high school days uncomfortable to revisit.

Alex leaned toward me; eyes tinted with concern. "I'm sorry you had to deal with all of that today. Your ex-husband sounds like a jerk."

"He is a violent, narcissistic piece of shit." I sucked in a breath of courage and revealed a few stories of the abuse I'd suffered at the hands of my ex, how things escalated toward the end, how he'd injured Lily, and how the judge in our divorce proceedings had, thankfully, believed me and only granted Keith one supervised visit with Lily per month once he'd completed a domestic violence awareness course. "Keith doesn't care about Lily. He's only angry because he lost."

Alex released a breath, shaking his head. "That's what it sounds like. But after hearing all that, I'm even more impressed with you now. You're so strong. So courageous." He touched my hair.

I remained still. "So, I hope you can understand why, after everything Lily and I have been through, I need to take things slowly between us."

"Of course, I understand." Alex stared at me, his face softening. "We don't have to rush anything. I'm sorry if that's how it felt to you."

I could feel my troubles falling away, my cheeks blushing as I gazed at Alex. Opening up to him was easy. "I'm still worried Keith will get to us somehow. Either in this apartment or at school."

"I'm not going to let that asshole get anywhere near you. Or Lily, for that matter." Alex's hand was on my leg, his fingers massaging my knee through my jeans. "Can I stay with you tonight?" He lifted his hand and motioned between us. "We don't have to *do* anything. I'll sleep on the couch, and I'll leave before Lily wakes up in the morning. I don't want you to worry anymore. I want you to feel safe."

Although I'd promised myself I wouldn't rush into a new relationship, I couldn't help feeling there was something different about Alex. I *did* feel safe around him. On top of the physical attraction, I enjoyed his company. Every time I peeled back another layer of his personality, I discovered something about him I admired even more. The process had been exactly the opposite with Keith. Where Keith had insulted and disap-pointed me, Alex delighted and lifted me up. "I would like for you to stay on the couch tonight if you don't mind." I smiled at him, and we kissed. His body pressed against mine, solid and pulsing, our heat melding.

Then, stopping himself, he pulled away and held my hand, giving me a wink. "For a second, I forgot we were taking it slowly."

I giggled and leaned into Alex, my attraction for him growing even as we pumped the brakes on our physical relation-ship. I was happy he was staying the night, watching over Lily and me from the living room.

* * *

The following week passed with Alex and I hanging out whenever possible, sharing stories from our day, or anecdotes from our childhoods. I'd only known him for a month, but it seemed we'd known each other much longer. Physically, we hadn't gone much further than kissing and lying next to each other on the couch, but the thrill of new love spun through me, the possibility of a healthy relationship distracting me from everything that didn't involve him. We'd spent most of the weekend together, Alex ordering pizza for the three of us on Friday night and treating Lily and me to a day at the Chicago Art Institute on Saturday. He slept on the couch some nights or went back to his place when he had running the next morning. We shared our hopes for the future with each other, excited to find more and more things we had in common. I was proud of myself for taking it slowly with Alex. Our connection felt rare, not something I'd toss aside just because Keith had scarred me. I no longer feared I was merely a rebound relationship for Alex or vice versa. Lily was still enjoying her new school, and there'd been no additional sightings of Keith—or Liz—since I'd spotted them in the beer garden.

So, there was a spring in my step the following Wednesday morning when I returned to the building on Roslyn Place after dropping Lily at Shorewood, ready to complete my tasks for the insurance company as quickly as possible. Henry greeted me and buzzed me through the glass barrier. Realizing I hadn't checked my mail the day before, I stopped at my mailbox, opening the tiny door, and pulling out a stack of catalogs and bills. I tucked the bundle under my arm and rode the elevator up with the Levys, who'd returned from a morning walk in matching black windbreakers. They asked after Lily before I exited on four and let myself into the apartment. I sat down, flipping through the papers as I waited for my laptop to fire up.

I tossed aside an ad for life insurance, uncovering a sky-blue envelope. The card's familiar shape and size sent a tremor across my skin. The address was handwritten, addressed to

Annie Turner, and, as before, the sender was Julia Turner in Australia.

I ripped it open, with no hesitation this time. My eyes swam over the blue ink.

> *Annie, where are you??? Please contact me! I called the police in Chicago, but they aren't doing anything. The school said you quit. I'm flying to the States as soon as I can. I'm so worried! Jules xx*

The paper shook as I held it closer to my face, rereading Julia's pleas. I'd told myself Annie was either traveling through Europe or was already back in Australia, that the first letter had crossed paths with her, and that she'd skipped town so mysteriously to avoid paying her remaining rent. But now I knew Annie still hadn't been in touch with whoever this relative was in Australia. I pulled my stunned gaze from the letter, my eyes traveling around the apartment, willing the walls to speak. I had no proof, but a dark knowing weighed in my gut. The security camera cord looped around the edge of the ceiling like a noose, the sight of it strangling my breath. I couldn't shake the feeling that Annie Turner was dead.

SIXTEEN

I pulled the keyboard closer, fingers tumbling over the keys. A search for *Jules Turner Melbourne Australia* turned up hundreds of results, myriad faces of various ages and colors smiling back at me. I tried *Julia,* instead, retrieving even more results. Most of the links connected to business accounts on LinkedIn, professional articles, and personal Facebook profiles. I scrolled through them, hoping something would jump out at me, but I had no idea which of these Julia Turners had sent the two envelopes from the other side of the world. Whether Julia was Annie's sister or some other relative, I didn't know for sure. I tried a different angle, typing in *Annie Turner Melbourne Australia.* This search resulted in even more hits, including Annas, Annes, and Annabelles. Turner was among the most common of surnames.

I leaned toward the screen, studying every entry as I scrolled, discounting each one for one reason or another. On page three, my eyes hovered over the image of a woman who looked to be in her mid-twenties—long, cornsilk hair, symmetrical features, a determined gleam in her hazel eyes. It was a Facebook profile for Annie Turner, hometown Melbourne,

Australia. It wasn't the woman herself who looked familiar, but the background image that drew my eyes inches from the screen. A second photo stretched out behind the woman's smiling head: the Chicago skyline. There was no mistaking the spires of the Hancock Building to the north and Willis Tower to the south; the angled, mirrored face of the Diamond Building; and the giant Ferris wheel adorning the touristy Navy Pier peninsula. The woman in the Facebook profile had to be the same Annie Turner from Melbourne who'd lived in my apartment.

I clicked into the profile, expecting more information, praying for a recent update about Annie's travels in Europe. I hoped to discover she had settled into a new apartment in Paris or Madrid, or to find that she had gone sightseeing in Iceland. But Annie's posts weren't visible to the public. She must have used her privacy settings so only her friends could see her information.

I clicked around for a minute, getting nowhere. The "Send a Friend Request" button hovered below Annie's name. We had zero mutual friends, but I sent the request, unsure if the woman would accept an invitation from someone she'd never met. But if she did, it would mean she was still alive. My mind would finally be at ease.

Tucking Julia's second letter next to the first one inside my desk drawer, I exited Facebook and returned to my login page with the insurance company. It was time to pull myself together and get some work done. But as I reviewed the first claim, my eyes flickered from the screen to the front window and the walls. My mind wandered to what this apartment might have looked like six or eight weeks earlier when Annie lived here. What pictures had she hung on the walls? Had she used the second bedroom for storage? Or to work out? How had she removed her things without anyone seeing? Surely, Annie would have had a couple of large suitcases with her, at the least.

Maybe even a trunk. Forty-five minutes passed before I realized I hadn't accomplished anything.

I tipped my head back, exasperated. The chair legs scraped across the wooden floor as I stood. I silently berated myself for being nosy, obsessed with someone I'd never met. I remembered the way I'd pored over the posts from Liz Meyer-Barnes on Facebook. Keith had gone out of his way to embarrass me by telling Liz about my infatuation with images of her seemingly perfect life in the city. I couldn't help wondering if my compulsion to study other people's lives was some sort of defect in my personality. I swiped my keys from the counter and headed down to the lobby.

Henry stood at his post, signing for a package from a FedEx worker. As the delivery man walked away, I approached the counter. Henry's eyebrows lifted above his watery eyes. "Good morning, Rachel. Heading out again?"

"No." I shoved my hands in my pockets and looked out the window. "I don't know if you have a minute, but I was just wondering about something and thought you might have some information."

The man's posture straightened. "Sure. How can I help?"

"Did you know the woman who lived in apartment 4B before me? Annie Turner."

"Well, yes. I met her a few times. She was Australian. Always coming and going. Very friendly." He looked down and tightened his lips. "It wasn't right what she did to Oliver, though. He was upset. And rightly so."

"You mean, breaking her lease?"

He nodded. "Annie didn't give him any notice at all. Oliver and his wife were about to leave for their house in California. They live out in wine country a few months out of the year. Anyway, he didn't want to take too long to find someone responsible to rent the place. But I suppose you already know this story. That's why you got such a good deal." Henry shrugged, a sheepish look on his face. "Oliver told me he dropped the price."

"Yeah. I lucked out. My realtor contacted Oliver after I called Lily's school. Annie used to work there and one of her co-workers told me she broke her lease and gave me the address." I paced to the other end of the counter. "But did you actually see Annie move out? You or one of the other doormen?"

Henry looked toward the elevator. "No. I can't say I did now that you mention it. But Robbie works a lot of the night shifts." He shook his head. "I don't even know exactly which night Annie left. It was like she vanished into thin air. Oliver only realized his tenant was gone when she wasn't home to open the doors for the worker he hired to re-caulk the windows. Annie had promised she'd be home to let the guy inside, but she wasn't. Oliver called her with a reminder—or several—but she didn't respond. Finally, he rescheduled with the worker and came over the following day to open the door for him. Anyway, when Oliver came back down to the lobby, he told me Annie had removed all of her clothes and personal items but left some pots and pans in the kitchen and a couple of rugs. He couldn't believe she'd skipped town like that."

"What happened to her stuff?"

"Oliver donated the items to charity. That was sometime in late March. Maybe March 26th or so. He never received the remaining months of rent from her either."

I laced my fingers together, thinking. Of course, if Annie had run away to Europe, she wouldn't have had room in her suitcase for cookware and rugs. "Are there security cameras in the elevators?"

"Yes. In this main one here." Henry pointed beyond the glass door.

"Is there any chance I can see the footage from around the time she moved out?"

Henry frowned. "I'm afraid not. We have an old system on

a hard drive. It gets recorded over every two weeks. And if Annie left out of the freight elevator, there wouldn't have been any footage at all."

"Why is that?"

"There aren't any cameras in the freight elevator."

I looked at my hands, stomach sinking. I was no closer to finding out the truth.

"Why are you so concerned about Annie?"

"Oh." I thought of the letters I'd illegally opened and Alex's assurances that Annie was on a secret trip to Europe. "It's nothing. I was just curious." I pressed my weight into my heels, deciding to dig for a different kind of information. "Do you happen to know if Annie and Alex were romantically involved?"

"Oh, boy." Henry held up his hands, chuckling. "I might have had a hunch, but I'm going to plead the fifth on that one. You'll have to ask Alex yourself."

I bit my lip and looked away.

"Rachel." Henry's voice was softer now, concerned. "I don't want to overstep my bounds, but a bit of advice, if I may?"

I nodded.

"I've seen you with Alex these last couple of weeks, coming and going. It's impossible not to notice how happy you look together. Like I always tell my daughter, don't make trouble where there isn't any." Henry smiled and gave a friendly wink. "You know what I mean?"

"Yeah, Henry. I do know what you mean." Lily and I had been so fortunate to land here, and Alex was proving to be a terrific confidant, boyfriend, and even something of a father figure for Lily. I didn't know why I kept trying to find problems or involve myself in other people's drama. Mom's face flickered in my mind, and I realized maybe I did know why I tended to see the worst in every situation. It was a habit she'd ingrained in me and one I was determined to break.

I thanked Henry and returned to my home office, immersing myself in insurance forms, descriptions of property damage, and estimates. It was almost a relief not to have to think about anything else.

Later that night, I clicked on a bookshelf I'd found on clearance and with free shipping. It would make the perfect addition to Lily's bedroom. Alex hovered in front of the stove, stirring vegetables in a soy-ginger sauce and cooking a pot of rice. "This stir-fry is one of my signature dishes." He looked over his shoulder and grinned. "I think even Lily will like it."

Lily was stoic, sitting at the table and writing out new words she'd learned at school. "I don't like broccoli."

"You can't even taste it." He removed his focus from the sizzling pan long enough to make a face at Lily. "How about I load you up with crispy tofu, peppers, green beans, water chestnuts, and carrots? I won't put any broccoli on your plate."

A smile cracked Lily's stone face. "Okay."

I leaned back in my chair, impressed not only that Alex had insisted on cooking dinner for us but that he could convince Lily to eat any vegetables at all. He was so health-conscious, always thinking about how his diet would affect his training and running times. I already felt his positive influence rubbing off on us.

But the discovery of the second letter from Julia weighed inside me as we ate. As soon as we finished eating and Lily ventured into her bedroom to play with her dollhouse, I pulled Alex over to the couch. "I have to tell you something."

"What is it? Not Keith again?"

"No. Another letter from Julia Turner arrived today. She still hasn't heard from Annie." I was already halfway across the room, opening the desk drawer. I slid the card from its hiding place and handed it to Alex, watching as he read it.

"Huh." He swallowed, studying the paper. "You know, you really shouldn't be opening these." Alex's voice sounded different, almost threatening. Under the harsh ceiling light, his skin was paler. I stopped breathing because, for a moment, he didn't look quite like himself. But the unsettling look passed just as quickly as it had appeared.

I angled myself toward him, hovering over the letter and ignoring his rebuke. "So, it seems like that first letter didn't simply cross paths with its recipient. This Julia person still hasn't heard from Annie."

Alex held up the envelope. "Yeah. But it's been two weeks since she mailed this one too. We don't know what's happened in the last fourteen days."

"But Julia was worried enough to contact the Chicago Police."

Alex sighed. "Rachel, this letter doesn't change anything. Annie is in Europe. She told Louise about her plans, swore her to secrecy. Also... to be honest, I got the feeling from Louise that Annie was being covert about her destination because she was running from something."

"Like what?"

"I have no idea. Responsibility? Maybe she decided Chicago wasn't quite what she thought it would be and bailed. Maybe she was embarrassed to tell her family that she failed at her mission, her book, or whatever."

"I found Annie on Facebook. I sent her a friend request." Alex peered at me, eyes bulging as if I'd just said something frightening. "Were *you* Facebook friends with her?" I asked. "We can check for updates."

He rubbed his forehead. "Nah. I don't even have a Facebook account anymore. I stay away from social media as much as possible."

"But you were friends with her. Right? In real life?"

"I'd say more like acquaintances. Neighbors." He lowered the letter and shifted his position.

"Don't these letters concern you at all?"

"Honestly, not really. It seems Annie didn't want the person who sent these letters to know where she was going. That doesn't mean Annie met some unfortunate end." He squeezed my hand. "Why are you asking so many questions about this? I thought we'd already moved on."

Henry's advice cycled through my mind: *Don't make trouble where there isn't any.* He was probably right.

"Yeah. I just wasn't expecting another letter to arrive. I hope Annie is okay."

"I'm sure she is." Alex rested his hand on my arm, fingers rubbing my skin.

We sat in silence for a minute before he spoke again. "You know, as much as I enjoyed cooking for you and Lily tonight, I'd love to take you on a real date. Without Lily. No offense to her, of course."

I chuckled. "That would be nice."

"How about Friday?"

"Oh, I can't. Remember that welcome dinner with Ben Brickman I told you about? We finally scheduled it for Friday. It's at Bistro Roma in Old Town."

Alex pulled back, his features suddenly rigid, the same ghostly expression he'd worn a few minutes earlier returning. "Watch out for Ben. He puts on a good show for all the parents, but he has a bad reputation around women, especially single women."

"Really?"

Alex sighed, tipping his head toward the ceiling. "I've heard rumors over the last two years. The guy is slick."

I thought of the way the principal had rubbed my back on the first day. Maybe I hadn't overreacted. But I shook my head.

"This dinner won't be like that. Ben's wife is going to be there too."

"Oh." Alex's body slackened. "That's good."

"I hate to ask this, but is there any chance you can hang out with Lily while I'm gone?"

"Of course. We can have an Uno marathon and eat some junk food."

"Thank you."

He glanced toward the window, then back at me. "How about you and I go out tomorrow then?"

I dropped my head. "I'm sorry. I already made plans with Bridget tomorrow night. She's going to the library with Lily and me. Then we might get ice cream afterward."

"Bridget?"

"Yeah. From upstairs? In 5B."

"Oh."

"Why? Don't you like her?"

Alex pressed his lips together, eyes downcast. "I don't really know her. She just seems a little—"

"What?"

"Never mind."

I nudged his arm. "What were you going to say?"

"I was going to say that she seems a little desperate."

"Desperate?"

"Yeah. Like some of my students who try a little too hard to get attention. But I realized that sounded harsh. I really don't know Bridget at all. She's probably a nice person. And I'm glad you're making other friends in the building."

I thought of my interactions with Bridget, her openness and razor-sharp honesty. "She's not desperate. I think she's just had bad luck with men recently. She welcomed me in immediately, and she's great with Lily. Did you know she's an attorney who helps wrongly accused people in her free time?"

Alex held up his hands. "See. That's why I stopped myself

from talking. I know nothing. You've already proved me wrong."
He smiled as he scrolled through his phone, pulling up his
calendar. "Okay. I'm not giving up on scheduling our date.
Saturday isn't great because I have my training on Sunday
morning. But I can take you out Sunday night?"

I nodded. "I'll ask Bridget if she can watch Lily on Sunday.
That will be fun. A nice dinner out."

"And Bridget can babysit. I like her better already. Do you
like Vietnamese food?"

"I have no idea. But I can't wait to find out."

Alex pulled me close and kissed my lips. I felt safe next to
him. The building was starting to feel like a community, people
greeting me in the elevator or the mailroom, making a big fuss
over Lily. Lily was already making friends at her new school. If
only I could get Annie out of my head. If only I could get Keith
to stay away from us. Then things would be perfect.

SEVENTEEN

At 7 p.m. on Thursday, long shadows stretched from the front window and across the hardwood floor, reaching toward Lily, who perched on the edge of the couch wearing her empty backpack. We'd have another hour or so of daylight before the sun plunged behind the urban skyline. I stepped into the living room, where the aroma of spaghetti sauce and the garlic bread I'd accidentally burnt filled the apartment. Breathing in shallow breaths, I pulled the door to my bedroom closed, taking a few steps to the side and clicking Lily's door shut too. I hoped sealing off our bedrooms would prevent any more of the odor from infiltrating our sleeping spaces.

Three knocks cracked at the door, and Lily ran toward the sound, opening the door. I grabbed my purse, noting that Bridget was right on time.

"Hi, guys!" Bridget stood in the entryway, her face clear and bright. She wore ripped jeans and a stylish jacket adorned with rows of angled zippers. "Ready for a night out on the town?"

I smirked. "It doesn't get much crazier than the library."

Bridget and I chuckled while Lily hopped out into the hallway. I locked the door behind us. As we rode the elevator down,

Bridget told us a story about her pompous boss only letting her bill five hours for the eight hours of work she'd done. She huffed out a breath and shook her head. "It's like three hours of my day didn't even count." She stopped herself and looked toward me. "Still better than my old firm, though."

We waved to Henry, who was chatting with the Levys as we left the lobby. Outside, the city greeted us with a cool breeze whipping off the lake and a symphony of noises—car motors grumbling, people talking loudly on their phones as they navigated the narrow sidewalks, live music pulsating through the open door of a nearby bar. Three blocks later, we'd landed at the bus stop where we boarded the number 74 bus, riding it west along Fullerton Avenue.

I stared in awe at my daughter's ease in navigating the bus ride, her posture straight and her chin held high as she climbed the steps, swiped her card, and found a seat near the window as if she'd done this a thousand times. Confidence radiated from her, so unlike myself at her age, and I realized I must have done something right. After several long and lurching minutes, we exited and followed Bridget past a row of buildings on the tree-lined streets of DePaul University's campus. Finally, we arrived at the Lincoln Park branch of the Chicago Library.

Bridget waved her arm. "Here we are. Now you know how to get here."

"Yay!" Lily's feet bounced as she slipped inside the front door. The room was high-ceilinged and brightly lit, smelling of paper and wood. Dozens of people, who I guessed to be college or graduate students, sat hunched over laptops at evenly spaced tables. Other than a few whispers, keys clacking, and someone who coughed twice, the place was eerily silent. I asked Bridget to lead Lily to the Children's section while I headed to the front desk to receive my library card.

As I filled out the form and handed it to a smiling woman with thick glasses, the smell of the library carried me back into my childhood, to the only safe place I'd known, a place where it was okay to dream, to want something better. In the spines of the books, I could envision thousands of possibilities laid out before me. I could retreat into the pages and escape Mom's rants, live other people's lives for an hour or two. Mom didn't like me reading in the house, said it "gave her the creeps" to see my head buried in a book all the time. But our barren backyard, although the size of a postage stamp, featured a single tree where I could rest my back and read when the weather allowed. And sometimes even when it didn't.

"Here you go." The woman behind the counter handed me a library card, her voice bringing me back to the present. I thanked her and located Lily and Bridget in the children's corner. Lily pinched her tongue between her teeth as she stacked a few books—spines aligned methodically—on a nearby table and then returned to the shelves

Bridget leaned in close, lowering her voice. "If you don't mind, I'm going to check out the non-fiction section. I'll be back in ten or fifteen."

"Sounds good."

I helped Lily select a few more books, then studied the posters on the walls as she flipped through her new treasures. An ad for a children's summer day camp at the library caught my eye. I pulled out my phone and looked up details on the website, finding the price nearly as outrageous as the camp Marnie's mom had told me about. Still, I saved the page to look up scholarship options later.

"Anyway, I work at a firm downtown if you ever have a question. I won't even charge you." An exaggerated laugh bubbled from Bridget's lips, cutting through the library's quiet.

I turned toward Bridget's voice, spotting her walking towards us next to a man with broad shoulders and a tangled mess of hair. She held out her business card to him.

He took the card, a strange smile twitching at his lips as if he wasn't sure whether he should be flattered or scared. "Thanks. Nice meeting you, but I've gotta run."

"Okay. See you later, Dan." Bridget faced me; her eyes lit up. "Did you see him?" she whispered. "He's totally hot."

"Do you know him from somewhere?"

"No. I just met him over in the photography section. I hope he calls me."

I pulled at my sleeve, unsure how to respond. Bridget's overtly flirty behavior didn't quite match my vision of her as a self-sufficient and professional single woman. I looked toward the books in Bridget's hand—one called *Urban Photography* and another called *American Criminal Justice Reform in the Twenty-First Century*. Her reading choices almost made me feel silly for the mystery novel I'd snagged from a nearby shelf while Lily occupied herself.

Alex's comment from yesterday forced its way through my head: *She seems kind of desperate.* I wondered if he'd noticed something about Bridget I hadn't. My new friend was intelligent, attractive, and driven, for sure. *But desperate?* I hadn't witnessed that until a minute ago. Then again, maybe if Alex had never said anything about Bridget being desperate, I wouldn't have thought twice about her interaction with a handsome stranger. She was single, after all, and fresh out of a relationship.

"Should we check our books out and go get some ice cream?" Bridget angled her face at me.

"Yes. Let's do that," I said, relieved to shift my focus. I told Lily to select her ten favorite books, which we took to the counter along with my mystery novel. Bridget checked out next to us.

By the time we stepped outside, night had descended. A streetlamp splashed a pool of light across the sidewalk, and windows glowed yellow up and down the street.

Bridget hiked her tiny backpack higher on her shoulder.

"There's a diner around the corner that serves really good ice cream and shakes."

Lily was all for it. We arrived a couple of minutes later, ordering at a counter and claiming a table near the back. Lily's feet kicked under the table as she slurped at her root-beer float and then removed an impossibly long spoon, licking off the whipped cream, her eyes shining with sheer delight. Bridget sucked on a straw poking from her caramel shake, then told me how her friend, Leo, had crashed at her place last night. "He left early this morning before I headed to work. I let him sleep on the couch once in a while when he's in a bind. I want to show him what he could have someday if he'd only finish school, that he still has a chance for a good future."

I gulped in a breath of air, which seemed to have expanded in my throat. While I admired Bridget's work with the Windy City Justice Project, it didn't seem wise letting a convicted criminal and someone who'd been accused—albeit, falsely—of murder sleep on her couch.

"But do you ever feel unsafe with him there? How much do you really know about him?"

Bridget lowered her gaze, grinning. "No. It's okay. Leo has made mistakes. I mean, he attempted to rob a liquor store at gunpoint when he was nineteen. But he never denied his involvement. He served his time and wants a different life. There's no way he did what they accused him of two years ago."

"What did they accuse him of?"

"Shooting a woman on the street over drugs. Leo didn't do it, and he doesn't sell drugs. Eyewitness accounts are notoriously unreliable." Bridget frowned, setting down her cardboard cup and crossing her arms in front of her. "The guy who ID'd Leo in the lineup had only seen the shooter in the dark from half a block away. I mean, come on. There's no way he could have seen anyone's face."

"Yeah. That's crazy."

"At least the judge agreed with me. Sometimes justice needs a little push in the right direction." She leaned toward me, tapping her nail on the table. "The truth is that Leo has been nothing but loyal and protective of me. I've never felt unsafe having him in my apartment."

"Oh. That's good." I shifted my chair, realizing Leo's presence in the building made me uneasy, even if Bridget had no qualms about it.

We changed topics, and Bridget raved about her favorite restaurants in the area.

I sat up at the mention of Vietnamese food. "Hey, that reminds me. Alex and I were hoping to go out for dinner on Sunday night. Are you still up for watching Lily for a few hours?"

"Yes. I'd love to. You can drop her at my place if that works. We can bake cookies." She winked at Lily, who burst into cheers.

Bridget must have noticed the unease on my face because she poked my arm. "Don't worry. Leo won't be there. He works at a pizza place on the South Side Thursday through Sunday."

"Okay," I said, feeling my muscles loosening.

"I'm so happy you and Alex are getting along. But you still need to do something for yourself. Remember?" Bridget crossed her arms and leaned back. "Tell me. What are you doing just for Rachel?"

I giggled and averted my eyes from her expectant stare. "What are you? A life coach?" I blinked, but she only tightened her eyes on me. "I don't have a lot of free time."

"I can watch Lily once or twice a week. You have no excuse." Bridget tilted her head, a mischievous twinkle in her eyes. "What have you always wanted to do but never had the chance?"

"I don't know. I'd like to learn more about art. It would be fun to work in a museum."

"That's easy. The Chicago Institute of Art offers painting classes."

"Well, I don't really want to paint, myself. I'd like to read more about other people's paintings."

"Okay, you can check out some art history books next time you're at the library." Bridget glanced at the ceiling, puffing out a breath. "Let's think of something more exciting."

I was about to tell Bridget there was nothing else I wanted to do when a vision galloped into my mind. First, it was the horses at The Farm in the Zoo, followed by memories of my classmate's horse show photos and Mom's ridiculing laughter when I asked if I could get a pony. I picked at my nail, confessing, "I've always wanted to learn how to ride a horse, like galloping and jumping. I just love horses—their big eyes and silky coats, the way they smell, the sound of their hooves..." I paused, my smile fading. "But I know it will never happen."

Bridget threw up her hand. "Why wouldn't it?"

"Too expensive, for one. And we live in the city."

My friend leaned forward. "I know of a place that gives riding lessons. It's in a suburb only twenty or thirty minutes north of here. One of my co-workers rides there every Sunday."

"You should do it, Mommy." Lily lifted her face from her root-beer float.

"I can't. Money is too tight. Besides, I don't have a car."

Bridget made a face as she fidgeted with her straw. "You don't even know how much it costs, and you can use my car. Or I'm sure Alex would let you borrow his."

"Alex doesn't have a car."

Bridget narrowed her eyes at me. "Well, I do."

"I'll think about it. Okay?" My answer seemed to satisfy Bridget, and she moved on to asking Lily about her school, prompting Lily to detail the best places to hide on Shorewood's playground during games of tag and hide-and-seek.

A man entered the diner and strode past us toward the

counter, where he placed an order for a chicken sandwich and onion rings. I wouldn't have noticed him at all except Bridget gasped at the sight of him, the whites of her eye showing like a frightened animal. She angled her chair away from the counter. "I have to go." Her voice was barely above a whisper.

"What?"

"I have to go. That guy." She tipped her head toward the man paying for his food. "We dated for a while. Things ended badly. I did some things I shouldn't have, you know, online."

I stared at her, wanting more information.

"They say revenge is the best medicine." She paused, "But sometimes it can backfire."

"Oh," I said, still not completely understanding.

"I'm sorry. Please forgive me, but I'm going to sneak out before he sees me." Bridget tucked a piece of hair behind her ear, hand quivering. The color had drained from her face. "Can you guys make your way back on your own?"

"Yeah. The 74 bus to Clark."

Bridget hesitated, eyes darting from me to the counter.

I waved her away. "It's fine. Go."

Bridget put her head down and scurried across the tiled floor like a mouse afraid of the light.

"Bye, Bridg—" Lily said, but stopped when I turned toward her, holding my index finger over my lips.

The man swiveled around, eyeing us. I smiled at him, struggling to act casual. He turned toward the door just as it closed, with Bridget darting into the night. Her cardboard cup remained on the table, dented and leaking. I wondered what she had done.

EIGHTEEN

Lily and I neared 420 Roslyn Place about half an hour after Bridget had dashed away from the man in the diner. Her sudden departure had left me feeling slightly off-balance. Or maybe that was merely caused by the backpack full of books straining my right shoulder and Lily yanking on my hand. As we approached the front double doors, I refocused on other things, like how beautiful our building looked at night, all lit up like a constellation. I stopped Lily, pointing at the lights lit within the buildings and apartments around us. There was the high-rise across the street, displaying a checkered pattern of gleaming windows. A squat greystone sat next door to our building, its solid walls flanked by two stone turrets, the mansion now divided into what I imagined were expensive townhomes. A few windows glowed warm and yellow inside.

I looked toward Lily. "Isn't our street beautiful at night?"

Lily's breath was heavy, her neck craned toward the night sky, and her round, pale face reflected like the moon. "Coo-ool." She stretched the word into two syllables, eyelashes blinking.

"So many different people following so many different

dreams." I gazed at the lights, imagining the stories all these strangers behind the windows were writing for themselves, the goals they'd set, the loves they'd found, the hardships they'd overcome. How many of their stories would have happy endings? I turned back to our building, which we viewed from the street corner. "There's our apartment." I pointed four floors above the lobby level to a darkened, three-paneled window, second from the left.

"I see it," Lily said.

Before I looked away, something shifted behind the windowpane, a vague outline moving from left to right. I rolled back on my heels, breath hitching in my throat as a car passed behind us. "Did you see something up there? In the window?"

Lily blinked, frowning. "No."

I stared at the opaque glass, finding no movement. Our living room window was quiet and still, nothing more than a darkened rectangle. My head swiveled over my shoulder as I searched the surroundings, then studied the exterior of our building again. The shifting shadow had passed in the same direction as our one-way street—east to west. "It must have been the headlights from the passing cars."

To the left, Alex's apartment glowed like a lit candle behind lowered shades. A floor above, Bridget's curtained front window was also aglow. I couldn't make out anything inside either one.

Lily tugged at my sleeve. "Can we go inside now?"

"Just a minute." Something inside me felt unsure about returning to the apartment. I wanted to breathe in the night air for a little while longer. "Let's look at the city lights for a second."

Lily stood patiently and gazed along with me at the sparkling lights against a black sky, pointing out stars and passing planes. When I'd taken it all in and centered myself, we walked back to the front door, entering the lobby.

Henry sat in his chair behind the counter, arms crossed and eyes closed. His head jerked up at the sound of the door, and I realized we'd caught him dozing.

"Welcome back," he said, pushing his glasses higher on his nose. He stood and smoothed down his shirt.

"Don't you ever go home?" I asked.

"Every once in a while." He chuckled. "Robbie is running late, so I'm covering for him." Henry ruffled a plastic bag behind the counter and held it up. "It's a good thing I'm still here because I wanted to make sure Lily got this." He handed her a paper shopping bag. "The Levys were at a toy store this evening and said they couldn't resist picking it up for you. They left it here for me to pass on when you returned."

Lily pulled out a stuffed animal about the size of a large house cat, except it looked like a cheetah, covered in spots and wearing a red collar. "Wow! It's so soft." She hugged the spotted toy to her face. "Thank you!"

Henry chuckled. "I'll tell them you liked it."

"We'll be sure to thank the Levys next time we see them. Right, Lily?"

Lily nodded, still entranced by the gift. We said goodnight as Henry buzzed us through the glass barrier to the elevator. When the doors opened on four, the sound of a growling dog greeted us. I flung my arm in front of Lily and peered down the hallway.

Our next-door neighbor, Marie, held Bingo on a tight leash. Her face held a pained look, her body straining with effort. Drake stood across from them, arms hanging at his sides, along with his oversized trench coat. Bingo growled and attempted to lunge toward the man with the spider face tattoo.

"Relax." Drake redirected his glare from the dog to Marie. "What's your dog's problem, anyway?"

"I'm sorry. He's not usually like this."

Drake huffed and darted past them, swerving to the right when he noticed us exiting the elevator. I gave him a curt nod, keeping Lily close as we passed his relentless stare. He stepped into the elevator, its doors faltering and closing.

We continued toward Marie, who wore a look of consternation. Bingo's rumblings transformed to playful jumping and a wagging tail as we approached.

"Bingo and Drake don't get along." Marie shook her head. "Every once in a while, my dog meets someone he doesn't like. Usually, there's no rhyme or reason to it, but Drake has a different vibe."

I raised my eyebrows. "I can't really blame your dog."

"He likes me." Lily held out her hand, and Bingo licked it several times before rolling over on his back to ask for a belly rub.

"He sure does. It must be something about your apartment. Bingo went nuts every time he saw Annie, the woman who lived here before you. We joked that she must have washed her clothes in chicken broth." Marie chuckled to herself, but the mention of Annie stoked my curiosity.

"Did you know Annie well?"

"Oh, no. Not really. Only in passing. She didn't live here very long."

"Did you happen to see Annie move out? It would have been sometime around March 26th. Maybe Bingo barked at something in the middle of the night?"

Marie shook her head. "Sheldon and I were at a ten-day conference in San Francisco the last week of March into early April. Bingo stayed with a friend in the suburbs. We must have missed her."

"Oh."

Marie twisted her lips to the side. "Why? Did Annie forget something?"

"No. I don't know." I hung my head, feeling silly for even asking. "I heard that some of Annie's family back in Australia were looking for her. I thought you might know where she went."

"I'm sorry. I have no idea." The woman pulled Bingo into a sit. "Alex might know. I saw him coming out of your apartment a couple of times when Annie lived there."

I swallowed back something hot and sour rising in my throat, possibly jealousy. "I already talked to Alex about it. He didn't see Annie leave either."

"Well, I bet it's nothing to worry about." Bingo pawed at Marie's leg. "I better get this guy outside. It was nice to see you."

"Thanks. You, too." I unlocked the apartment door as Lily yelled goodbye to the neighbor's dog.

We stepped inside, where the faint aroma of burned garlic bread still laced the air. I heaved the backpack full of books onto the floor, my shoulder aching and my stomach gurgling with the bowl of ice cream I'd eaten.

"Mommy, can we get a dog?"

I paused, looking down at Lily, her eyes glinting with hope. I remembered how Mom had ridiculed me when I'd asked for a pony, how it had felt like someone had stomped on my soul with a heeled boot. I crouched down next to my daughter, meeting her eyes. "Someday, I'd love to get a dog. That would be fun, wouldn't it?"

Lily nodded, mouth opening.

I touched her arm. "The thing is, it's a lot of responsibility. We'd have to take him for walks every few hours, even when it's cold and raining outside. And it costs money to take dogs to the vet. And we're still getting settled here. So now isn't the right time. But maybe, in a couple of years, we'll be in a better position to do that. I'd love to rescue a dog from the shelter."

"So would I."

"Let's save this dream for another day, okay? When it will be easier on us. Right now, you can play with Bingo."

"Okay." Lily bit her lip, and I could see her trying to hide her disappointment.

"Hey. I love you."

"I love you too." She wrapped her little arms around me and I rested my chin on her head.

"Go get your jammies on and brush your teeth. I'll read you one of your library books before bed."

Lily scampered toward her bedroom, winding her way around the couch. I stood up, glancing around the apartment. My arms dropped to my sides as I registered something amiss, a breath of terror prickling along the back of my neck. My bedroom door remained closed, just as I'd left it. But the door to Lily's bedroom, the one I'd pulled shut before we ventured out with Bridget to the library to prevent the odor of burnt garlic bread from permeating her sheets, was now slightly ajar. The movement I thought I'd glimpsed in the window a few minutes earlier shifted through my mind. Maybe someone *had* been inside here while we were out.

"Lily, wait!" I spun around, searching for an intruder hiding in a corner or behind the couch. But no one was there.

"What?" Lily looked at me, confused.

"Go out in the hallway for a minute. Leave the door open."

She followed my orders. Her movements were rushed as she scurried out into the hallway.

I thought back to our first night in the apartment, to the footsteps I'd thought I'd heard, the cupboard or drawer thumping shut, the beam of light swooping beneath the crack in the door, the unsecured top lock on the door to the hallway. *What if those events hadn't been in my head? What if someone had been in our apartment that night, and what if they'd returned?* I pulled out my phone and pressed 9-1. My finger hovered over the second 1 as I yanked the door to Lily's bedroom open and jumped back.

Lily's twin bed sat in shadows; a silhouette of toys lined up along the wall. I flipped on the light, relieved to find no one there. I checked the closet, then the one in my room, marched to the bathroom, and peeked behind the shower curtain. When I was satisfied that we were the only ones in the apartment, I called Lily back inside and double-locked the door.

"Why did I have to go out in the hallway?" Lily's lower lip stuck out as she peered around the apartment.

"Sorry. Mommy got scared for a second. I thought I closed our bedroom doors when we left earlier, but yours was open a little."

"Who opened it?"

"I don't know." I rubbed my forehead, wondering if I'd gone crazy, become over-the-top paranoid about Annie's disappearance. In my rush to leave, maybe I hadn't pulled both doors all the way shut. The last thing I wanted to do was scare Lily. "Maybe the latch isn't secure. Sometimes that happens, and doors fall open all by themselves."

"Oh." Lily peered into her bedroom. "Can I get ready for bed now?"

"Yes." I stood frozen in place as Lily entered her bedroom. I wondered why anyone would want to break into our apartment. My thoughts kept returning to Annie Turner, my eyes again finding the wire that once led to a security camera. With a sudden rush of adrenaline, I leaped toward the desk, pulling open the top drawer, finding both letters from Julia Turner exactly where I'd left them. I closed the drawer, dropping my head in my hands.

A thud sounded from above the ceiling, followed by creaking and the faint echo of Bridget's laughter. I wondered how long ago she'd returned, what she'd been doing, and how she could be laughing after the near-miss with her ex-boyfriend and her tension-filled exit from the diner. I pictured Bingo baring his teeth at Drake in the hallway and Drake's previous claim that he'd been friends with Annie. Had they been close enough that she'd given him a key to 4B? Had Drake been in here looking for something? I'd never asked Penelope if Oliver had changed the locks between tenants, but I guessed he hadn't wanted to add to his expenses by hiring a locksmith. Then there was Marie's observation that she'd seen Alex leaving Annie's apartment a few times—the same thing Drake had mentioned. But Alex hadn't mentioned anything about having a key. He had no reason to sneak in here because I let him inside whenever he liked.

Everyone in the building had been so friendly and welcoming. I didn't want to think the worst, especially of Alex, but there was Mom's voice again, eroding through my positivity like acid: *Watch out for people who are a little too friendly. It means they want something from you.*

I inhaled, exorcising Mom's poisonous mindset from my head. But just as I started to feel better, a more terrifying option tore through me, leaving an inescapable black hole in its place. I closed my eyes, seeing a flicker of Keith's face, his grotesque smile, his refusal to let me move on to a better life. I pictured the way Henry had been dozing off downstairs. Was it possible Keith had weaseled his way past the doorman, had figured out how to secure an extra key from the building? Or the owner? My eyes blinked at the thought. No. He couldn't have pulled that off.

A text beeped through on my phone. It was from Alex: *Did you have fun at the library? Want me to come over?*

I focused on the message, grateful for the distraction. Part of me did want to see Alex, but it was late, I was exhausted, and my stomach sloshed with undigested ice cream. I didn't feel like explaining my paranoia to him tonight, especially with zero evidence to back up my suspicion that someone else may have entered the apartment.

I wrote back: *It was fun, but Lily and I are tired. I'll see you tomorrow. Xx*

Ok. I missed you today. Sleep well.

I gave his message a heart and wandered toward the bathroom to brush my teeth. I read Lily a book and kissed her good night, turning on her sound machine and leaving her in the dark as she hugged her new cheetah stuffed animal to her chest. My body gravitated back toward the front door, eyes studying the two locks I'd already secured—top and bottom. I used separate keys to open them, so someone would need both to get inside.

A movie I'd seen years earlier surfaced from my memory. The main character feared someone had been entering her house while she was at work, so she placed a piece of paper in the crack. Hours later, she returned home through a different door and found the paper on the floor, confirming her fears.

I rummaged through my desk, retrieving a piece of white copy paper and cutting it into a narrow strip, which I then folded into a square and wedged in between the door and the frame at about knee height. The square fit snuggly, barely jiggling at all when I tried to move it. But if someone opened this door tonight, the paper would fall to the floor. A poor woman's security camera. Still, it was better than nothing, and I realized it was unlikely for an intruder to return again the same night.

Retrieving my phone, I located Oliver's email address and typed out a message.

Dear Oliver,

The apartment is great, but I'm concerned about my security, and I'd like a locksmith to replace the locks on our door

ASAP. Please let me know when you can have someone out.
Thank you.

Rachel Gleason

I powered off my phone and set it on the charger. I glanced again at the paper in the door as I turned off the lights and headed to bed. I'd try to get some sleep and check it in the morning.

NINETEEN

The square of paper had remained wedged between the door and the frame when I'd awoken early on Friday morning. The sight of the paper resting in the exact place I'd left it was a relief, along with a response from Oliver waiting in my email inbox.

Is there something wrong with the locks?

I wrote back, explaining that the locks worked fine, but I worried the previous tenant had given out too many keys and I didn't feel safe.

I'm in California, but I'll call around and try and find a locksmith, Oliver replied a few minutes later.

I turned toward my coffee maker, wondering exactly how long it would take him.

The rest of the day was spent shuffling Lily to and from school in between hours of reviewing claim forms and flinching at every noise that sounded beyond the walls of my apartment. Despite my nerves, the day passed uneventfully.

Now it was 6 p.m. Lily nibbled on a slice of pizza while I slipped into a simple black dress, adding a cardigan and a couple of understated pieces of jewelry. I assumed business-casual was the appropriate dress code for dinner with Shorewood's principal and his wife. I only hoped the dinner wouldn't be as awkward as I imagined, and that I could get through it without saying the wrong thing.

I moved to the bathroom, where I brushed my hair and freshened my makeup. A text beeped through on my phone. I raised the screen to my face, finding a message from Mom, one of the only ones she'd sent since we'd moved to the city: *Please get the rest of your stuff out of my basement this weekend. My house isn't your storage area. Let me know when you're coming.*

A breath of annoyance hissed from my mouth. I set the phone down, struggling to control my reaction. Mom was abrasive, always skipping the niceties and possessing the emotional warmth of a TSA worker. I should have expected this behavior by now, and I knew she was angry that I'd left my marriage and moved away, but her message stung like a slap. She hadn't bothered to ask how Lily and I were doing or how the new apartment was working out. The same painful realization always came hurtling back at me—Mom didn't care about us. She only cared about herself.

I picked up the phone and typed: *I don't have a car, but I'll see if I can borrow one. Lily and I are doing great BTW.*

"Bitch," I added under my breath but didn't write it. I could feel my relaxing weekend going up in flames, colliding with an endless traffic jam on I-290, followed by several more hurtful comments from Mom. I only hoped Bridget would let me borrow her car to make the trip. I texted her to ask for the favor, and she responded immediately.

You can have it on Sunday. It's a Honda Pilot with tons of miles on it, but you should be able to load lots of stuff in the back.

I thanked Bridget as several soft knocks sounded at the door. Lily opened the door for Alex, who entered, seemingly eager for his babysitting duties. His eyes landed on me, widening. "Wow. You look beautiful." He kissed my cheek. "I wish you were going out with me instead of the Brickmans."

"Yeah. Me, too."

Alex noticed Lily standing there and changed his tune. "But we're going to have tons of fun here. Aren't we, Lily? Your mom and I have our own dinner date on Sunday."

"Yeah." Lily held up a colorful deck of cards. "Do you want to play Uno?"

"Sure thing. Maybe we can watch a movie too." Alex held up a flattened bag. "I brought microwave popcorn."

"Yay! Popcorn."

"Lily ate already," I said, as Alex nodded along. "Bedtime is at nine, but hopefully I'll be home by then." I checked the time. "I better get going in case the bus is running late."

"Okay. I hope it's not too bad. Don't worry about us. We're fine."

"Bye, Mom." Lily hugged me.

I kissed her warm forehead and forced myself out the door, hearing the lock click behind me.

Fifteen minutes later, I approached the Italian restaurant in Old Town, daylight dwindling around me and sidewalks bustling with the weekend crowd. I entered the lobby, my eyes adjusting to a dim interior and walls that replicated a cavernous wine cellar. The space held the luscious aroma of garlic and basil simmering in olive oil. Ben was already there, standing by the wall across from the host stand and looking sharp in his freshly pressed shirt.

A smile spread across his face as he stepped forward, clasping my hands in his. "Rachel. I'm so glad this worked out."

"Yes. Me too." I looked around for Mrs. Brickman. "Is your wife at the table?"

"Oh. I'm so sorry. Whitney couldn't make it tonight after all. She gets terrible migraines once in a while. She sends her apologies."

"That's too bad." I looked away to hide my disappointment. "I hope she feels better soon."

"I'm sure she will." He squeezed my arm. "So, you're stuck with me."

A warning darted through me, as fleeting as a shadow drifting through a dark alley. I followed the young hostess, the principal's hand resting near my back as if he felt the need to guide me toward the table. His closeness was uncomfortable, and I stepped faster to escape it. I slid into a private booth in the corner of the restaurant, forcing a smile across the table.

"Have you eaten here before?" he asked as the hostess set down two menus and walked away.

"No. I haven't had a chance to try too many restaurants yet."

"This is one of my favorite spots." He glanced at his menu, thick cardstock with swirling black print, then refocused on me. A candle flickered between us, casting strange shadows across his face. "You look beautiful in that dress, by the way."

"Thank you." My mouth had gone dry at his inappropriate comment, my appetite vanished. I tried to come up with an excuse to leave, but I couldn't think of a way to do it without being obvious. A busboy traveled toward us, filling our water glasses. As soon as he left, Ben spoke again.

"I hope it wasn't too difficult to find arrangements for Lily tonight?"

"No. Alex Ballard lives next door as I mentioned the other day. He and Lily get along well."

The principal stared at me, eyes steely. "That's great." There was something artificial in his voice. I suspected the principal had witnessed the attraction between me and Alex, the way we smiled at each other and stood too close. I remembered what Alex had told me about Ben, about the rumors of him using his position of power to take advantage of women. I hoped that wasn't what was happening here. Ben had been nothing but kind to me, and I determined to form my own opinions and give him the benefit of the doubt.

I cleared my throat, getting the conversation on track. "Lily is really enjoying Shorewood. She's already made a good friend, and Ms. Lisle is a terrific teacher."

"That's wonderful to hear. The kindergarteners will be getting a visit from the Museum of Science and Industry next week. It's part of the 'Focus on Science' initiative."

"It's never too early to learn about science." I rambled on about a science experiment I remembered from elementary school, a volcano of baking soda erupting. My nerves had taken over, and I had no idea what I was saying. I stopped talking, clenched my teeth, and scanned through the menu, deciding on mushroom ravioli.

"Good evening, folks. Can I get you some drinks?" A scare-crow-like waiter peered down at us, an earnest look on his face, a notepad in hand.

"Yes," Ben spoke first. "Get my friend here a glass of wine." He looked at me. "Red or white?"

"White, please."

He motioned his thick hand toward me. "A glass of what-ever your best white is. And I'll have a Grey Goose martini on the rocks with two olives."

"Will do." The waiter dipped his head and hurried away.

The busboy returned, setting a basket of steaming bread on the table. I sat still, stunned. Even pig-headed Keith had never been so presumptuous to order for me as if I wasn't capable of thinking and speaking for myself. I pulled in a slow breath, reminding myself that Ben was a good fifteen to twenty years older than me, half a generation. Perhaps he'd missed the messages from the #MeToo movement and merely needed a refresher course on what was and wasn't appropriate in his interactions with women.

I tried, again, to steer the conversation in the direction I wanted it to go. "We're so grateful for the scholarship. I feel like Lily's future is limitless now."

"Well, it is. She'll have dozens of colleges and universities to choose from by the time she graduates. Shorewood opens doors for its students."

The conversation about Shorewood facilities, curriculum, and scholarships continued as our drinks arrived and we ordered our food. This time I spoke up before Ben could interrupt, "I'll have the mushroom ravioli, please."

A different server set down our drinks. Ben raised his glass, something hungry surfacing in his murky eyes. "To you, Rachel."

I lifted my wine glass. "And Lily," I added.

The food arrived a few minutes later. Ben dug into his lasagna Bolognese as I explained about the court order against Keith and how it limited his face-to-face interactions with Lily to one supervised visit per month. I pulled up a photo of Keith's face and truck on my phone to remind him to be on the lookout.

"Keith and Liz Meyer-Barnes were high school acquaintances. I don't think I told you that before. Anyway, they recently reconnected, and I'm worried she might let Keith sneak through the gates behind her."

Ben took another bite and swallowed. "Rachel, we're on top of it. Lily's teacher and Louise in the office have received the information and the photos. Everyone knows to only release Lily to you." He set down his utensils, reached across the table, and squeezed my hand. "You aren't the first Shorewood parent to have custody issues. We have protocols in place. Please, don't worry."

His words reassured me, but I didn't like the feeling of his palm weighing down my hand. I slid my hand away, changing the subject to Ben's wife, Whitney, and their summer travel plans. Ben mentioned Greece again, describing the crystal waters of the Greek isles, the white stucco houses, and detailing some sights they planned to visit. But he suddenly dropped his gaze, mouth flattening. "You know, to be totally honest, being married to the same person for so many years can become a little... tiresome. I can't help wondering how much more exciting it would be to travel with someone vibrant and full of life like you."

I nearly dropped my fork. "I'm sure your wife wouldn't appreciate that."

His smile was sideways, creepy. "I don't think she cares."

I balanced my fork on the edge of my plate, unsure what to say. "I'm sure that's not true."

"Can I bring you another round of drinks?" The waiter appeared next to us again, and I could have hugged him for disrupting the uncomfortable conversation.

"Yes," Ben said, eyeing my empty wine glass. "Another round."

Before I could disagree, the waiter was already gone.

I pressed my hands into the seat cushion, feeling trapped in the enclosed booth, like the room was spinning around me. "I'm going to run to the restroom for a minute. I'll be right back."

Ben nodded as I slipped away. I navigated between tables on my wobbly legs, finding my way to the women's bathroom back near the kitchen. Once I'd shut myself inside, I inhaled several long breaths and leaned against the wall, relieved to get away. I checked my phone, finding no new texts. I typed out a message to Alex: *Everything okay?*

A few seconds later, he responded: *All good! Watching Zootopia and eating popcorn. Are you coming back soon?*

Hopefully in 20-30 minutes.

Alex gave a thumbs up. I hadn't told him that Whitney Brickman hadn't shown up. Clearly, Whitney wasn't home in bed with a migraine. Ben probably hadn't even told her about this dinner. He'd duped us both. I washed my hands and found my way back to the table, hoping to end the night soon.

Ben was already well into his second drink. He nodded toward my wine. "Let's enjoy the evening."

I forced a friendly expression onto my face and took a tiny sip of wine.

"Rachel, I have a confession to make."

"You do?"

"Yes. I noticed you right away when I saw your application video, how pretty you were. I thought, that's the kind of woman I'd like to have at Shorewood."

I pinched the cloth napkin on my lap, momentarily stunned into silence. "Hopefully, that wasn't the only consideration," I hardened my voice. "Lily is a capable and smart little girl. She's been through a tough time and deserves the opportunity."

"Yes. Of course. I'm only saying, all things being equal, I wanted to give Lily the scholarship because of you." He rapped his knuckles on the tablecloth. "Nothing comes for free, but I'm sure you already know that."

This time I gulped a mouthful of alcohol, feeling it burn down my throat as Ben's words pinned me to my seat. "As I said, we're very grateful for the scholarship."

"You know, Rachel. We're both adults. We don't have to play games. There's a hotel right down the street. Let's head over there for a nightcap. It'll be more comfortable."

"I'm sorry. I have to pick up Lily soon."

He tapped a finger against his glass. "As long as Lily is with your next-door neighbor, I can walk you back to your apartment. We can be quiet, no one will ever know I was there."

I sat back, pressing my spine against the booth and wishing I could push myself through the rustic stone wall. "No."

"It could be fun. You and me."

"No. I don't... This isn't why I came here tonight."

The corner of his lip twitched. "You know, Lily's scholarship isn't guaranteed."

I could almost feel my temperature drop, my primal instincts to protect my daughter taking over as my fangs came out. "You wouldn't. I'll sue you. I'll tell the other parents."

He tilted his head. "That wouldn't be a smart move."

I glared at him.

"Lily's scholarship is conditional on my approval, plus the approval of a handful of people on the scholarship committee, all of whom I hold in the palm of my hand. Anyone turns on me, and I'll make sure their kid doesn't get into the university of their dreams. It's not pretty, but that's the way it works. My say is the last word." He lowered his gaze. "On the other hand, none of the parents or committee members have any allegiance to you." His eyebrows lifted. "Let's just cut loose and have a little fun. Like I said, no one will ever know."

My mouth went dry as I realized Ben Brickman played by a different set of rules, the kind of rules reserved for those with money and power. I lifted my chin, finding my voice. "Alex Ballard is my boyfriend. I won't cheat on him."

The principal's face changed, his features falling. "Ha. I was afraid you'd say that." The man rubbed his eyes. "Alex Ballard. What a catch. Surely you can do better than him."

I looked at my lap, cheeks burning.

"Has Alex told you what he's done?" Ben tipped his glass back and slurped his drink as he waited for me to respond.

I shook my head, confused. Whatever else this sleazy man wanted to tell me, I didn't care to hear it. "Thank you for dinner, but I need to get home to my daughter now." I slid to the edge of the booth and stood, avoiding eye contact.

Ben's gruff voice followed me as I turned away. "Listen to me, Rachel. I'll give you another chance because you're new here and I have your best interests at heart. I meant it when I said that Shorewood is like a family. And a quick internet search will tell you all you need to know about Alex."

I paused, eyeing him.

"When you get home, google 'Michael Ballard, Silver Meadows school district.'"

"Who's Michael Ballard?"

"Michael is Alex's real first name. Alex is his middle name."

"I don't understand." I rolled back on my heels. "Why?"

"You'll understand after you read the article. Then you can tell me what you think of your boyfriend."

With my purse pinned beneath my arm, I darted toward the door, having no idea what he was referring to. Still, nausea swirled in my stomach. Ben knew something about Alex that I didn't. Alex seemed too good to be true, and I wondered now if I'd been so charmed that I'd overlooked something, an obvious red flag. I hadn't even known his real name. I could almost hear Mom's voice chirping among the clinking glasses and scraping silverware as I rushed toward the exit: *Remember Rachel, the higher you climb, the harder you fall.*

TWENTY

I unlocked the door to 4B twenty minutes after escaping the Italian bistro and the advances of Ben Brickman. My blood pulsed through my body. I couldn't quell my nerves.

"Hi, Mommy!" Lily jumped up from the couch and hopped toward me. "We watched *Zootopia*. Alex said I could stay up until you got home."

"That sounds like fun." I checked my phone—it was five minutes after 9 p.m. I looked toward Alex, searching for something dark and mysterious in his eyes, a secret hiding behind his shiny pupils. But only a warm smile spread across his stubbled face.

"Lily, why don't you brush your teeth? I'll tuck you into bed in a couple of minutes."

"Okay." She scampered off.

Alex tilted his head. "You don't look happy. Everything okay?"

"Yeah." My response was automatic, a lie. Lily's scholarship to Shorewood suddenly felt fragile and breakable, completely dependent on how carefully I tread.

Alex patted the couch cushion, coaxing me to sit next to him. "I'm glad you survived. Was it horrible?"

"Kind of." I swallowed against my parched throat, lowering myself next to him. "Whitney didn't show up."

The smile faded from Alex's face, his black pupils sinking like two dark stones into the water. "It was just you and Brickman? Are you okay?"

"Yes. But it was horrible." I lowered my voice, making sure Lily wasn't within range. "Ben wanted me to go to a hotel with him, said we'd be more comfortable there. He basically threatened to take away Lily's scholarship if I didn't." I felt hot tears building behind my eyes, but I blinked them back. "I couldn't do it. I got up and left."

"Oh my God. That bastard." Alex looped his arm around me. His muscles were tense, and I noticed the way he'd set his jaw. "You did the right thing. I'm so glad you didn't leave with that dirtbag."

"Do you think I should report him? To the police?"

"No." Alex straightened up, a flash of fear on his face. "You can't do that. The guy has an army of lawyers. He'll destroy you, your reputation, Lily's future. Everything."

I slid my palms down my thighs, balancing my weight. I remembered what the principal had said about his influence over so many others at the school, and what Bridget had said about justice not being the same for everyone, that those with the most money and power had an advantage. It seemed she was right. Ben Brickman was like a wrecking ball smashing through the life I'd been so carefully constructing.

Alex pulled me closer. "I'm so sorry, Rachel. I shouldn't have let you meet him without me. Unfortunately, I think the best thing you can do is to put your head down and keep your distance from him."

I dug my toe into the floor. Life was unfair. The sexual harassment from Lily's principal was troubling enough, but then there was the possibility that taking action would only make things worse. On top of that, I couldn't shake that last thing Ben had said as I fled the restaurant, urging me to google Alex. *Or Michael.* I hadn't done any online research on my new boyfriend, and maybe I was naive not to have done it sooner. *Has Alex told you what he's done?* Ben had laced his words with venom; his question lurked in my mind. I didn't want to imagine what the search would reveal. I hoped it had nothing to do with Annie Turner.

"How about I stick around after Lily goes to bed?" Alex smoothed my hair back. "There's so much more I should tell you about Brickman."

I flinched at his touch, causing him to pull away.

"Rachel. What's wrong?"

"Nothing. I'm just not feeling well. The food was so rich, and the whole thing with Ben. I kind of want to go to sleep and start over tomorrow."

Alex peered at me, not speaking.

"I'm sorry," I said. "I'm so tired. We'll hang out later this weekend."

"Okay. We're still on for Sunday, right?"

"Yes. Of course."

He stood, firm hands massaging my shoulders. "I hope you get some rest and feel better."

"Thank you for watching Lily. That was super nice of you."

"I enjoyed it."

We said good night, exchanged a quick kiss, and he left. After double-locking the door, I found Lily in her bed, a tangle of wheat-colored hair spread across her pillow. She'd turned on her white noise machine, which whirred atop her nightstand. After she detailed her fun night with Alex, I kissed her good night and returned to the living room, closing her door behind me.

I rested on the couch for a moment, staring into space, gathering the courage to approach my laptop. Competing voices screamed within me: *Do it! Don't do it!* Ignorance was bliss, but the pull of my curiosity was too strong. I needed to know the truth, especially if I was going to leave Alex in charge of Lily occasionally.

With a few clicks, I pulled up a search bar, then typed *Michael Ballard Silver Meadows school district*. It only took a moment for the results to appear, but it took much longer for my mind to register the headline, the words underneath.

High School Teacher Suspended after Breaking Student's Arm and Jaw

Michael Ballard, a ninth-grade social studies teacher at Robertson High School in Silver Meadows, was suspended indefinitely after a physical altercation with a student. Multiple witnesses reported seeing Ballard grasp fourteen-year-old Billy Riley by the arm and slam him into a nearby locker with such force that Riley suffered multiple bone fractures in his arm and jaw. The incident happened between fourth- and fifth-hour, with dozens of students flooding the hallway and witnessing the altercation. The school district and the parents of Riley are likely to press civil charges while authorities investigate whether criminal charges are warranted. Neither Ballard nor his attorney could be reached for comment.

My eyes swam through the words, each new revelation ripping through me. My lungs struggled for breath and I had the sensation of drowning. I remembered the fist pounding against the drywall on the other side of my bedroom two weeks earlier, and Alex's claim that he wasn't a violent person. The force of Keith slamming me into the wall would live in my psyche forever. Maybe I attracted a certain type of man—violent and abusive.

My stomach folded in on itself, pressure building in my head. I'd left Alex with my daughter, no questions asked, so easily drawn in by his strong jawline and twinkling eyes, his kind words and volunteer work. What if he'd gotten angry with her? What might have happened? I stepped across the creaky floor and peeked in on Lily, who was already fast asleep. She looked like an angel in the rectangle of light cast from the living room.

I closed Lily inside her room, retrieved a glass of water from the kitchen, and returned to the computer. I scanned more articles related to the Silver Meadows incident, finding that the victim's parents had decided not to press charges, but the school had terminated Alex's contract. A judge had sentenced him to probation and a series of anger management classes. That was three years ago. My feet pressed into the floor as I tried to make sense of everything I'd read. I couldn't fathom how Alex had earned his prime teaching position at Shorewood Academy with this incident marring his record, but I guessed that was where the name change came in. Maybe the parents at Shorewood simply didn't know about his past. Still, Ben Brickman was clearly aware of Alex's real story.

Our plans to hang out tomorrow and dinner on Sunday now felt like a trap, another step into a sticky web. I couldn't ignore what I'd discovered. It was too late now, but tomorrow I'd ask Alex to explain himself.

My body felt hollow, my insides scraped clean, as I stumbled toward the door, questioning everything I thought I knew. I retrieved the square of paper from the shelf and wedged it between the door and the frame.

TWENTY-ONE

I awoke on Saturday, haggard and worn, gasping in horror when I glimpsed myself in the mirror, my face colorless with purple half-moons under my eyes. My only comfort was the sight of Lily hopping around the apartment and the paper square wedged in the door, clinging to the same spot where I'd left it. I deliberated over my next move as I sipped a cup of coffee, rereading the articles from the night before. Finally, I'd texted Alex: *Can you come over for a few minutes? I need to talk to you about something.* I wanted there to be an innocent explanation, something that would make perfect sense of what I'd read and what I already knew of Alex. It was only fair to hear his side of the story.

I'd situated Lily inside her bedroom, door closed, with an oversized pad of paper and a new box of crayons. Now, Alex sat across from me at the kitchen table, his eyes downcast in the gray morning light.

I pulled up the article on my laptop and showed it to him. "Ben alerted me to this last night."

Alex shook his head, resting his forehead in his hands and releasing a long breath. "Of course he did."

"Why didn't you tell me?"

"I was going to tell you about this when the time was right. This article isn't the full story." He paused, a grimace on his lips. "You have to believe me. I would never hit anyone, especially a student, if there wasn't a reason."

I leaned back, stunned. "What reason could there be to slam a fourteen-year-old into a locker so hard that he broke his arm and jaw?"

"Rachel, that kid, Billy Riley, he was the worst kind of bully —good-looking, naturally athletic, but with low grades and uninvolved parents. I watched Billy torment this other boy, Nathan Benson, every day. Nathan was the opposite of Billy. He was smart and kind. He was artistic, thoughtful, and tried to mind his own business. But Billy and his crew relentlessly taunted Nathan, calling him a loser and a freak. And much worse." Alex clenched his teeth, closing his eyes and opening them again. "Billy would take things from Nathan, a baseball hat, a coat, a book, his lunch, whatever, and throw it in the trash while his idiot friends stood behind him, laughing. This torture went on for months. Nathan never fought back. He never reported any of it because he knew that would only make things worse. But I saw what was happening. I saw how much Nathan was hurting, how he looked like he'd rather be anywhere else in the world than at that school where a group of thugs ridiculed him day in and day out. I told the counselor about the bullying, and she called Billy to her office once or twice, gave him a slap on the wrist. Nothing changed." Alex laced his fingers together, staring toward the window, the cloudy morning outside. His eyes held a distant look, and he seemed to have drifted somewhere else.

I leaned toward him. "What happened that day, Alex?"

Alex's gaze returned to me. He placed his palms on the table as if to brace himself for whatever was coming next. "That day, I heard a couple of kids laughing in the hallway a few minutes after the fourth-hour bell rung. They said that Billy had cornered Nathan in the boys' bathroom, that Billy had held Nathan down and made him drink toilet water. I didn't want to believe it. But a moment later, I saw Nathan walking toward me with his head down, looking like he might vomit. His eyes were red, and his shirt was wet around the collar. Billy was a few steps behind him, snarling. He said something to Nathan about walking faster. He asked Nathan if he was still thirsty. A switch flipped inside me. I couldn't let it happen anymore."

I shook my head, my heart aching for this boy, Nathan, who I'd never met.

"I stepped in front of Billy. I told him if he thought he was so tough, then he should fight me. He started laughing like he thought I was joking. I grabbed Billy by the arm—not to fight him, but only to drag him to the principal's office. That's when he tried to punch me in the face. I reacted out of self-defense without thinking. I flung him into the locker. I didn't mean to do it that hard. I swear."

"Oh my gosh." I reached across the table and squeezed Alex's hand. His eyes glistened, and I could see that revisiting that day was painful. The situation hadn't been as black and white as the article depicted.

"I'm proud of you for standing up for that poor boy."

Alex chuckled but it sounded sad. "You know what? I've had so much time to think about this. Even with the fallout, even with losing my job and getting probation, having to use my middle name as my first name to avoid identification by people at Shorewood, I would do the same thing again. Nathan needed someone on his side. He needed someone to fight for him."

"And Billy's parents didn't sue you?"

"No. Not when they realized how it would look for their son, how disgusting his behavior was. They knew my claim of self-defense was legitimate, even if they wouldn't admit it."

"Wow. And you still got the job at Shorewood just by using your middle name?"

Alex rubbed his arm. "No. Not exactly. That was a bit trickier."

"What do you mean?"

"I had the support of my department chair at the previous school. She knew the full story about the bullying and promised to give me a glowing referral. But, even so, there was a permanent black mark on my record." Alex paused, looking down. "My parents have a friend who graduated from Shorewood years ago. He's done well for himself and has become a major donor to the school over the years. Before I interviewed for the position, my parents asked this man to write a letter on my behalf. It may have implied that his future donations were tied to me being hired." Alex's eyes flicked toward me, then away. "I'm not proud of the tactic I used, but I didn't have the luxury of doing things differently. If anything, I was overly qualified for the position. I love teaching, and I needed a job."

I stared at Alex, seeing the shame flashing across his face, his struggle to keep his chin up. "It's okay. I understand. Sometimes life doesn't give you a choice."

He leaned back. "The school—which was Brickman and a small committee he controls—needed to keep the donations flowing. They agreed to hire me, but only if I went by a different name so that none of the parents would make the connection if they happened to Google me. Alex is my middle name, but I've gotten used to it as my first name now." He sighed. "So, now you know the whole story about my dark secrets." He tilted his head, studying my reaction. "I understand if you want to take a break from seeing me. But please believe that I wasn't trying to lie to you. I just didn't know the right time to bring this up."

I shook my head, amazed he'd gotten my reaction so wrong. "Alex, the story you just told me makes me like you even more.

You stood up for that boy when no one else would. Thank you for telling me. I want us to be honest with each other."

Alex tilted his face, staring at me with wonder. "You know, as long as we're clearing the air, there is one other thing I haven't been completely honest about. But I want to tell you now."

"What is it?"

"You've been asking a lot of questions about Annie Turner."

I sat up at the mention of her name.

"The truth is that I knew Annie better than I've let on. We weren't dating, but she was a friend."

"Okay."

"She got involved with Brickman. It sounded a lot like what happened to you last night, except Annie went back with him to the hotel. At first, she seemed to enjoy the attention, like she thought it was all some kind of big joke. I even heard Brickman here—through the wall—a couple of times."

I shuddered, realizing Brickman had been in my apartment. With Annie.

Alex continued. "I warned Annie about him, but she said it was just for fun, something scandalous she could add to her book. But after a few weeks, Brickman became controlling. He didn't take it well when she tried to end it."

"Oh my God."

"I never would have let you go to that dinner last night if I'd known Ben's wife wasn't going to be there."

"I know you wouldn't have." I intertwined my fingers, piecing together the information.

"Anyway, I haven't even told you the worst part yet. Annie swore me to secrecy on this, so I need you to promise to keep it a secret too."

I nodded, but the air felt thick in my mouth.

"The reason Annie left this apartment so suddenly was that she found out she was pregnant. She suspected it was Brickman's, and she told him so. Brickman was furious and told her to get an abortion, but Annie came from a strict Catholic upbringing. She was conflicted. She didn't want a child, but she didn't know what to do. I helped her come up with a last-minute plan to leave in the middle of the night. She was going to call a ride to the airport, catch a flight on standby, and disappear to Europe for a while to figure things out. She needed time to think about her options without Brickman breathing down her back, threatening her, without her older sister, Julia, preaching to her. She didn't want Brickman to find her. That's why she left without a trace. That's why her sister, who sent her those letters, hasn't heard from her."

"Oh, wow." I leaned forward, cradling my head in my hands. It all made sense. The story Alex told me added up with everything I'd discovered.

"What about Annie's parents?"

"She said her father died years ago, and her mom was in poor health." Alex pinned his lips together. "I don't know the details."

"And Annie didn't report Brickman?"

"No. Annie felt like she was partly to blame. She wasn't as... cautious as you. I wanted to report him, but I couldn't. I knew he'd fire me. No other school district will ever hire me after what happened at Silver Meadows."

"I promise I won't tell anyone." I stood and went over to him. Alex met me halfway. His embrace felt stronger and warmer than it ever had before. He wasn't a violent abuser. He was a good man who helped people. "Thank you for telling me the truth."

"Thank you for understanding." He rested his chin on the top of my head. "Rachel, there's one other thing I've wanted to tell you. And I really hope it doesn't scare you away."

"What?" I asked, muscles tensing as I wondered what else he could possibly reveal.

He pulled away, gazing into my eyes. "I think I'm falling in love with you."

It took a second to take it in, to realize not only that my world hadn't shattered but that it was coming together better than I could have imagined. I leaned into Alex, comforted by the heat of his body. "I think I'm falling in love with you too."

TWENTY-TWO

At just after 3 o'clock on Saturday afternoon, the intercom buzzed.

"Hello?"

"Hi, Rachel. It's Henry. You have a delivery here. A very large box."

"Oh, yeah. It must be the bookshelf I ordered. I'll come get it."

"No, no. I'll bring it up. It's quite heavy and I have a cart that makes it easy."

"Are you sure?"

"Of course. I'll be there in two minutes."

Henry arrived a minute later, towing the bookshelf, which was still in the box. He looked past my shoulder. "Where do you want it?"

"Over here." I led him to Lily's room, where we unloaded it as Lily bounced up and down, telling Henry about her library books. The older man seemed enthralled by her every word.

After Lily had described each one of her books, we stepped back into the living room, where Henry paused, looking around.

"Well, this place sure looks a lot better than the last time I saw it."

"When was that?"

"Right after Annie skipped town, I helped Oliver carry down some boxes of her leftover belongings. The place was pretty bare-bones." His eyes paused on the framed photos of Lily outside her new school. "You've done a nice job with it."

"Thanks. We've been working to make it feel like ours." I remembered the email I'd finally received back from Oliver late last night about my request to change the locks. He told me his regular maintenance guy had retired and suggested I ask Henry to line up someone. "Before you go, I'm looking to get the locks on my door replaced. Oliver said for me to ask you to find someone, and he'll foot the bill."

"Sure. I have a guy." Henry eyed the door handle, giving it a jiggle. "Looks fine, but people are always coming and going in buildings like this. You're smart to get the locks replaced."

"Yeah. Better safe than sorry." I swallowed, realizing I sounded just like Mom. Still, I imagined how relieved I'd be with a new set of locks, instead of relying on my paper square trick. It seemed Annie had given multiple people access to this apartment at one point or another, and I had no idea how many spare keys were floating around.

Henry waved as he let himself out. "I'll get back to you."

On Sunday morning, Bridget's car rattled down the road leading to Mom's subdivision. It felt strange—almost too easy—to drive again after weeks of walking and public transit. The familiar suburban surroundings caused my chest to tighten as we approached Briar Lane. I glanced in the rearview mirror, finding Lily picking at her thumbnail in the back seat. I'd buckled her atop her booster seat, the one I'd retrieved from the locker this morning, sneaking in and out of the damp and shadowy storage room as quickly as possible.

"Can I see Natalie?"

"I don't think we're going to have time for that today." I held a breath in my lungs, my eyes flickering toward my daughter. Natalie had been fine—a good friend to Lily in preschool—but there was nothing I'd want to do less than reuniting with the girl's parents, Keith's awful friends, even if only for a few minutes.

Lily's lower lip protruded.

"I'm sorry, honey. But we'll grab our Halloween decorations, the little Christmas tree, our bag of winter clothes, and your bike. Okay? Then we'll head back home. We have plenty of room in our storage locker. Maybe I'll take you and Marnie for a bike ride in the park sometime soon."

Lily nodded, staring out the window. We rolled past rows of tiny brick houses; some kept up better than others. The driveway leading to my childhood home appeared in front of my bumper, cement buckling and weeds sprouting from cracks. I continued past it, parking next to the curb, so Mom wouldn't complain about how I'd blocked the garage. I let Lily out and approached the front door, eyeing the slatted fence that encircled the backyard where I'd spent hours a day reading as a kid, escaping through books into other worlds. But I felt no nostalgia for the years I'd spent in the tiny brick house. Instead, I had the sensation of nearing a poisonous plume of smoke. Best to hold my breath and get in and out without breathing in Mom's emotionally noxious fumes.

Before knocking on the door, I bent down and whispered to Lily, "Remember to tell Grandma how much you like your new school. And we're not going to mention Alex, okay?"

She nodded her little head as the door opened. Mom hovered in the opening, wearing sweatpants and an oversized Minnie Mouse shirt, a mop of wiry hair propped on her bony shoulders, and a cigarette dangling from the corner of her mouth.

"Well, here you are. A little late, but I'll take what I can get."

I glanced at my feet, knowing we were only ten minutes later than the estimate I'd given her. I waved toward the curb. "I had to borrow my friend's car. It took a few minutes."

Mom shook her head, tapping her cigarette ash into the bushes. "What a hassle. Poor Lily, growing up in that concrete jungle, people shooting each other in the streets."

"Hi, Grandma," Lily said, her voice no more than a squeak.

"Hello, pumpkin." Mom finally acknowledged her.

"We're enjoying the city, Mom." I sharpened my voice. "You need to stop believing everything you see on your Facebook feed. Downtown is full of interesting people and opportunities. Not at all like this place."

Mom grunted, her mouth sagging. "I hope you're not being overly friendly with strangers. You've always been too trusting. You'll get burned, for sure."

"I love my school," Lily blurted out, throwing me a furtive glance. "My teacher is nice."

Mom huffed but widened the door, letting Lily and me inside. The scent of stale cigarettes permeated the air, making it difficult to breathe. The living room was dusty and unkempt, as usual. I glanced toward the kitchen, where a pile of dirty pots and pans spilled over the edge of the sink. Mom didn't have me around to clean up her mess anymore, and despite her complete lack of empathy, I couldn't help feeling a bit sad for her.

Mom snuffed her cigarette into an ashtray, smoke swirling in front of her face. "Your stuff's in the basement where you left it. I can't keep it for you anymore. There's simply not enough room."

"That's why I'm here." My jaw tightened as I turned toward the basement stairs, flipping on the light and struggling to block out a blur of memories. Lily and I had resided in the gloomy, cold space for months, staying down there as much as possible to avoid run-ins with Mom. It had been our only option, and I probably should have been thankful for the safety net, that we hadn't been thrust into homelessness, landed in a shelter, or forced to stay in an abusive relationship. But Mom lived in her own version of reality, where it was better to stick with the misery you knew, rather than making a change and risking ending up with something even worse. She'd made my breakup with Keith even more difficult than it already was. *You need to go back to your husband. You made a commitment, and you can't just walk away when it's not fun anymore.* She said that whenever I said or did something she didn't like, seemingly ignoring the fact that Keith had abused me, that he'd harmed Lily. It was obvious Mom's real issue was with my dad, more than me, that she somehow equated my actions to the way he'd walked out on her so many years earlier, but that didn't make her comments any easier to handle.

My feet hurried down the steep steps, Lily trailing behind me. We'd cleared out the space when we moved, but a few things sat in a darkened corner—Lily's purple bike, our little Christmas tree, a plastic jack-o'-lantern for Halloween, a compact box of books, two jigsaw puzzles, a garbage bag bursting with our winter clothes, hats, and mittens. I wondered what pained Mom so much about housing this little pile of belongings. Why reminders of Lily and me in a room she never used bothered her so? But Mom wasn't rational, and there was no making sense of her behavior.

"I'm so glad we have our own place now," I said to Lily, keeping my voice low.

"Me too."

A door closed upstairs, a second set of footsteps sounding from the floor above. I peered up the stairway, wondering who else would be here. Mom didn't have many friends.

"Why don't you carry these two puzzles out to the car?" I handed Lily the two partially collapsed boxes. "I'll come right behind you with your bike. This won't take long at all."

Lily climbed the stairs, balancing the boxes in her arms. I grasped the bike by the frame, readjusting my grip a couple of times so the training wheels wouldn't scrape my leg.

"Daddy!" Lily was upstairs now, and I was still in the basement.

I dropped the bike, realizing I'd been tricked. Mom and Keith must have planned this ambush. Anger surged through me, along with a fierce natural instinct to protect my daughter. It was an instinct my own mother had always lacked. I raced up the stairs, finding Keith crouched down, hugging Lily.

Mom watched them, her face creased with righteous indignation. She turned to me, frowning. "It's not right to keep a child from her father. Poor Lily."

"You have no right!" I hissed at her, hoping Lily wouldn't hear. "This is not okay. Keith beat me. He injured Lily. That's why a judge ruled his visits with Lily must be supervised by a social worker. How dare you put my daughter in danger like this."

Mom flung her head toward the ceiling. "Oh, Rachel. Always so dramatic."

Lily turned to me, lips trembling and eyes focused on the puzzles she'd set on the floor.

I looked at her. "It's okay, Lily. None of this is your fault."

Keith stood. Something resembling desperation spread across his face. "Rachel. Come on, just let me spend the day with my daughter. I'll even drop her back to you in the city later."

"No." I widened my stance, ready to fight back this time if he hit me.

Keith turned to Lily. "You want me to take you to Dairy Queen, Lily? Then we can hit the playground?"

Lily's head popped up, hope dancing in her eyes.

"No. That's not allowed." My heart broke for my daughter. "I'm sorry, Lily."

"Look, I'm prepared to pay you. Whatever I need to do to make this happen. How about five-hundred dollars for me to spend the day with Lily? The judge doesn't have to know."

"You don't have five-hundred dollars."

"I got a few new clients over in Elmhurst. I have the money. I'm sure you can use it."

I crossed my arms, looking toward the wall. The truth was I could have used that money. It was enough to pay for two weeks of Lily's summer camp. But taking it from Keith felt wrong, dirty. I wouldn't let Keith demean me again. "Your visitation day is only a week away. You'll have to wait. Now, you have thirty seconds to leave before I call the police."

"Oh, for the love of God." Mom leaned against the wall, rolling her eyes.

"And stay away from our apartment too."

Keith's eyebrows furrowed as he stepped toward me. "Rachel, please. Think about this."

"Men who hit women and children don't get my sympathy. Leave." I pulled out my phone, showing him I was ready to dial.

Keith set his mouth in a flat line. "Bye, Lily." He tousled her hair. "Sorry, your mom is such a horrible, petty person. I'll see you next weekend. I thought we'd go to Navy Pier and ride that big Ferris wheel."

Lily shifted her feet, face uncertain. "Okay."

I put my arm around Lily as Keith nodded toward Mom and stomped out the front door. A few seconds later, his truck engine rumbled outside, slowly fading into the distance.

I glared at Mom in disbelief. "Please stay away from us while I clear out our things. After today, you won't ever have to see us again."

"Don't be a drama queen." She let out a cackle, deep and

throaty. "You'll be back as soon as something goes wrong in the city. I'd bet my life on it."

I stared her down. "We are never coming back here."

Mom must have sensed the conviction in my voice because a look of shock flashed across her face. I grabbed Lily's hand, scooped up the puzzles, and rushed outside, throwing the boxes in the back seat. I asked Lily if she wanted to wait in the car while I retrieved the rest of our things, and she nodded. Mom peered down her nose at me as I made four more trips down the stairs and out to the street, shoving the items into the back of Bridget's SUV, thankful that Lily's bike was so compact and the fake Christmas tree broke into three pieces.

Mom hovered in the front doorway, muttering about how she was only trying to help, how a child needs two parents, and how I was being selfish. My foot pressed the accelerator as I kept my eyes straight ahead, silently vowing I'd never return. I pulled into the street, picking up speed and squealing away.

TWENTY-THREE

We returned to our building barely two hours after departing for the suburbs. I parked in the loading zone, throwing on the flashers and texting Bridget to tell her I was back. Lily had been quiet on the ride home, and I knew the altercation with Keith had been stressful and confusing for her.

"How about we go to the Pancake House after we get all this stuff unloaded? I think we deserve a special treat."

Lily nodded. "Okay."

I craned my neck over the seat. "I'm sorry about what happened with your dad. It shouldn't have to be like that. We both need to follow the rules that the judge set."

"I know."

"You'll see him next weekend, okay? I bet you'll have fun at Navy Pier."

Lily nodded again but her eyelids drooped. She looked sad. I promised myself I'd get her to open up further over pancakes.

Bridget approached from the building's front door, waving and smiling. I climbed out and handed her the keys. "Thanks so much for letting me take your car."

She eyed the items piled behind Lily. "Looks like you packed a lot in there."

I opened the door for Lily, and she stepped next to me on the sidewalk.

Bridget opened the back. "I'll help you unload. Then I'll take this pile of metal back to the parking garage."

We unloaded our belongings, extricating the bike pedals from the bag of clothes and fake tree branches. I wished Alex had been there to make things go faster, but he was likely still running along the lakeshore with his marathon training group. Bridget carried everything into the lobby as fast as I unloaded.

Pedestrians hurried past without any notice, and cars rumbled westward along Roslyn Place. As I heaved out the box of books, I noticed an attractive woman standing across the street, facing us. She was older than me—maybe in her mid-forties, with deep frown lines etched beside her mouth. Her highlighted hair fell in wavy tendrils to her shoulders, skimming her tailored jacket. I got the feeling she was watching us, although I couldn't tell for sure because of her mirrored sunglasses. When I stared back at her, she turned to the side, edging closer to a city bus stop sign.

"Is that everything?" Bridget returned from the lobby again, her hand resting on the open hatch.

"Yep," I said, grabbing Lily's booster seat from the back seat. "That's it. Thanks again for your car and all your help. I owe you."

"No problem at all. I'm glad someone's using it. I pay so much for the parking spot." Bridget fiddled with her keys. "I'll take it back to the garage. Or did you want me to help you carry your stuff down to the storage room first?"

I waved her off. "No, Lily and I can handle it."

Bridget fluttered her fingers in the air and drove off. I glanced toward the woman on the opposite sidewalk, who was now entranced by something on her phone. A young couple stood near her, chatting, and I realized she was only waiting for the bus. She'd probably been looking at Lily because many people weren't used to seeing six-year-olds in Lincoln Park.

Lily and I returned to the lobby, where the other doorman, Robbie, stood guard. He'd been there when we'd left a couple of hours earlier, too.

"You can use the freight elevator if you'd like. It's open."

"Sure. That would be great."

"Let me give you a hand." Robbie had never been overly friendly before—not the way Henry had been—but to my surprise, he gathered up the pieces of our fake tree and the bag of clothes. I lifted the box of books and rolled Lily's bike toward the glass barrier beyond the sitting area. Robbie buzzed us through and made another trip to help us load the rest of the items into the elevator. We thanked him and pushed the button for the lower level, watching him disappear behind the doors.

A few seconds later, the metal door lurched open into the basement's stark hallway. I stepped out into the cool air to get my bearings. We were in an alcove around the corner from the regular elevator, somewhat hidden. A dryer spun in the distance, the artificial scent of fabric softener freshening the air.

"Hold the doors open, Lily."

Lily kept her finger pressed against the button that held the doors ajar while I slid everything out into the hallway, motioning for Lily to exit too. I stared at the pile and then toward the darkened doorway to the storage room down the hall. The cage-filled room gave me the creeps, and I hesitated to approach. Instead, I inched down the hall and poked my head into the laundry area opposite the storage room, finding a few loads of laundry going but no people.

"Should we put this stuff in the locker, Mommy?"

Lily's voice made me jump, and I turned toward her, a nervous giggle escaping my mouth. "Yes. Let's do it." I gathered up the plastic tree branches and asked Lily to roll her bike behind me. We wove between the cages in the dim light. Other than a hiss and groan emanating from the utility room, the place was silent. We located our locker and loaded our belongings, making two more trips and deciding to take the bag of winter clothes upstairs for me to sort through. I released a breath when everything was locked away, and we were back in the main hallway. I hoisted the bag toward the elevator but stopped moving when I noticed a door beyond the freight elevator labeled EMERGENCY EXIT. We were standing below street level, and I wondered where the door led.

"Just a second," I said to Lily, who'd been about to press the elevator's call button. I hoped opening the emergency exit door wouldn't set off any alarms, but no one had posted any warnings about that. I stepped closer and grasped the industrial metal handle, turning it down and pushing. I held my breath, thankful to be met with silence instead of the blare of an alarm. Peeking through the crack, I could see a shadowy, cement stairway leading up toward a bright sky. A car rolled past above me.

"Hold this door open for a second. Don't close it. Okay?"

Lily nodded. I darted up the steps, blinking into the daylight and poking my head out. I found myself in the alley running along the side of the building. Two large dumpsters sat on either side of me, sour smells filling the air. I ducked back down, noticing a key slot but no handles outside the metal door. No one could enter this way; it was solely for people to leave.

"Where did you go?" Lily slipped back inside after me, letting the door close with a thud.

"Oh, nowhere. That's the alley up there. I don't think anyone is really supposed to use that door, except for emergencies. I was just curious."

"Oh. Can I press the button now?"

"Yes."

I raised the bag of clothes, glancing back at the door, and remembering Henry's comment that there were no security cameras in the freight elevator. Annie Turner had managed to disappear in the night, many of her belongings in tow, without anyone seeing. I had a hunch this door into the alley was how she'd done it.

A Sunday crowd packed the brunch spot, which stood a few blocks south of our apartment. Lily dug into her second pancake. We'd had to wait twenty minutes for a table, and I was ravenous by the time our food arrived. Our little table perched near a window overlooking Lincoln Avenue, where a steady stream of walkers, joggers, and young mothers pushing strollers passed out front. After a few minutes of talking about the encounter with Keith this morning and reminding Lily, again, that she'd done nothing wrong and we both loved her, the sparkle had finally returned to her eyes.

"Want to check out that playground down the street after we eat?" I asked.

"Are there swings there?"

"I don't know. We'll have to find out, I guess."

Lily returned to her pancakes as I glanced outside, almost spitting out the gulp of water in my mouth. The woman who'd been staring at us outside of our building now sat on a bench across the street from the restaurant. It had been nearly an hour since I'd noticed her watching us a few blocks away. I'd thought she'd been waiting for a bus. But why bother riding a bus for only three blocks, especially on a nice day? I supposed maybe she lived in the area and wondered if her presence was merely a coincidence. She sat with her arms crossed, mirrored sunglasses still shielding her face.

"Do you know that woman? Is she from your school?" I pointed outside.

Lily leaned forward, squinting. "I don't think so."

"Huh." I watched the stranger for a minute as she remained

motionless. I couldn't tell exactly where she was looking, but she faced the restaurant. She could have been waiting for someone. Lily began telling me about a couple of science experiments her teacher had demonstrated for the class last week and about the upcoming visit by some people from the science museum. The mention of it caused a memory of my dinner with Ben Brickman to spear through me, but I blinked it away, focusing on Lily. The waiter came by, cleared our plates, and gave me the bill. I laid down enough cash to cover the food and a tip, and we stood to leave. I glanced across the street again. The woman had disappeared. I shook my head, realizing that maybe she hadn't been following us after all.

The playground whirled and squealed with a Sunday afternoon crowd of children and parents. After a few minutes of pushing Lily on the swings, holding her up as she traversed the monkey bars, and watching her take several trips down a twisty slide, we headed home. Something in the air felt heavy, and I couldn't shake the feeling of someone watching us. I kept turning back and looking for that woman lurking behind a tree or in the shadows, but she wasn't there.

"Are you looking for Alex?" Lily asked after I turned back for the third time.

"Oh. No." I smiled at her. "But I am going out on a dinner date with Alex tonight. Remember?"

Lily nodded. "And I'll stay with Bridget?"

"Yes."

Lily hopped over a crack. "Cool! I like her."

"Good! I know she likes you too."

We entered our building, nodding toward Robbie, who buzzed us through. Once back inside the apartment, we rambled around for a while. Lily eventually settled on the couch to watch a cartoon. I sifted through the bag of clothes I'd retrieved from Mom's house, removing a light sweater and jacket. The rest could go down to storage.

"Hey, Lily. I'm running this bag down to our locker. Promise me you won't open the door for anyone. I'll be back in two minutes."

"I promise," she said, without removing her focus from the TV.

I left, locking her inside and taking the elevator down to the building's lowest level. I stepped into the corridor, noticing a man folding clothes in the laundry area as I passed. As I entered the shadowy storage room, a door creaked open along the far wall, the sound of a toilet flushing. I edged around the cages, finding Robbie, emerging from the staff room. I glimpsed a couple of utilitarian metal desks inside the room before he flipped the light, realizing there was a bathroom in there too.

He gave me a curt nod. "My five-minute break."

"Of course." I smiled, but panic rippled through me at the thought of the vacant doorman station in the lobby, even if it was only for five minutes. I'd seen the long hours the doormen worked, and I supposed they needed a breather once in a while, even if it was just to use the bathroom. I reminded myself that no one could get through to the elevators without a keycard.

Even so, I hurried over to my locker, threw in the bag of clothes, and relocked it. A minute later, I joined the man holding his laundry basket as we waited for the elevator, making small talk about the beautiful day outside. At last, the doors lurched open, and we rode the elevator up, the other man exiting on the third floor and me going one level higher.

My eyes followed the diamond-patterned carpeting as I walked down the hallway, but a swish of movement drew my gaze upward. I stopped, my limbs suddenly heavy and unable to move. The woman I'd seen earlier—across from our building and again near the restaurant—now squared her shoulders in front of my apartment door as if to block it. She'd propped her glasses on top of her head, providing a full view of her hardened gaze, the deep creases around her mouth.

"Can I help you?" I asked. A fleeting hope blew through me that maybe the woman was here for my neighbors in 4C, a client of their web-design business who wasn't sure on which door to knock. But when she glared directly at me, I knew it was me she wanted.

"I know who you are." She spoke through clenched teeth, jutting out her chin. "You're a homewrecker."

I shook my head, stunned. "I have no idea what you're talking about."

"You slept with my husband."

"You must have me confused with someone else. I don't even know who you are."

"Ha." She tipped her head toward the ceiling, rolling her eyes. "I'm Whitney. Ben's wife."

My mouth opened, but no words came out. It made sense now that I knew. I'd never seen Ben's wife before, but this woman with her manicured fingernails and tailored clothes looked like she fit the part.

"I saw you go into that restaurant with my husband on Friday night. I know about his nights at the hotel." She frowned.

I shook my head. "No. I'm not involved with your husband. I left the bistro as soon as we ate."

"You're lying. You're just like that other whore who used to live here." She blinked, stepping closer. "I thought my troubles would be over when I got rid of Annie, but now you're here."

"Got rid of her?"

Whitney pursed her lips. "Well, she's gone. Isn't she?"

"Did you do something to her?"

"Sometimes a little threat goes a long way." Whitney's hand slid into her purse, and I didn't want to know what she had in there. *A knife? A gun?* "Stay away from Ben. I'm warning you." This was a woman who'd been pushed to the brink. She seemed to be balancing on the edge of something dangerous, and I couldn't allow her to lose her footing. I didn't know what she was capable of.

"Please, don't do anything stupid." I stumbled backward, envisioning Lily on the other side of the door and hoping she was absorbed in her show and not hearing any of this.

Whitney leaned forward, pink splotches forming on the delicate skin around her neck. "Don't you dare try to turn this around on me. *I'm* the victim here. I'm doing what's necessary to protect my family."

I heard the crack in the woman's voice, desperation visible on her face. Although she frightened me, I couldn't help feeling sorry for her. Ben Brickman had shattered the foundation of his marriage. He had tried to cheat on his wife again with me, but I'd run the other direction.

I held my palms in the air, calming my voice. "I'm sorry for what your husband has done, but I swear I'm not involved with him. I have no interest at all. Ben assured me you were going to be dining with us on Friday. That's the only reason I agreed to go. But when I got there, he said you couldn't make it, that you had a migraine. I left before the bill was paid. I had to get back to my daughter."

Whitney's features sagged, realization flickering in her eyes.

"My boyfriend, Alex, lives right here." I pointed to the door of 4A. "He's the only man in my life. I promise."

The woman slid her hand from her purse, fingers empty. Her shoulders slumped as she gave me a couple of slight nods. "I see," she said, speaking barely above a whisper. "I've made a mistake. A big mistake."

"It's o—" I started to say, but she rushed away from me, slipping into the stairwell without looking back.

I stayed there for a minute, drawing in a few deep breaths, regaining my composure before entering my apartment. I unlocked the door, and went inside. Lily lounged in the living room watching her show just as I'd left her.

She hugged her knees to her chest. "Someone knocked on the door, but I didn't answer."

"You did the right thing. Good work." I double-locked the door behind me and paced toward the front window, looking down toward the street. After a minute, Whitney darted out onto the sidewalk, arms close to her sides. She hurried east and turned the corner. I wondered what she would do next. Confront her husband? File for divorce?

"Who was it?" Lily asked.

"No one." I shook my head. "A woman. She was lost."

I turned toward our locked door. Whitney had gotten inside the building with no trouble. She'd merely waited for the doorman to leave his post for a minute or two. She must have slipped in behind someone else as they passed through the door from the lobby to the elevators. Another resident probably noticed the attractive and well-dressed middle-aged woman hurrying towards the door and held it open for her, no questions asked. Keith could put on a good show too, and I feared someone might do the same for him.

TWENTY-FOUR

At 7:30 on Sunday night, Alex and I sat across a white-clothed table from each other, the aroma of lemongrass and basil filling the air. The restaurant had a romantic atmosphere. The lighting was dim, and a votive candle and flower petals floated in a bowl of water between us.

Alex looked up from a shrimp spring roll nestled in a bed of microgreens, his eyes traveling over me. "I'm glad I finally get to take you on a real date."

"This is nice." So different from the uncomfortable dinner with Ben Brickman two nights earlier. I sipped my wine, crossing my legs beneath my silky dress, one I hadn't worn in over two years. The Vietnamese restaurant was fancier than I'd expected, located on Chicago's Gold Coast. We'd taken an Uber to our current location after I'd gotten Lily settled with Bridget.

"Not that I don't want Lily here." Alex reached across and squeezed my hand.

"Adults only," I said, smiling. "I've never eaten a lotus root salad before. It's delicious." I glanced toward the nearly empty plate in front of me. It was one of a few appetizers we'd decided to share off the unique menu, making a meal out of them. Our waitress appeared and cleared the salad as another server set down two more colorful dishes.

We tasted a spicy noodle dish as Alex told me about his morning run, how between miles seven and eight, another guy in his group twisted his ankle. They all had to stop and help the injured runner hobble to a nearby street to catch a cab home.

"I guess we've both had an eventful day." I leaned forward, recounting a watered-down version of our visit to Mom's house and the ambush by Keith.

"I'm so proud of you for not caving into him. You did the right thing."

"Thank you." I set down my fork. "Something else strange happened after Lily and I got back from brunch."

"What?"

I described the woman I'd seen twice earlier in the morning and how she'd been standing in the hallway when I'd returned from the storage room. "It was Whitney Brickman. She was so angry. She thought I'd slept with her disgusting husband."

"Wow." Alex placed his palms on the table, leaning back. "She followed you?"

"Yeah. But I told her that she'd misunderstood, that Ben led me to believe she was going to be at the dinner too, and I had no interest in him."

"And then she left?"

"Yeah. She seemed flustered; said she'd made a big mistake."

"Man." Alex let out a breath. "Hopefully some of Ben's actions will finally catch up with him."

"It's creepy that she got past the doorman so easily, though. Isn't it? It makes me feel like our building isn't that secure." The unsettling nighttime noises from my living room creaked through my mind, the square of paper in the door. Henry hadn't been working today, so I didn't know where things stood with a locksmith. But nothing had dislodged the paper square since I'd started the routine, and maybe I was simply paranoid.

Alex took a sip of his drink, shrugging. "I see people slipping into the elevator area behind other people once in a while. I've done it too, held the door open for someone who looks like they might live in the building, or even if they say they're visiting someone. I don't want to be rude."

"Yeah. I see how it can happen." My eyes wandered to a nearby table where an older couple clinked their glasses together.

Alex followed my gaze. "That could be us someday."

Something tingled inside of me at the thought. "Yeah. I hope so." A few sips of wine pooled at the bottom of my glass, but I wasn't ready to drink it, I wasn't ready to abandon the previous topic. "I can't shake something else Whitney said."

"What?"

"She knew Annie lived in 4B before me. She knew all about Ben's trips to the hotel and their affair."

"Well, I guess it's not surprising. Ben is a total narcissist. I can't imagine he's great at hiding his extra-curricular activities." Alex studied my face, perhaps seeing my distress. "Listen, if Whitney ever shows up again, knock on my door or text me if I'm not home. I'll tell her she's out of line and to step aside. I've always got your back, Rachel. Always."

"Okay. Thanks."

"It sounds like you've handled it already though, so I'm not too worried."

I nodded, thankful to have Alex in my life. A few months ago, I couldn't have imagined sitting in this romantic restaurant under the city's glimmering lights, eating food I'd never tasted before with a man who was turning out to be the best kind of partner.

The discussion veered toward our plans for the coming week and some difficult parents of a couple of kids in one of

Alex's classes. Even as the conversation flowed effortlessly, I struggled to blink away memories from a few hours earlier. Whitney Brickman's scowl had etched itself in my mind, the way she'd slid her hand inside her purse. *What had she been grasping inside the leather bag?* I pushed away the possible answers, remembering what Alex had said; I'd handled the situation.

After another round of drinks, two more appetizers, and a Vietnamese version of crème brûlée for dessert, Alex discreetly paid the bill. He escorted me outside with a sturdy arm wrapped around me. I leaned my weight into him as we made our way toward Michigan Avenue, his lips finding mine every few minutes. As we strolled along the Magnificent Mile, window shopping, I checked my phone. It was 9:15, and there were no messages from Bridget. Still, it was a school night, and Lily usually went to bed by 9 p.m.

"I hate for this night to end, but we should probably head back. I have to pick up Lily."

Alex made a face, shoving his hands into his pockets. "We can head home, but the night doesn't have to end. How about I come over after you get Lily tucked into her bed? I'll leave before she wakes up."

I shifted my weight, wanting nothing more than for Alex to spend the night with me. Maybe I wouldn't encourage him to sleep on the couch tonight. "Okay. Let's do that."

Alex pulled me close again, then raised his arm to hail a taxi. Ten minutes later, we were back at Roslyn Place.

I knocked lightly on Bridget's door, which opened a few seconds later.

"How did it go?" Bridget whispered.

"It was great," I said, matching the low volume of her voice. "The restaurant was amazing. And then we walked along

Michigan Avenue for a while. I hope I'm not too late." I peeked over Bridget's shoulder, finding Lily sprawled across the couch, eyes closed.

"Not at all. She fell asleep twenty minutes ago, but we had lots of fun before that." Bridget waved me inside and closed the door with a soft click. Her phone buzzed from nearby, and she picked it up. "I'm sorry. I have to take this. I'll go in the bedroom, so I don't wake Lily up. You can gather Lily's things. Her bag is there." Bridget pointed to the reusable grocery bag we'd brought over. It had been filled with games and books but now sat empty.

"Okay."

As Bridget darted into the bedroom, I retrieved Lily's belongings from around the living room. One of the hardcover picture books sitting on Bridget's bookshelf slid out of my hand. I jumped to catch it before it hit the floor. My fingers closed around the book, stopping the crash, but my elbow bumped a canvas-lined box on a nearby shelf, tipping it over. The contents spilled across the wooden surface, squares of shiny paper with black-and-white images fluttering to the floor. They were some of Bridget's photographs.

I set down the book and picked up a photo that had landed face down, turning it over and doing a double take at the subject. In the photo, Alex pumped his arms, mid-stride, as he ran past the photographer. I turned over another one, gasping at the image. It was Alex again, running along the lakeshore path, the close-up of his face highlighting the stone-cold determination in his eyes. A third photo had been taken from further out, capturing Alex's entire running group. But Alex was the focal point with the rest of the faces out of focus and the lake spread out behind them. My hands moved, frantic, as I flipped over more photos, finding Alex framed in black and white each time with a variety of urban backdrops behind him. I couldn't make sense of what I'd found. Why had Bridget taken so many photos of my boyfriend? Bridget's voice sounded louder from behind the bedroom door as she wrapped up her phone call.

I scooped all the photos off the floor and shoved them back into the box, replacing the lid and returning the box to its original spot. My pulse pounded in my ears, and I knew I'd seen something I shouldn't have. I picked up Lily's bag and threw her picture book into it, heading toward her other belongings on the floor.

"Sorry about that." Bridget stood behind me now, rubbing her hands together. "I never know when it's a real emergency with Leo. Turns out, it was nothing."

I couldn't make eye contact with Bridget as I gathered the rest of Lily's things. I thanked her for watching Lily and touched my daughter's arm to wake her. She blinked up at me, taking a minute to remember where she was. I guided Lily's narrow shoulders out the door, eager to leave.

The myriad images of Alex barraged my mind as we took the stairs one flight down. I couldn't make sense of what I'd seen. As my feet hurried down the steps, a troubling realization struck me. In each image, Alex appeared completely unaware that Bridget had been taking his picture.

* * *

"How well do you know Bridget?" I kept my voice quiet and glanced toward the ceiling, conscious of thin walls and vents. Lily was asleep in her room. Alex sat next to me on the couch, his eyelids heavy.

Alex shook his head. It was after 10:30 p.m., and he looked as tired as I felt. "Not well. She's only someone I see in the elevator from time to time."

"Oh." I dug my toe into the floor, relieved to be free of my heeled shoes. "Are you sure that's it?"

"Yeah." He yawned and massaged his forehead. "Now that

I think about it, Bridget joined my running group a while back. I didn't realize she lived in the building at the time. Not until she told me. She dropped out of our group a couple of weeks later. Once the runs got past three miles, she couldn't keep up. That's happened with a few people now." He lowered his gaze toward me. "Why do you ask?"

"Nothing." I ran my fingertip over the stitching on the throw pillow, debating how much to share. I remembered the first time I'd gone to Bridget's apartment, how she'd confided in me about her crush on Alex. Bridget had even told me about joining the running group, but she'd quickly realized Alex hadn't felt the same. She'd seemed embarrassed about the whole thing and had sworn me to secrecy. Bridget must have taken those photos of Alex back then, around the time she'd joined the running group, perhaps just before. Maybe she'd held on to the images because she was proud of her photography. From an artistic standpoint, they were stunning portraits, well-composed and filled with emotion. Even during the brief glimpse I'd had of them, her talent was obvious.

Bridget seemed genuinely happy for my budding romance with Alex, and I didn't believe she still had feelings for him. She'd been dating someone else from her office building when I met her. There'd been the man she'd accosted at the library, plus the other ex-boyfriend she'd avoided at the diner. It seemed Bridget fell hard and fast for people, that some of her short-lived relationships had suffered tumultuous endings. Still, she'd been a good friend to me, welcoming Lily and me to the building, taking us to the library, babysitting for Lily, and letting me borrow her car without a second thought. I would ask about the images in the box another time, but it didn't feel right to tell Alex about the photos until I spoke to her first. Bridget would be humiliated if Alex knew about them.

Alex stretched his arms above his head and flopped back into the cushions. "Did things go okay with Lily?"

"Yeah. Everything was fine." My eyes gravitated toward the locked door. There was no need to place the paper in the door with Alex here, nor did I want him to know how paranoid I'd become. I yawned, causing Alex to do the same. "It's just been a long day."

Alex rested his hand on my knee. "Let's go to bed." He moved toward the front closet where we kept the bedding for the couch.

"Wait," I said, my insides fluttering. "I don't think we need to do this couch thing anymore."

Alex stared at me for a moment, then smiled as I angled my head toward the bedroom.

TWENTY-FIVE

When I'd dropped Lily at Shorewood on Monday morning, I feared finding her scholarship pulled and her chair removed from the classroom, but everything appeared to be the same; Ms. Lisle had welcomed her in the doorway and asked about her weekend. The several pick ups and drop offs that followed had been hurried and stressful, but there'd been no sign of Principal Brickman on the school grounds, and, thankfully, no sign of Whitney either. I'd made a point to keep my head down, merely smiling toward Alex from a distance and making no effort at small talk with the other parents. My only goal was to fly under the radar and get in and out as quickly as possible, so Lily's education could proceed uninterrupted.

Now it was Wednesday morning, and I kissed Lily's head and stood near the fountain, watching her run into the north entrance of Shorewood Academy, Marnie skipping by her side. A warm wind gusted past me, fanning my hair across my face. I pushed my locks away, spotting Alex waiting near the south entrance, greeting students. The courtyard was clearing out, so I wandered over to him. After a romantic and intimate night together on Sunday, we'd missed each other the last two nights, and I wanted to say a quick hello as long as Ben Brickman wasn't around.

Alex dipped his head as I neared. "Hello, Ms. Gleason."

"Hi." I peered around, searching for anyone watching.

"You look even more beautiful than you did yesterday."

I smiled, shaking my head. "Any sign of Brickman?" I asked, lowering my voice.

"No. He's out of the office this week. At least, that's what our internal email said this morning."

I released a breath. "Thank God."

"I'm guessing he's taking time off to save his marriage. But only you and I know about that."

The shrill ring of the school bell sliced through the air, causing me to jump. Alex lifted his hand. "Sorry, but I've gotta go. I'll see you later, hopefully."

"Sounds good."

Alex disappeared through the doorway, a late student scuttling through the opening behind him. I turned toward the gate, my eyes trained on the brick pathway. As I walked, my skin bristled with an innate awareness, some primal instinct left over from caveman times, letting me know that someone was watching me, hunting me. It was the same sensation I'd gotten a few days earlier when Whitney had been following me. I swung my head around, surveying my surroundings, worried the principal's wife would jump out from behind a tree and falsely accuse me of sleeping with her husband in front of dozens of parents. But she wasn't there.

My vision snagged on something beyond the wrought-iron fence, a familiar black SUV parked on the opposite side of the street, the driver's window partially lowered, revealing Liz Meyer-Barnes. To anyone else, she'd appear as a concerned parent, watching her child enter the school, but I knew her eyes were fixed on me. I shot a forceful stare right back at her, wondering why she lingered on the street even after the bell rang. For some reason, this woman had aligned herself with my ex-husband, and I imagined she was reporting back to him, just waiting for me to do something wrong. Anger tightened inside me. I strode toward her, ready to tell her what I thought of her and where she could go. But she raised her chin and pulled out into traffic.

I bit back my frustration at the spiteful woman as her brake lights disappeared around the corner. As I continued through the gate and away from the school, a sickening feeling expanded in my stomach. Only four days until Keith's visit with Lily. It was clear by the recent stunts he'd pulled that he wasn't okay with our custody arrangement, that he would slither into any available cracks to gather false evidence and prove his point. Sunday would be horrible for me, but it was important for Lily to understand that her dad hadn't abandoned her. At least the social worker would supervise the visit.

A few minutes later, I arrived back at our building breathless from my hurried walk. Henry sat at his usual post. "Hi, Rachel. I finally heard back from the locksmith. Unfortunately, he's booked solid for the next few weeks. I guess there's been a rash of break-ins in the area."

"Few weeks?"

"Yeah. I went ahead and scheduled him for June 19th, but I have a call out to another company. I'll keep you posted if I can get someone over sooner."

My stomach sank as I thanked him. He buzzed me through, and I waited for the elevator as the Levys wandered up next to me, wearing matching sneakers, cardboard coffee cups squeezed within their thick fingers.

"Good morning, Rachel." Mrs. Levy grinned. "How's life in 4B?"

"Fine, thanks. Lily and I have been meaning to thank you

for the adorable cheetah toy. Lily just loves it. She's called it Champ."

"It was our pleasure." The older woman smiled at me with her coffee-stained teeth. "We had so much fun picking it out."

"Have her knock on our door if she wants to play checkers again. I'd like a rematch." Stan chuckled and sipped his coffee.

"She enjoyed playing with you."

"When is Lily's birthday?" Mrs. Levy angled her body toward me. "I need to put it on my calendar."

"Not until November."

"We'll get her something for the last day of school then. When's that?"

"June 14th. But you really don't need to get her anything else."

The elevator doors opened, and we moved inside. I didn't know whether to be flattered or alarmed by their over-the-top interest in my daughter, but I decided they were harmless, just an older couple who yearned for a grandchild of their own. We chatted about the coffee place down the street. I said goodbye as the doors opened onto the fourth-floor hallway. As I turned the key in my lock, another door creaked open down the hall, Drake's eyes peering through the crack. I huffed out a breath, having lost my patience with the strange man-child who always seemed to be lurking nearby, always standing too close.

"Can I help you, Drake?" My voice flung out more forcefully than I intended.

"Annie's gone."

"I know. She's in Europe." I closed my eyes, remembering Drake didn't know the whole story. "At least, that's what she told some people who she worked with at the school."

"Have you heard from her?"

"No. Why would I? Have you?"

He frowned. "No."

I shrugged. "That's the way some people are. They don't

want to be found." My fingers tightened on the door handle. "I'm sure she had her reasons. Sorry, but I've got to get to work."

Drake stepped toward me, staring. "Has your boyfriend slipped up? Said anything? He must feel guilty."

"You've got it wrong, Drake."

Drake ran his tongue over his pale lips, tilting his head. "I don't think I do. Be careful, Rachel. Alex has a type."

I shot him a look.

"He's drawn to single women making a fresh start. Most serial killers have habits and patterns. I've read a lot about it."

"Have a nice day." I turned my back to Drake, slipped inside, and closed the door, thankful to be away from him. My finger turned the deadbolt, double locking myself inside the apartment.

"When can I ride my bike?" Lily stood in the living room, hand on hip, a ray of afternoon sun creasing her eyes. "Marnie rides her bike on the path by the zoo."

"Oh." I tugged at my shirt. After my two weird incidents in the morning, I'd been so thankful for a non-eventful afternoon school pick up that I'd all but forgotten about the bike. I pictured the storage locker, the bike's deflated tires. "How about I bring it up here so we can put air in the tires? I bet Alex has an air pump. I can take you to the path after school on Friday if the weather is nice."

Lily hopped up and smiled. "Yay!"

"Can you wait here and not open the door while I go get it?"

"Yes!"

I made Lily promise to stay in her bedroom. Then I locked her inside the apartment and headed down to the lowest depths of the building. A smiling woman joined me on the third floor, both of us staring at the elevator doors. I hoped she was also going to the storage room, but she pushed the button for the lobby. She exited, leaving me alone as I continued down, drawing in a breath as I ventured into the dim corridor.

Bridget's familiar voice caught my ear. "There's nothing to feel guilty about, Leo. We had no choice."

"That's bullshit, and you know it," a deep voice said.

"I can't ignore someone who needs help." It was Bridget who spoke again.

My insides twitched, aware I must have overheard something private. I halted, unable to stop myself from eavesdropping. But before they said anything else, Bridget emerged from the storage room.

Her eyes popped. "Oh. Hi, Rachel."

A muscled man stood behind her, holding a large cardboard box in his arms. His dark hair shaved so close to his head that I could see his scalp. His clothes were baggy—jeans and a black T-shirt—and his small eyes held a vacant look as he angled his gaze away from me. It was the same thick-necked man in the framed picture on Bridget's living room table.

I nodded. "Hi. I thought I heard you in there."

Bridget opened her mouth, then closed it. She glanced at the man. "This is my friend, Leo. He's just helping me with a heavy box." She motioned in my direction. "This is Rachel. She lives in the apartment below mine. 4B."

"Hi," I said.

Leo tipped his head without looking at me. He repositioned the box, his sinewy arms straining.

"Do you need help carrying anything?" Bridget asked.

"No. I'm only grabbing Lily's bike. Thanks, though."

"Okay. See you later. And tell Lily I said hi."

"Will do." I continued toward the shadowy room as they left in the opposite direction. The shiny black-and-white images of Alex fluttered through my mind, sour acid churning in my gut. I wanted to question Bridget about the invasive photos I'd spotted in her apartment, to tell her how unsettling it had been to find dozens of photos of my boyfriend in a box on her shelf. But the timing hadn't been right. Not with Leo standing there.

I wasn't sure if Bridget's charity case was guilty of any of the crimes he'd been accused of, but he seemed to lack social skills. On the other hand, Leo probably hadn't had any good role models until Bridget came along. Still, I was expecting someone different—a charming smooth talker or a grateful shy kid. Leo was more hardened than I'd envisioned. I wondered if he and Drake would hit it off, and I almost giggled to myself until I remembered the proximity of both men to Lily.

I sucked in a breath and ventured through the maze of cages, looking over my shoulder as I unlocked mine and rolled out Lily's bike. The strange noises in the room gave me the creeps—faint creaks and moans emanating from pipes in dark corners. I got out of there as quickly as I could, returning to Lily upstairs.

I leaned the bike against the wall over by the window. As Lily inspected it, we talked about making tacos again for dinner. Back in the kitchen, I opened a couple of cupboards, retrieving our leftover taco shells, a can of pinto beans, and a can of black olives. Heavy footsteps landed upstairs, followed by Bridget's laughter. I wondered again about the photos, and about what she and Leo were doing. What was inside that heavy box? What had she and Leo had no choice but to do?

The intercom buzzed, interrupting my thoughts.

"Hello?"

"It's Robbie. There's a woman here that says she needs to talk to the current tenant of 4B. Her name is Julia Turner."

Julia Turner. My blood ran cold as my brain registered the name. "Julia Turner?" I repeated, confirming I'd heard him correctly.

"Yes. Should I let her in?"

My hand hovered over my stomach, and I felt as if I might throw up. My eyes darted toward the desk drawer where I'd saved Julia's letters. Annie Turner's sister had traveled all the way from Australia to search for answers. Now the worried woman was downstairs in the lobby.

I swallowed against my dry throat, debating how much I should tell her. *How many of her sister's secrets were mine to reveal?* Facing the intercom, I rolled back my shoulders, knowing I'd never sleep again if I didn't meet with her.

"Tell her I'll come down to the lobby in a minute."

"Okay."

I popped into the hallway and knocked on Alex's door.

He opened the door, his smile flattening when he saw my face. "What's wrong?"

"Can you watch Lily for ten or fifteen minutes?"

"Sure. Why?"

"Julia Turner is here from Australia. She's looking for her sister."

TWENTY-SIX

With a queasy stomach, I made my way down to the lobby, finding a woman perched on the edge of a chair in the sitting area. She looked about my age, with vaguely familiar features. Her hair was slightly darker and shorter, her face rounder, but she bore a mild resemblance to the photo of Annie I'd seen on Facebook.

I nodded to Robbie and stepped over to her. "Hi. I'm Rachel Gleason. I live in apartment 4B."

"Hi. I'm Julia Turner." Her voice carried the relaxed inflections of an Australian accent. The smile she forced into the corners of her mouth didn't match her watery eyes. "Thank you for meeting with me. I know you don't know me, but my sister, Annie Turner, used to live in your apartment. No one's heard from her since she left. I'm running out of leads and thought someone here might be able to help me."

I looked over my shoulder, realizing there were too many people coming and going, too many ears that could potentially overhear our conversation. "There's a coffee shop around the corner. Maybe it's better if we talk there."

Julia nodded and followed me out the door. When we

entered the café, she said she didn't want anything, so I bought a bottle of water and we sat at a small table near the wall.

Julia hugged her arms around herself, her gaze wandering around the shop as if she were fearful of something. She leaned forward and fastened her deep blue stare on me. "My sister is missing. I haven't heard from her in over two months. No calls or texts. Nothing." Julia bit her lip.

"What about social media?" I asked, remembering Annie's Facebook page.

"Annie blocked me from all her social media accounts last year." Julia shook her head. "I didn't approve of some of the content she was posting, or how she handled her relationships with men. I guess blocking me was her way of dealing with my criticism." The woman drew in a long breath. "Annie's love life was a sore spot between us, but she's never just not responded to me. It's not like her. We'd been talking once every two weeks until she stopped answering."

"I'm so sorry. I can understand why you're worried."

"I finally got in contact with the man she rented this place from, Oliver, and he told me Annie skipped town in the middle of the night."

I nodded. "Yes. That's what he told me too."

"Outside of that small piece of information, I'm getting no help from anyone. Even the police said there's nothing they can do about a grown woman cutting off contact with her sister. I was hoping, by some miracle, I'd find her here. Or that someone in the building could offer a clue, something concrete I can take to the police." Julia tightened her lips, blue veins visible beneath the pale skin of her neck. "Do you mind telling me when you moved in?"

"April 16th. Lily and I have been here about six weeks. My realtor said your sister moved out two or three weeks before that. Oliver wanted to get the place leased before he left town for a few months. That's why I got such a good deal."

She dipped her head. "Oliver mentioned several times that he had to lower the rent. Do you happen to know if any of the neighbors helped Annie move out? If they know where she went?"

"I'm not sure. From what I've heard, it sounds like she vanished in the middle of the night."

"Can you tell me if Annie left any of her things behind in the apartment? I'm just so worried. And, like I said, the police don't even seem concerned, especially after they learned Annie had already blocked me on social media. They think she's avoiding me."

"I haven't found anything. I'm sorry." I gazed toward the counter, shifting my weight in my chair. "The apartment had been cleaned before I got there. The furniture belonged to the owner."

Julia laced her fingers together on the table, hands shaky. "I talked to Annie every couple of weeks. She told me a little about her part-time job at the school, the sights she saw, and restaurants where she ate. She was always searching for material for her book."

"What kind of book was it?" I asked, pretending like I knew nothing.

"She was really into true crime and dreamed of uncovering a crime or a scandal that she could write about. The last time we spoke—March 24th—she sounded different though, scared or sad. I don't know. She was vague, but she told me she needed to leave right away. She felt like someone was stalking her, threatening her, but she wasn't sure who. She swore someone had broken into the apartment when she wasn't home because her notebook was in a different place than where she'd left it. But Annie was always so dramatic. I didn't take her seriously at the time." A sad smile formed on Julia's lips. "Now I'm scared someone's done something to her." Julia leaned forward, blinking rapidly and whisking her tears away with the back of her hand. "She's my little sister."

The woman's raw emotion caused something inside of me to shatter; the secret Alex had shared with me, leaking through the cracks. "Listen, I can see why Annie freaked herself out living in that apartment. Sometimes I think I hear footsteps in the living room at night, but it's just because the walls are so thin." I thought of the paper square I inserted in the crack every night, the one that was always in the exact place in the morning. Apparently, I wasn't the only one who heard things.

Julia flattened her lips, her gaze flitting across the walls, and pausing on the window. "I just feel like there's more to it. A feeling in my gut that something horrible has happened. That last time I spoke to her, Annie mentioned she'd found something in the basement that scared her. It was something she shouldn't have seen, something in a box."

The recent memory of Leo lugging a box upstairs for Bridget popped in my mind. Then, I thought about the bustling laundry area, the creepy storage room with the rows of cages, and the secret door to the alley beyond the freight elevator. "What did she find?"

"I don't know. Annie wouldn't tell me because she was convinced someone was listening to her." Julia waved her fingers in the air. "Like there was a microphone hidden somewhere in the ceiling. My guess is that she planned to include whatever illicit information she'd stumbled across into her book. I thought Annie was exaggerating about the stalker, but maybe someone really did find out about her discovery, and then tried to stop her."

I thought of the wire that used to connect to a security camera in the hallway. Julia was correct that her sister had been paranoid, but she'd imagined a completely different scenario than what had most likely transpired. It was more plausible that Brickman or his wife had been the ones harassing Annie. I watched the way Julia clenched her jaw and wrung her hands as she perched on the chair. Julia was a woman who was suffering from the unknown, imagining the worst.

I pulled in a breath. "Listen, Julia. It's probably not my place to tell you this, but I do know a little bit more about where your sister might be."

Julia widened her eyes.

"My daughter goes to Shorewood Academy. We're new to the school. Lily just started kindergarten there on a scholarship."

Julia's shoulders lifted. "That's where Annie worked!"

"Yes. And it seems Annie told one of the other women in the office there that she was going to Europe."

"Europe? Where in Europe?"

I looked at my hands, then refocused on the woman across from me. "I don't know any specifics, only that she planned to break her lease and skip town so she wouldn't have to pay."

Julia's narrowed her eyes. "But why would she do that? Annie had plenty of money. We each got half of our grandparents' estate when they died. She wouldn't think twice about paying for a few months' rent." Julia tightened her jaw. "It must have something to do with that book she was writing."

I glanced away, realizing Julia wasn't going to swallow my half-truth so easily.

Julia crossed her arms, her face pinched. "Annie told me, 'The more scandalous, the better.' She was always poking her nose into places it didn't belong, searching for a shocking crime that hadn't been investigated yet for some book that was probably never going to be published. The last time we spoke—when she was acting so weird—she told me she'd finally found a good subject for her book, that the building was full of people who seemed normal but weren't. Whatever she'd found must have been related to the contents of that box she'd stumbled across. She didn't want to tell me any details, wanted me to go in blind when it was finally time for me to read it. But she must have stepped too close to something dangerous. I just know it."

Julia's suffering was painful to witness. My heart told me to spill everything I knew, but my brain slammed on the brakes. As much as I wanted to reveal more, I didn't want to involve Alex or Ben Brickman in Julia's quest for answers. Brickman would surely seek retribution for anyone who exposed his affair with Annie, not to mention the pregnancy. There was too much at stake—Alex's career, for one, plus Lily's scholarship. I angled my shoulders toward her, struggling to find the thin line between truth and lies. Anything to help this woman and to let me sleep at night. "There was something else I heard, but I don't even know if it's true. It might explain why Annie hasn't been in touch with you."

"What is it?"

I lowered my voice. "I heard Annie was pregnant, that she didn't want the baby. Apparently, she wasn't sure how you—or the rest of her family—would react. She needed to disappear, so she'd have time to think."

Julia's mouth dropped open. "What? Pregnant? Who was she involved with?"

"I have no idea." Ben Brickman's face surfaced in my mind, but I blinked it away. "This all happened before I moved here. I've never met your sister."

Julia stared at me. "Then how do you know any of this?"

"My boyfriend, Alex. He lives next door. He told me how he heard Annie crying one morning. He knocked on the door, asked her if she was okay. She confided in Alex about the pregnancy but never told him who the father was. They weren't that close." I glanced at the wall, hating that I was protecting Brickman. But I had to do it for Lily's sake. "Anyway, only a couple of days later, Annie had moved out without telling Alex or anyone else."

Julia's chest rose and fell as she registered the information.

"Wow. If that's true, I feel horrible that Annie didn't think she could tell me." She leaned closer. "Can I talk to Alex?"

"He's not home today," I lied. "And I'm certain he doesn't know anything more than what I just told you. He swore me to secrecy and he'll be angry that I mentioned this at all."

Julia clasped her fingers together again, still staring at me.

I pulled my gaze away from her. "Maybe Annie just needed to get away for a while, without people pressuring her to make one decision or another. It makes sense given what you told me before, about her knowing you didn't approve of her relationship choices."

Deep lines creased Julia's forehead. "I hope that's what she's doing. I still think she'd send a text to let me know she's okay. This isn't like her."

"I'm sorry. I really hope she contacts you soon."

Julia shifted in her chair, frowning and clearly disappointed that all her questions hadn't been answered. "I'm in town for twelve days. Then I've got to get back to my daughter and husband in Melbourne." She pulled a scrap of paper and a pen out of her purse and scribbled on it. "I'm staying at the Days Inn, a few blocks north of here. Here's my number." She handed it to me. "Can you please contact me if you think of anything else?"

"Yes. Of course."

She began to stand but paused, reversing course and retaking her seat. "Are you sure you didn't hear who Annie was dating?"

"No. I don't know."

"Would you be willing to ask your boyfriend again? Even if it's just a guess, so I can follow up?"

"I'll ask him, but he said he didn't know."

Julia blinked rapidly, eyes watering. "Please have him contact me if he remembers anything else."

"I will. I'll give him your number."

"Is there anyone else you can think of in the building who knew Annie?"

I shook my head, even as Drake's face flashed in my head. The last thing I needed was for Drake to mislead Annie's sister and suggest Alex was responsible for her disappearance. "I'm sorry I can't be of more help. People in the building tend to keep to themselves. When I first moved in, I asked a few neighbors if they knew why the previous tenant had moved, and they all said they didn't know. They seemed just as surprised as you that she'd left."

Julia looked at the floor as she stood and slipped her purse strap over her shoulder. "I see. Well, thank you for your help."

"I'll definitely let you know if I hear anything else." I watched Julia leave, stepping out the door and onto the sidewalk. I was glad to have offered a bit of reassurance to Annie's sister, to provide a viable theory she could follow all the way to Europe. I'd been so worried about Annie's fate since reading the letters, and now, after meeting Julia, I felt more confident that Alex's story about Annie leaving for Europe to contemplate her pregnancy options made the most sense. An unwanted pregnancy wouldn't be the type of thing Annie discussed with her sister, who she'd already blocked from social media to prevent lectures about her relationship choices. I'd done what I could to put Julia's mind at ease, but my plate was full with everything else going on in my life. I'd step aside and let Julia take over the search for her sister.

TWENTY-SEVEN

"Have fun, Lily." I gave my daughter one last hug, resting my lips on the crown of her head and inhaling the scent of her hair. No matter where we were, she always smelled like home.

I steadied my feet on the sidewalk as Keith took Lily's hand and pulled her closer to him. "We're going to ride that big Ferris wheel and eat junk food." He looked only at Lily, avoiding all eye contact with me. I rested my hand on my hip, preferring Keith's cold shoulder to the fake good guy act he'd performed last weekend.

Lily hopped up. "Okay."

The social worker was the same rosy-cheeked woman that had supervised Keith's last visit. She wore a kind smile and had looped a colorful silk scarf around her neck. Her arm pinned a canvas messenger bag to her side. "We'll meet you back at this location at 5 p.m." She appraised me, surely sensing my discomfort. "Don't worry. I'll be supervising them the whole time."

I gave a slight nod, still feeling uneasy. It was May 31st, Memorial Day weekend, and there were sure to be larger than normal crowds at Navy Pier. They climbed into Keith's pickup truck, parked illegally in front of a fire hydrant. The truck veered into traffic, eventually disappearing from sight.

Feeling lost, I forced my feet around the block. The sky held a low layer of clouds, and even my shadow had faded from my side. The usually vibrant city now appeared monochrome, everything layered in shades of gray. I passed the neighborhood café, noticing the aroma of roasting coffee beans. As much as I wanted to treat myself to a steaming frothy drink, I kept moving. For weeks, I'd been skipping even the smallest of extravagances to save money. Hot tears formed in the corners of my eyes, but I faced straight ahead, staring into the wind, refusing to let them win. I wished I could give Lily a simpler life, an emotionally stable father. But some things were out of my control.

A text buzzed through from Bridget. I paused at the sight of her name as memories of the shiny photos of Alex fluttered through my mind. *Why did she have them?* She seemed to be well over any past attraction she may have had to Alex. I'd avoided questioning Bridget about the photos because I knew she would be embarrassed by my discovery, that perhaps her little crush on my boyfriend when she first moved in had been more intense than she'd suggested. It seemed like the type of delicate topic I had to approach in person and at the right time, if at all. Given all that Bridget had done for me, and how quick she was to forgive the flaws of others, maybe it was best to let the whole thing drop. I focused on my phone and read Bridget's message: *Hey girl! Here's that riding stable I was telling you about. Call them to set up a lesson. You can use my car.*

I can't afford– I started typing but stopped. Instead, I double-clicked on the link for the Lakeside Equestrian Center. It opened into a window of colorful photos of gorgeous horses jumping over obstacles or standing in groups, smiling riders on their backs. My insides pulled with a yearning I rarely felt. The truth was I'd always loved horses, and I *did* want to take a few riding lessons. I rarely did anything just for myself. Here was my friend, Bridget, making it easy for me, handing me up the opportunity on a platter. Despite her other flaws, Bridget was thoughtful and generous. I studied the website, finding no prices listed for lessons.

I would have thought I'd have nothing remaining in my bank account after our first six weeks in the city. But somehow, I'd managed to save nearly three hundred dollars on top of the twelve hundred I'd already stashed away while living in Mom's basement. Lily and I made our groceries last for the whole week, every week. Alex had been incredibly generous, covering our outings and many of our meals out. With the deal I'd gotten on the apartment, plus not having the expenses of a car, I'd stretched my money further than I'd thought. Sure, there'd be summer camps and unforeseen expenses to cover, but with all the other cuts I'd made, maybe treating myself to a riding lesson a couple of times a month wasn't so crazy.

Up ahead, I spotted an open bench at the edge of a park. I strolled over and sat down, calling the number. A woman on the other end gave me the information I needed. The first lesson would be private and only thirty minutes, but then I could join a group lesson and save money. If I only went every other week, it could fit within my budget. I set up my first lesson for a week from today at 10 a.m. with someone named Heather. Pushing aside my misgivings about Bridget's secret box of photos, I texted her to confirm that I could borrow her car and she could watch Lily at that time. She sent me back a row of thumbs-up emojis followed by several more smiley faces, horses, and hearts. I walked back home with a spring in my step that hadn't been there a few minutes earlier.

An hour later, I sat on Alex's couch, staring at the screen on my phone.

"I'm sure Lily is fine." He patted my knee, having observed

my obsessive-compulsive phone checking since I'd arrived. "The social worker is with them. Right?"

"Yeah."

"Okay. Let's put the phone down and hang out." He slid his arm behind me, lips landing on my cheek. "You hungry? I have eggs and veggies. I can make us a couple of omelets."

"Sure. Thank you. I haven't eaten much today."

As Alex chopped onion and green pepper and cracked eggs into a bowl, I sat at his kitchen counter, telling him about how I'd scheduled a riding lesson. He said he was proud of me for doing something for myself, and confessed he'd been terrified of horses ever since taking a trail ride when he was eight years old when a barn-sour horse had galloped away with him. Alex poured the mixture into the pan, butter sizzling beneath the eggs.

I'd already recounted all the details about the surprise visit from Annie's sister, Julia, right after I'd hurried home from the coffee shop the other day. Alex had been shocked, but he'd understood why I had to reveal part of Annie's secret to the worried sister.

I turned my phone face down. "I was just thinking about Julia again."

Alex stopped stirring, looking up at me. "Yeah."

"Has she been poking around Shorewood at all?" I asked. "She was definitely on a mission to find answers."

"No. But I don't hang out near the office much. At least Brickman wasn't around last week."

I leaned forward, resting my elbows on the counter. "There's nothing else about Annie's disappearance you haven't told me, right?"

"I told you everything I know." Alex looked at me, setting his jaw. "You know, now that you mention it, I really wish you hadn't mentioned my name to Julia. Only because it could get back to Brickman, and who knows what he'll do if he thinks I ratted him out."

"I'm sorry. I made it clear that the two of you weren't close. It broke my heart to see how worried Julia was about her sister. I couldn't think of how else I would have known about Annie's pregnancy. It's not exactly the kind of information I'd overhear in the parent pick-up line."

Alex turned his back on me, facing the stove. "Yeah. I get it. She put you on the spot. Hopefully, Annie will get in touch soon, and this whole ordeal will blow over."

"Yeah."

Alex slid two perfectly cooked omelets onto our plates. As we ate, Alex's phone buzzed with a text. He stared at it for a minute, set it down, then picked it up again.

"Who's that?"

"Oh, nothing. My friend, Brian, has an extra ticket to the Cubs game this afternoon. He asked if I could go." Alex took a few bites, staring straight ahead.

"Are you going?"

"Nah. I know you're having a hard time with Lily being with Keith today. I want to be here for you."

I set down my fork. "I'm fine. Really. Go to the game with your friend. The weather's getting nicer already."

"It's okay. I need to clean this place. It's a mess."

I glanced around the apartment, which looked a little dusty, but not too bad otherwise. "I'll clean it up for you. It's the least I can do after all you've done for me. And it will keep my mind off Lily. I want you to go to the game." I nodded toward his phone. "Text him back."

"Really?"

"Yes."

"Okay. You don't have to clean my place, though. I can do that tomorrow."

I smiled at him as he texted his friend the good news.

"I've got to leave in about fifteen minutes. I'm going to change." He stood up and moved his plate to the sink.

"Do you have an extra key so I can lock up when you leave?" I asked.

"Sure."

"And if you don't mind, I'm going to throw away the hair products and makeup that your ex left behind in your bathroom." I winked at Alex.

Alex dropped his head. "Sorry about that. I didn't even realize her stuff was still in there. Go ahead and throw away whatever you want."

Several minutes later, Alex was gone. The apartment felt different without him in it, a little mysterious. But it was comforting to be surrounded by his things—the books, artwork, clothing, and furniture he'd selected. I washed the dishes first and put them away. Then I wiped the dust from the shelves, dresser, and nightstands. Trash bag in hand, I retrieved half-empty cans of women's styling mousse, leave-in conditioner, and shampoo from the bathroom cupboard and tossed them into the bag. A small wicker basket shoved into the back corner held lipstick, eyeshadow, and tinted moisturizer. I threw the whole thing into the bag, my body lightening as I banished each reminder of Sarah.

I ducked down to the cupboard again, spying a lump of sheer red fabric. It must have been wedged between the basket of makeup and the corner of the cupboard. I pinched the item between my thumb and index finger, pulling it toward me as the lacy cloth fell open, rumpled and nearly see-through. A skimpy pair of lace-lined panties hung near my face, a piece of women's lingerie that didn't leave much to the imagination. My stomach lurched as images of Alex removing them from his previous flame tumbled through my mind. My eyes flickered away from

Alex's ex-girlfriend's panties, but not before noticing they were about my size with the word "Maidenly" stamped in black across the back seam. I wasn't familiar with the brand. The piece of clothing felt toxic in my hand and I tossed it into the trash bag, wondering if I should invest in some sexier underwear.

Then—before I could stop myself—I sat on the couch and googled Alex's former girlfriend, entering the name he'd mentioned once with a sour look on his face. *Sarah Lewiston Chicago*. Images of Alex's ex appeared on my screen. She was thirty years old, pretty, a community planner employed by the city, a graduate of the University of Chicago. Everything I found matched what Alex had told me. Sarah had dumped Alex and then wanted him back. He'd had enough self-respect to say no. Alex was mine now. I closed the browser on my phone, putting the past behind us, and carried the bag out to the garbage chute in the hallway.

TWENTY-EIGHT

I nearly ran into someone as I exited Alex's apartment, eager to throw away reminders of his ex.

"Oh. Excuse me." Mrs. Levy placed her hand on her chest, her face white. "I wasn't expecting you to pop out of there like that."

"Hi." I lowered the bag. "Sorry. I was just helping my friend clean up his place a little."

"I see." The woman raised her over-plucked eyebrows at me, eyes darting from my door to Alex's.

I could feel my cheeks burning. "What are you doing on the fourth floor?" I asked, eager to shift her probing stare away from me.

Mrs. Levy raised her chin. "I'm on the condo board. I do weekly checks of the hallways to make sure everyone is following the rules. No holiday decorations or political signs in the common areas. That sort of thing."

"Oh." I couldn't help glancing to the spot above my door where Annie Turner had installed a security camera. "What about security cameras?"

Judith shook her head, disapproving. "Not allowed. We don't want people to think the building is unsafe."

It was clear the woman standing next to me was the one who'd reported Annie's breach of the rules, forced her to take the camera down. The policy seemed unnecessarily harsh, especially for a single woman who may have been worried about her safety. I recalled how easily Whitney Brickman had slipped past the lobby security and I was sure others could do it too. But maybe the lack of cameras had helped Annie disappear in the end. I thought of the creepy documentary I'd been watching about the hotel in L.A. where the Canadian tourist disappeared. Many believed the building was cursed or haunted, explaining the building's murderous past. I faced Judith, the woman who'd lived in this place longer than anyone else. I couldn't help wondering what secrets resided at 420 Roslyn Place. "Has anything bad ever happened here? I mean, in the years you've lived in the building?"

"What do you mean?"

"I don't know. Maybe a robbery or a murder somewhere in the building."

The woman shook her head. "No. Nothing like that. A woman got mugged out front on the street once. That was about five years ago, but it was three in the morning, and she'd been walking alone, not paying attention. Come to think of it, she wasn't even a resident here."

"Huh." I looked down. A random mugging outside wasn't exactly the bombshell I'd been searching for.

"That's exactly why there's no need for individuals to have security cameras. Can you imagine the eyesore? And how alarming rows of security cameras would be to prospective buyers?"

"I guess." I glanced away to hide my total disagreement. "Well, our hallway looks pretty clear to me."

"Yes. Everything looks fine here. I should head down to the

third floor." She searched up and down the long hallway. "Is Lily home? I'd love to say hello."

"No. Lily's visiting with her dad today. They went to Navy Pier."

"I see." Judith pushed her frown into a smile. "Well, Lily is just a little angel. It's wonderful to have her in the building."

I smiled back, lifting the bag off the floor. "Thank you. Enjoy the rest of your day."

She nodded and wandered to the stairwell as I stepped toward the trash chute.

That night, I lay in bed, grateful the day was over. Keith, Lily, and the social worker had met me on time at the pick-up spot. Lily's face was sticky with the remnants of cotton candy, but other than that, she was no worse for wear. She even seemed happy. I was relieved she'd had a positive experience with her dad, but I hated the jealousy that crept through me. At least, it would be another month before I had to face Keith again.

I heard the muffled sound of a closet door opening and closing on the other side of the bedroom wall, and I knew it was Alex getting ready for bed. He'd spent the afternoon at the Cubs game, followed by dinner out with his friend. He'd stopped by for a few minutes after he'd returned home, thanking me for cleaning his place, asking about Lily's day, and telling me about the game. I gave him a rundown of my day, deciding to leave out the part where I'd unearthed Sarah's lacy lingerie in his cupboard. Alex's marathon training had been canceled this weekend because of the holiday, but he had his own run planned for the next morning, which was Memorial Day. He wanted to sleep in his own bed to rest up.

I pulled the covers up to my chin, staring through the darkness, eyes entranced by the lights of other buildings outside my window. The yellow and white lights were beautiful, twinkling like stars. Two cars honked at each other somewhere in the distance. Laughter boomed from the sidewalk. Several blocks away, a siren whirred. This cacophony of sounds had become my urban lullaby. I let my head sink into the pillow, my eyelids growing heavy as I drifted to sleep.

I sat up in bed, gasping. A surge of adrenaline shot through me because a noise had yanked me from my slumber. *What was it?* I held my breath, afraid to breathe or blink. For a moment, I could have sworn someone else had been in the bedroom with me. My eyes searched through the blackened room but found nothing amiss, nothing moving. I was alone. *Had a floorboard in the living room creaked?* Angling my head toward the door, I listened for footsteps. But only silence met my ears. I waited, frozen. A man yelled from somewhere outside. Someone else shouted in response. Maybe they were the ones who'd woken me up.

The clock on my nightstand glowed with the time: 3:27 a.m. I remained still, listening. Two minutes passed. Then five. There was no movement, not even the faintest hint of a sound from the living room. I exhaled and lowered my eyelids. The people outside had been yelling while I was asleep. That must have been what had woken me so abruptly. Rolling onto my side, I hid beneath my pillow and returned to my dreams.

Lily scampered around the kitchen, plucking the last two donuts from the box and setting them on two plates. "Can we get more of these?"

"We can look for them at the store later." I poured myself a mug of coffee and sat at the table, making a mental list of things I needed to get done before the work week started—wash a couple of loads of laundry and shop for groceries, for starters.

Lily blinked at me, looking so sweet in her pink jammies. "Can I ride my bike today?"

"Yes." I'd borrowed a hand-held air pump from Alex yesterday after spotting it on a shelf in his closet next to some tools, boxes of nails, and a couple rolls of duct tape. "We'll go to the trail this morning. Your tires are as good as new."

"Yay!" Lily flailed her arms, nearly knocking over her orange juice.

I moved her cup further away and stood up, heading toward the window to see how the weather looked. My head was hazy with sleep, but as I reached halfway across the living room, something popped in the corner of my vision. My body went rigid, panic prickling over my skin. I struggled to gulp down air, turning toward the out-of-place object. A few inches in front of the door, the white paper square gleamed back at me from the floor.

I gasped, inching toward the tiny white square. I'd wedged the paper into the crack last night and locked the door. Someone must have opened the door, been in the apartment as we slept. The memory of being startled awake in the middle of the night tunneled through me. My fingers grasped the metal handle, jiggling it. The door was locked. I stepped back, confused. I plucked the paper from the floor and returned it to its keeping place on the console table.

"Mommy, what's wrong?"

"Nothing, sweetie." I rotated away to hide my lying face. Something was very wrong. Someone outside had a key to my apartment, had crept around in the dark as we slept, and locked the door behind them when they left. *Who would do that? And why?* Alex had a key because I'd given him my spare one, but he wasn't a creeper. Had Annie given a key to someone else? Drake? Maybe even Ben Brickman? I shuddered at the thought of either of those men having access to my apartment. But how would Brickman have gotten past the doorman at three in the morning? There wouldn't be anyone coming and going at that time.

Julia Turner's words edged into my mind: *Annie thought someone was stalking her... She thought someone was listening like there was a hidden microphone.*

I recalled Judith Levy's odd behavior, along with her statement that she'd watered Annie's plants when Annie had gone out of town. Did Judith still have a key to 4B? I reconsidered the woman's unusual interest in my daughter and her policing of security cameras. Suddenly, a terror ripped through me as I pictured the stuffed animal she and her husband had given Lily. I darted into Lily's bedroom, picking up the cheetah, turning it over. I'd seen stories of people hiding cameras inside of clocks or teddy bears to spy on their nannies and I feared this was what the Levys had done. I squeezed the toy, checking the stitching for any irregularities. I inspected the vinyl collar and squeezed the eyes, which were nothing more than solid beads of plastic. There was no camera built into this toy.

"What are you doing with Champ?" Lily frowned.

"Oh, nothing." My breath was jagged as I handed the toy to her, wondering if I'd gone mad. Lily stared after me as I returned to the living room and looked around. Nothing appeared out of place. Even the twenty-dollar bill I'd left on the kitchen counter remained as I'd left it. I opened my top desk drawer, finding the letters from Julia Turner in their place. I picked up my phone to call Alex, but remembered he was already out running. Instead, I texted him: *You weren't in my apartment last night, were you?*

Maybe there was a more straightforward explanation, something much less sinister than what I was imagining. I recalled the spare key I'd given Alex the first time he'd watched Lily. I'd thought it was good for him to have a key in case they wanted to go somewhere or run down to the lobby for something. I hadn't asked for the key back and Alex had never mentioned it again.

Perhaps Alex had remembered in the middle of the night that he'd left something he needed for his run and hadn't wanted to wake us. Or maybe no one had been inside our apartment at all. The paper square could have fallen out on its own as one of my neighbors stomped down the hallway.

I walked over to the intercom and called down to the front desk.

"This is Henry."

"Hi, Henry. It's Rachel in 4B."

"Good morning, Rachel! What can I do for you?"

"I just wanted to follow up on getting my locks changed. Have you found anyone that can come sooner?"

"Yes. As a matter of fact, I located another locksmith who can get it done a week from Thursday, so I canceled the other guy. I was going to let you know the next time I saw you."

A week from Thursday sounded like an eternity to me. Still, it was better than waiting three weeks for the first company. "Okay. Thank you."

Henry must have heard the disappointment in my voice because he paused, exhaling. "Your ex-husband really has you on edge, huh?"

"Yeah. You could say that."

"We're all keeping a close watch on the front door. I can promise you that."

"Thank you, Henry. I appreciate it."

"Sure thing. Enjoy your day now."

"I will." But as I stepped away from the intercom, unease seeped through me. Something had yanked me from my sleep last night, and I still didn't know what it was.

TWENTY-NINE

Later that morning, Alex knocked on my door. I opened it, finding him sweaty and still in his running clothes. He held up the message I'd sent him on his phone, narrowing his eyes. "I would never let myself into your apartment without asking you first."

"I'm sorry. I know, it's just that I thought I heard a noise last night. I wondered if you forgot something." I stepped back to let him inside, but Alex remained in the hallway.

He flung his hand in the air. "There's always noises in the middle of the night in this building. It doesn't mean someone broke into your apartment. Especially not me! Why would you even think that?" His words were clipped. I'd offended him. "Was anything missing or out of place? Did you see anyone?"

"No. I didn't. I was half asleep."

Alex frowned.

"I'm sorry I suggested it might have been you. It was probably nothing."

He crossed his arms. "Anyway, it turns out I can't hang out today. My run killed me. I'm exhausted and going to take the day to rest. Maybe knock out a few errands later."

I nodded, feeling like I'd screwed up. I'd all but questioned his integrity. "Okay. Maybe I'll see you tomorrow then."

"Yeah." Alex lowered his chin and turned away.

If someone had been inside the apartment the night before, I was sure it wasn't my boyfriend. But the fact that I'd considered the idea had opened a rift between us.

On Wednesday, I sat at my desk, clicking through mind-numbing forms and thinking about the school drop off earlier that morning. Lily had been so excited to go to school because of the visit from the people from the science museum; a traveling field trip, they called it. As soon as she'd bounded through the entrance, I'd turned toward the fountain, stomach dropping as I spotted Principal Brickman chatting up a group of moms in the distance. We'd made eye contact for a moment, and I'd quickly looked away. But I'd seen how he'd turned away from the other women and started marching toward me. I'd hustled in the opposite direction, slipping beyond the school gates before he reached me.

Alex had been giving me the cold shoulder for a few days now, and I felt broken inside. It seemed odd he'd been so offended by my single question, and I wondered if there was more going on. Whatever it was, I needed to make things right, to get him to talk about it. I flipped over my phone and texted him: *I'd love it if you could join Lily and me for dinner tonight. I'm making my famous spaghetti and garlic bread. I'm sorry again about the other day.*

My message sat unopened for a couple of hours as my hope deflated. At 12:15, his response popped through: *That sounds nice. I'll be there.*

All at once, my entire body felt lighter and a smile tugged at my lips. All was not lost.

·   ·   ·

A few hours later, Alex arrived from next door, his freshly shaved neck pink with razor burn. He dressed in jeans and a navy shirt that brought out the blueness of his eyes. Squeezing my arm as he entered, he surprised me with a peck on the cheek.

"Thanks for the invitation." He picked at the stitching on his jeans. "I'm sorry for the way I've been acting."

"I'm sorry, too."

I served up the salad, pasta, and bread as Lily told us all about the visitors from the science museum and described the experiments they did in class, where they looked at various objects and invisible ink under a black light to see how differently they appeared. "Some things glow. And some things that you can't even see without the light look black." Lily's eyes were wide and bright, and I was happy she was this excited about the things she learned in school. "I got to bring the black light home today. Marnie got the other one. Everyone gets it for one night." Lily jumped up and unzipped her backpack, removing something that looked like an oversized flashlight. "Don't shine it in your eyes."

"That's really cool, Lily." I nodded toward her. "You should turn off all the lights in your bedroom and see what your room looks like."

"Yeah!" Lily carried the light into her bedroom, closing the door. A minute later, she bounded from the bedroom. "My bedspread looks cool under the light. I'm going to check the bathroom now."

"Okay."

The door clicked closed. "Whoa! Mommy, look at the wall in here!" Lily's muffled voice sounded from behind the enclosed space.

I stood up and crossed the room, opening the door to join Lily in the darkened bathroom. As I shut us inside, she turned on the black light again, pointing at the wall behind the toilet. "Look!"

It took a second for my eyes to register the sight on the wall, where a gruesome pattern appeared, as if someone had splattered a pot of black ink across the tiles. Except I'd watched enough TV to know the mess wasn't ink. It was blood.

My hand flew to my mouth, and I nearly fell to my knees, feeling like I might vomit. I remembered the overpowering scent of bleach that had clung to this room for days after we'd moved in. The blood had been cleaned, but here under the harsh rays of the black light, I couldn't deny the brutal truth. Someone had been attacked—possibly murdered—right here in our bathroom. And I knew, in the pit of my gut, that the victim had been Annie Turner.

THIRTY

I opened the bathroom door, struggling for air. "I think it's blood spatter."

Alex stepped into the opening, his face falling. He looked exactly the way I felt—like he was going to throw up.

"Lily, go play in your room." I could barely force the words from my mouth.

"Why? I want to see this wall again." She clicked the light on and off, oblivious to what she'd discovered.

I clutched her bony shoulders. "Lily, I need you to go to your room now. Just for five minutes. Then I'll come find you."

"Fine." She dropped her head and dragged her feet into her bedroom, hugging the light to her side.

Alex's eyeballs bulged. "That was blood."

"It smelled like bleach in there when I moved in. Someone must have tried to clean it."

"The owner? Oliver?"

"Maybe." A previous conversation with Oliver surfaced in my mind, and I shook my head. "No. I don't think so. Oliver said the only thing he liked about the tenant before me was that she'd left the place spotless. I always wondered why someone leaving in such a rush would take the time to clean."

"Brickman did this." Alex spoke through clenched teeth. "He must have been angry about Annie's pregnancy and killed her. Or maybe he didn't want to let her leave." Alex covered his face with his hands. "Oh my God. I really believed that Annie escaped from here, that she was hiding."

I rubbed Alex's back. "You didn't know. You couldn't have known."

"That fucking bastard! When will his actions ever catch up with him?"

"We need to call the police." I reached for my phone, but Alex grabbed my arm.

"Rachel, wait. If we're wrong, or if the charges don't stick, I'll lose my job, for sure. No one else will hire me."

I stared at him, disbelief expanding inside me. "Alex! This isn't about you. If we're wrong, Brickman could take away Lily's scholarship too. We need to think of Annie, think of her family. A woman—your friend—was probably killed, and we might know who did it. We have to do the right thing."

Alex sighed, pacing toward the window and back, fingers laced behind his head. "Okay. Yeah. You're right. Sorry. Sorry. We should call the police."

Thirty minutes later, red lights flashed from outside, loud voices echoing from the street. I stepped toward my living room window, spotting four police cars parked below, one or two officers emerging from each one, and a crowd of onlookers gathering at the corner. I buzzed down to Henry, letting him know I'd called the police because of the blood spatter we'd discovered, giving permission to let the officers up to my apartment, and assuring him we were okay. I'd already deposited Lily with Bridget, and given Bridget a rundown of recent events as her face turned a greenish shade of white. I'd called Julia too, who'd just arrived with a stunned look etched on her face.

Two minutes later, a half-dozen police officers gathered at my door. A silver-haired man wearing a suit and badge appeared to be in charge, and he introduced himself to me and Alex as Detective Monroe. I led him to our gruesome discovery in the bathroom. Julia stood at the edge of my living room as we showed the officers how the wall looked under the black light, told them what we knew of Annie's disappearance and her involvement with Ben Brickman. The officers sprayed luminol on the wall, making the spatter glow with a bluish hue and getting a much more detailed view of the crime scene than we had with only the black light. They inspected every inch of the bathroom, measuring the trajectory of the droplets and taking photos. Julia kept her distance, pacing near the front window as she wiped away her tears. Whenever our eyes connected, she crossed her arms, and raised her chin in disgust because I hadn't told her the whole story, hadn't mentioned anything about her sister's involvement with Ben Brickman. I tried to explain why I'd omitted part of the truth, but Julia didn't want to hear it.

"Something definitely happened here." Detective Monroe motioned to another officer. "Cordon off this apartment with crime tape. We need to get everyone out of here and start collecting evidence. Have Dan identify anything we might be able to test for DNA."

"Annie was murdered in here, wasn't she?" Julia stood at the detective's side, her bulging eyes peering into the bathroom.

"I don't like to jump to conclusions. We can't tell yet how long that blood has been there or who it belonged to." He hooked his thumbs in his pockets.

"Yes, but my sister has been missing for over two months. She's from Australia but was visiting the US for a year. This was the last place anyone saw her."

The detective pressed his lips into a flat line. "I agree, it doesn't look good. We'll see if we can test any of the blood residue, but the bleach has most likely destroyed any DNA evidence, and it'll take a few days to get the results back from the lab. We won't know for sure until that happens."

My voice faltering, I repeated Julia's concerns about no one having heard from Annie in weeks, that she may have been pregnant, and about the strong smell of bleach when I'd moved in.

"We'll cover all the bases and get to the bottom of this," Detective Monroe said. "Unfortunately, most of the crime scene has been compromised already because you and your daughter have been living here for two months. But we'll do our best and I'll be paying Ben Brickman a visit as soon as I leave here."

Another officer took my name and phone number, along with Alex's and Julia's, and reassured us the detective would keep us updated as new information emerged.

Julia started asking another question, but the detective held up his hand. "I know this is very upsetting, but I'm going to have to ask all of you to step out into the hallway while we do what we need to do in here. It's going to be another couple of hours. We'll have plenty of time tomorrow to take statements from you down at the precinct, as needed. But right now, we need to collect physical evidence."

Alex waved us ahead of him out into the fourth-floor hall-way. To my surprise, a group of neighbors stood near the elevator speaking to each other in low voices—Stan and Judith Levy, Drake, and Marie and Sheldon from next door. Alex and I walked toward them, but Julia stopped.

"I'd like to be alone," she said, before heading in the oppo-site direction, to the far end of the hall.

"What happened, Rachel?" Judith asked. "Are you and Lily okay?"

"Yes. We're fine." I glanced toward Julia, who stood at a

distance with her back to us. "That's Julia. She's Annie Turner's sister."

"Annie's sister from Australia?" Drake looked from Julia to me, his small eyes pinning me in place.

Judith shook her head. "But why is Annie's sister here? And why is there a whole police squad out front? All this commotion looks terrible for the building."

I glanced at Alex. "Lily had a black light and discovered some blood spatter on the bathroom wall."

"We called the police when we saw it," Alex added.

Marie gasped. "Oh my gosh. Do they think something happened to Annie?"

My eyes darted toward Julia, who cradled her head in her hands at the far end of the hallway. My mouth had gone dry, and I couldn't manage an answer.

Drake grunted, kicking the carpet with the toe of his combat boot. "I knew it." He closed his eyes. "Annie wouldn't have left without telling me."

I scanned my neighbors' shocked faces, finding my voice. "We think Ben Brickman, the principal at Shorewood, might know something." I angled my face toward Drake. "Annie was dating him. But you probably knew that already."

"I never saw any school principal around here." Drake looked away, giving me a clear view of the spider legs clawing toward his eyeball. "You know who I did see leaving Annie's apartment? That guy." Drake jabbed his finger toward Alex, a sneer forming on his lips. "You're hiding something. I know it."

Alex squared his shoulders, a muscle pulsing in his jaw. "You've got it wrong, Drake. The police will probably arrest Ben Brickman before midnight. I was helping Annie escape, unseen, so Ben couldn't follow her. That's why you saw me leaving her apartment."

Drake smacked his fist into his opposite palm. His face

twitched, and I could see that behind the ink and bravado, the news of Annie's death was painful for him.

I touched Drake's shoulder. "Hey. I'm really sorry about your friend."

He jerked his head up, his pained eyes scanning up and down the hallway. "Are they going to search everyone's places?"

"I don't think so. At least, not without a good reason."

Drake shoved his hands into his pockets, eyes on the floor.

Alex stepped toward him. "Why, Drake? What are you hiding in there? Drugs?"

Although I suspected Drake did keep drugs in his apartment, I didn't like the tone of Alex's voice, like he was goading Drake on.

Drake sneered. "Never mind. It's nothing."

Judith Levy glared at Drake. "We have a zero-tolerance policy for illegal substances in this building. It's in the bylaws."

"Fuck all of you." Drake lowered his face and turned away, disappearing into his apartment.

Judith gasped.

Marie shook her head, looking at Sheldon. "I can't believe something like this happened right next door."

Her husband shrugged. "We were out of town. How could we have known?" A second later, they pulled their eyes from each other and turned toward Alex. "You didn't hear any screams or fighting back before Annie left?"

Alex closed his eyes, head falling forward. "No. I must have been asleep. My bedroom is on the other side and my fan is loud."

"Stan sleeps like a rock too," Judith said. "Not me. I wake up at every little bump."

Behind Judith, the stairwell door barged open. Bridget stood in the opening with Lily leaning next to her leg. "Oh my gosh. I can't stand being up there and not knowing what's going on." Bridget looked at me. "Is it okay for us to be here?"

I nodded and held out my hand. Lily jumped toward me. "The police are taking photos and collecting evidence. It's going to be another couple of hours before we can go back inside."

"Have they figured out anything?"

"Not yet."

We stayed in the hallway for a while longer, listening to the muffled voices sounding from within my apartment. Bridget approached Julia and encouraged her to stand with us. She tried to make conversation with Julia about her family back in Australia, but Annie's older sister seemed to be in shock, unable to answer the most basic questions.

A few minutes later, the Levys insisted on calling a cab for Julia to take her back to her hotel, and the crowd in the hallway dispersed. Lily and I waited inside Alex's apartment until I received a text from the detective saying they'd completed their search and we could return. We stood in the hallway as Detective Monroe removed the crime-scene tape. He said they had collected the remaining physical evidence, mostly from the bathroom, and would get the tests going as soon as possible. They would also secure the building's camera footage, and question Ben Brickman and others. Detective Monroe promised to keep me and Julia informed of any developments.

At last, we were back inside our apartment, the night turning black outside my windows. My insides felt hollow, my bones brittle, like a building about to crumble. Alex pulled me into a hug, resting his chin on my head. "I should stay here tonight. Who knows what kind of stunt Brickman will pull next?"

"Okay." I eyed the lock on my door which was still over a week away from being updated. It was late, and I didn't want to be alone. "Let's get to sleep."

THIRTY-ONE

The next day passed in a blur. Alex, Lily, and I walked to school together, thankful for no sign of Brickman. I wondered if the police had arrested him already and who would take over for him as principal. Hopefully, Brickman's replacement would be someone with a stronger moral compass, someone who recognized Lily was worthy of her scholarship. My mind spun with questions and imagined scenarios. *Were the police raiding Brickman's home? Questioning his wife? How had he disposed of Annie's body and cleaned the mess without anyone seeing?* The hours passed this way, with me checking my phone every few minutes, my molars clenched so tight I thought they might crack.

Finally, it was time to retrieve Lily from school. Tomorrow was Friday, and then I'd have the weekend to regroup.

Twenty minutes later, I guided Lily home from school, Alex flanking our sides. There'd still been no word from the police about an arrest. As we crossed the street, Alex's phone buzzed. He looked at the screen, feet abruptly stopping.

"What's wrong?" I asked.

He shook his head, eyes downcast. "I knew it. That slimeball."

I leaned over his phone to see what he was talking about. A text message read: *Good luck finding a new job.* It was from Ben Brickman.

Alex shoved his phone into his pocket, refusing to look at me. "He's going to get away with this just like he gets away with everything else. He's already sending threats. My teaching career is over."

"Maybe he's just lashing out because he knows he's about to get arrested."

We started walking again, but Alex stared straight ahead, his eyes glazed and movements rigid. He gave me the silent treatment the rest of the way back to our building. We entered the lobby.

Henry nodded toward us. "That was quite a commotion last night. Is everyone holding up okay?"

"Hi, Henry. We're fine," I said, while Alex stood silently next to me.

"Hopefully, this is all a misunderstanding. I'd hate to think anything bad happened to Annie."

"I know. Me too."

Henry stopped talking, probably sensing the tension between me and Alex, and buzzed us through to the elevators.

"Want to come over and talk?" I finally asked Alex as we reached the fourth floor.

"Nah. Sorry. I need to be alone."

I stepped in front of him, forcing him to look at me. "Alex, things are going to be okay."

"Maybe for you." His face was sad as he stepped past me and unlocked his door. He darted inside without looking back.

Feeling rattled by Alex's attitude, I entered my apartment with Lily by my side. I felt terrible about his situation. After all, he'd just found out his friend had likely been murdered as he slept next door, and his teaching position was in jeopardy. Still, it seemed as if he was blaming me for Brickman's threatening message. I didn't regret alerting the police to what we'd discovered in the bathroom, but it seemed Alex did. But his concern about the future of his career was valid, and I worried about him. In an instant, Brickman could reveal the black mark on Alex's record to the committees at Shorewood, expose the violent incident between teacher and student in Silver Meadows years before. Brickman had hired Alex and gone along with the cover-up of Alex's past to keep the donations flowing from Alex's family friend who was one of Shorewood's major donors. Yet, there was no doubt the principal would spin the facts in his favor, say he knew nothing about it, if the truth about Alex ever emerged.

I flopped onto the couch, staring at the ceiling as Lily unpacked a few books from her backpack. Angry banging and slamming noises echoed from next door. If I was completely honest, Alex's behavior scared me a little. Maybe I'd been so entranced by the idea of a new and improved partner that I'd been too trusting of the first handsome and charming man I'd encountered. I'd been conscious of taking things slowly, but Alex had been so easy to be around. Still, there was a lot about him I didn't know. Keeping my distance from him for a few days was probably the wise thing to do. I'd try to keep to myself for a while. Once things settled down with Annie's disappearance, we could dip our toes back in, get ourselves reacquainted, and pick up where we'd left off.

I awoke on Friday morning still feeling out of sorts and uncertain. Lily and I walked to school without bothering to knock on Alex's door first. Although Lily hovered nearby, brushing against my skin as we trekked along the sidewalk, loneliness descended on me. A black crow flew overhead and landed on a spindly tree. Hazy clouds loomed low in the sky. There'd still been no word from Detective Monroe, and I wondered how it could possibly be taking so long to make an arrest.

I deposited Lily safely to her classroom, drawing a curious smile from Ms. Lisle. I exited against a tide of students, pausing at the fountain to survey the surroundings. Nicola approached from the sidewalk, pulling Bryce in a red wagon as Marnie skipped next to her. "Bye, Mom!" Marnie darted past me and disappeared through the north entrance.

Nicola waved. "Hi, Rachel."

"Hi." I managed a smile. "Taking over drop-off duties today?"

"Our nanny took the day off." She pushed the wagon back and forth, which seemed to please Bryce. "Marnie would love to have Lily over for another playdate soon."

"That would be great. Thanks. We'll have Marnie over at some point too. Maybe I can take them to the bike path."

Nicola said something else about summer camp applications, but I didn't register the words because a circle of women stood on the other side of the walkway, whispering and shooting furtive glances toward me. My knees almost buckled at the sight of Liz Meyer-Barnes perched in the center of the group. I locked eyes with her but quickly turned back to Nicola. "Maybe you can text me the camp information." I didn't want to be rude to Nicola, but my body pulsed with the overwhelming need to flee.

"Okay. I'll send—"

"Hi, Rachel." Liz stepped next to me, so close I could smell her flowery perfume. She grinned toward me and Nicola, but there was something evil glittering in her eyes. "Is it true that your apartment is a crime scene?"

I opened my mouth, but no sound came out.

"I heard a woman was murdered in your bathroom right

before you moved in." She blinked. "How did you not notice all the blood stains?"

My eyes found Nicola, who'd stared at me with a stunned look. "Is that true, Rachel?"

"Yes. I mean, no." I closed my eyes, shaking my head. "Lily brought a black light home from school and when she shone it on the wall, we saw a stain that looked like blood spatter. I called the police because the woman who rented the apartment before us has been missing."

"Oh my God."

"We don't know anything for sure yet." I looked around to see if Principal Brickman was lurking nearby, listening. But there was no sign of him. "Who told you about it?"

Liz shrugged. "The rumor mill, I guess."

I glanced at the women who hovered nearby, clearly eager for Liz to report back to them. I wondered if the principal or his wife had told one of them about the investigation.

Liz leaned closer, smirking. "Your apartment sure doesn't seem like a safe place for a child to live."

I took a breath to stop myself from punching Liz in her perfect teeth. She was clearly going to report the events back to Keith if she hadn't done so already. He would figure out a way to use it against me. I leaned close to Liz's face. "My apartment is perfectly safe. This has nothing to do with me or Lily, so stay out of it."

Liz raised her palms in the air and backed away. "Jeez. Someone's a little testy," she said as she spun around, returning to her clique.

Nicola stared at me as she jiggled the wagon. I couldn't tell if she was scared or stunned. "I wish you'd told me about that, Rachel."

"I'm sorry." I dropped my head. "It only just happened. I'll let you know as soon as I find out anything else."

"Are you and Lily in danger?"

"No," I said, although I didn't know for sure. Ben Brickman's creepy grin flashed in my mind. I hoped he was already in handcuffs somewhere, but it didn't feel right to say anything before I knew all the facts. There was a chance he'd walk free. My mouth went dry as I refocused on Nicola. "Honestly, right now, I have no idea what's going on."

THIRTY-TWO

It was a sunny Saturday morning, the first weekend in June. Birds chirped outside, joining the sounds of chattering people and zooming cars on the street below. After my uncomfortable encounter with Liz yesterday, the rest of the day had passed in a state of uncertainty, with Lily and I holed up in the apartment all night. I hadn't seen Alex at Shorewood, and I wondered if he'd called in sick. I texted him to ask if he'd heard any updates, but he hadn't responded.

I forced my feet into an old pair of sneakers and tied back my hair, dreading the visit to the riding stable. Scheduling the lesson had been a mistake, and I wanted more than anything to cancel. It was supposed to have been a fun activity, but the thought of driving to the suburbs and leaving my daughter behind was only causing more stress. It was too late to back out, though. Doing so would be like throwing money in the trash. I had to keep my scheduled commitment and make the best of it. Tomorrow, I'd tell everyone I'd decided not to continue with the lessons.

I dropped Lily upstairs with Bridget, whispering a brief update on the investigation to my friend as Lily unpacked her toys. After retrieving Bridget's SUV from the parking garage, I followed my GPS to my destination. A sign for Morton Grove stood near the exit, and I realized the riding stable was located in the same suburb where Alex had said he'd grown up. A sense of longing shot through me and I wished I could call him up and tell him where I was, hear his candid take on his boyhood home. But Alex was still obviously furious at me—at the situation—and I guess I didn't blame him.

I parked Bridget's Pilot in the dusty lot outside the stables, a wad of cash stuffed in my pocket. A bubbly woman who looked about my age introduced herself as Heather and led me to a sleepy-looking bay gelding named Chester. Heather demonstrated how to groom the horse. As she lifted Chester's front hoof and picked out the mud, I cleared my throat.

"My next-door neighbor mentioned that he grew up in this suburb. I didn't realize where I was until I saw the sign."

She glanced up at me. "What's his name? I grew up here too. I probably know him."

"Alex..." I started but corrected myself, "Michael Ballard."

"Oh, yeah. I remember Michael. He went to my high school but was a year older. He was a nice guy. I think everyone our age remembers him." Heather released the horse's leg, her features shifting. "It's just such a shame what happened to his girlfriend."

The dusty air filled my mouth. My legs felt unsteady as I forced myself to utter the next question. "What happened to his girlfriend?"

"She died in a car accident. Her name was Peggy Neuman. It was the fall of my junior year, senior year for them. I think Michael was driving them both home from a party." Heather handed me the hoof pick and picked up her phone, typing something and reading. "Yeah. Here's an article about it. It doesn't mention Michael by name, but he was the driver." She handed me her phone and I took it, my eyes skimming across the shocking headline and the words underneath.

> *Teen Girl Killed in Crash – The victim has been identified as seventeen-year-old Peggy Neuman, an Honor Roll student at Jeffries High School in Morton Grove, IL... returning from a party with her boyfriend when they hit a tree at high speed... the driver appeared to have lost control of the vehicle... It is unknown at this time whether the seventeen-year-old driver will face criminal charges resulting from his reckless driving... Peggy's family, friends, and the surrounding community are devastated by the loss of this rising star.*

"Oh my gosh." I sucked in a breath and steadied my arm as I passed the phone back to her. Heather's story was true. I was stunned Alex had never mentioned anything about the tragedy to me, just as he'd never mentioned the incident at his previous school. This car accident must have been a pivotal event in his life. Maybe he was only waiting for the right time to share it. "Did anything happen to Michael?"

"No. I mean, he wasn't injured or anything. He was only seventeen, so it's not like they sent him to jail. He might have taken a turn too fast, but obviously he didn't intend to kill anyone. It was just a horrible accident." Heather picked up a bristled brush, sweeping clouds of dust off the horse's coat. "We've all broken the speed limit from time to time. Right?"

"Yeah. Right." Acid rose in my throat. Things Alex had said over the past several weeks took on a new meaning. *I haven't driven in years...* I thought he'd been referring to the hassle and cost of owning a car in the city, but there'd been so much more to the story. *Small towns are so claustrophobic. People know too much...* If I'd only known what he'd really meant.

Heather sighed. "Michael was devastated. He missed so much school after the accident that everyone kind of thought he'd dropped out. But then he just showed up again one day. I can't even comprehend how he made up all that work."

"Did you know Peggy?"

"Not really. Only in passing. She was new to the school the year before. I remember she was smart, always winning academic achievement awards. The whole thing was really sad." Heather lowered the brush and shook her head. "How's Michael doing now?"

"Oh. He's fine. Still a nice guy. He's a teacher at a private school in the city." I smiled and looked away, realizing how little I knew about him.

"Cool. I'd say to tell him I said hello, but I'm not sure he would remember me."

We finished tacking up Chester, and Heather lent me a spare helmet. She led the horse to a small outdoor ring, where she tightened the girth and helped me get on as the information about Alex spun in my head. I spent the next thirty minutes struggling to sit tall in the saddle and push my heels down. Chester plodded in circles, occasionally veering toward the fence to steal a mouthful of weeds.

"Use your legs to keep him going straight."

I squeezed my calves around the horse, but he ignored me, probably sensing my distracted thoughts. At last, we picked up a trot, and I nearly bounced out of the saddle as we endlessly circled the ring.

"Stretch tall. Keep your heels down. Don't flap your elbows," Heather repeated from a bench on the side of the ring again and again.

My back ached, and my legs burned. Chester was barely going through the motions. The activity wasn't nearly as fun as I'd envisioned. Maybe horseback riding wasn't my thing after all.

Heather glanced at her watch. "Well, that's our time. Good

job!" She pointed at my sneakers. "Maybe buy some paddock boots for next time."

Chester veered toward the fence, where Heather grabbed the reins, and I jumped off. Even though my legs wobbled, I was grateful to be back on solid ground.

I paid Heather and said I'd call to schedule the next lesson, although I doubted I'd return. She helped me remove the saddle and bridle and put Chester back in his stall. I gave him a few pats on the neck and thanked him for the ride as he munched on a pile of hay.

I slumped behind the wheel of Bridget's car, parched, sweaty, and covered in dirt. The information about Alex's car accident—an accident that had resulted in his girlfriend's death —amassed in my mind, slowing my thoughts. My phone buzzed on the seat next to me just as I turned the ignition. It was the detective.

"Hello."

"Hi, Rachel. This is Detective Monroe. I'm following up on the blood spatter we looked at the other night."

"Yes."

"We interviewed Ben Brickman and his wife, Whitney." He sighed. "We're not going to arrest either of them."

It felt as if my insides had turned inside out, my hands and feet turning ice-cold. "Why not?"

"Because they were attending a conference in Toronto the last week of March. We've corroborated their whereabouts through personal interviews with their colleagues and security footage from the hotel where they stayed. If something happened to Annie Turner, they weren't involved."

"Are you sure?"

"Yes. The alibi is solid. Brickman admitted to having an affair with Annie Turner, but he and his wife were in another country when Annie went missing. We've checked flight manifests and, so far, we haven't found any record of Annie Turner boarding an international flight from O'Hare during that time. We still might get results from the bathroom wall sample if the bleach missed even a tiny spot. The lab is working on it but, unfortunately, it's not sounding promising. It could take a few more days before we know for sure. Just wanted to keep you informed."

"Okay. Thank you." I gripped the steering wheel, staring toward an empty paddock. Thick dread weighed down my limbs as a question edged its way into my mind: *If Ben Brickman didn't kill Annie, then who did?*

THIRTY-THREE

I drove back to the city in a trance, turning off the ignition once I reached Bridget's reserved space on the third floor of the parking garage a few blocks west of our building. I had no idea how I'd arrived there. My brain couldn't process the heap of alarming information I'd recently learned: Brickman hadn't murdered Annie, and Alex had been responsible for the death of his high school girlfriend, a bombshell he'd never shared with me. I reminded myself we'd only known each other for two months. Perhaps it wasn't realistic to expect someone to share all their darkest secrets in such a short time frame. Still, I didn't know what to make of any of it.

Now, I entered the lobby, slipping past Robbie as he accepted a package from a delivery person and scanning myself through the glass barrier. I took the elevator up to the fifth floor to retrieve Lily, grateful that no one else climbed inside the enclosed space with me. My hair stuck to my head in sweaty clumps, dust clung to my clothes, and I was sure my body held an unpleasant smell.

I knocked on Bridget's door, and she opened it, her wide smile falling when she saw me. "What happened to you?"

"It was rough." I handed her the keys.

Bridget giggled. "Did you fall off?"

"No. I think I wasn't in the right mindset. I'm not sure I'm going back."

"Bummer."

"Thanks for getting me to try it, though. Now I won't feel like I'm missing out on anything." I looked past her toward Lily, who was painting with watercolors on a yellow legal pad.

Bridget shrugged. "It was the only paper I could find."

"Hi, Mommy. I'm painting the zoo."

"That's wonderful. You can bring it back with us and finish it in our apartment." I thanked Bridget for babysitting and for letting me use her SUV again. Once Lily slipped past me into the hallway, I poked my head back inside, catching Bridget's attention. "The detective just called me, by the way. I can't believe it, but they cleared Brickman and his wife. Turns out they were in Toronto that last week of March. Also, there are no records of Annie boarding any flights from O'Hare."

Bridget tugged at the ends of her hair. "No way. So, who do they think—?"

"They don't know."

Bridget paced toward her front window, staring at the floor. When she turned back toward me, her face had gone even paler, and she looked like she might be sick. "This is crazy," she said, rubbing her hands together. "Keep me posted. Okay?"

"Yes. I will." I stepped into the hallway but not before I'd glimpsed the linen box on Bridget's shelf, sitting in the same place it had been before I'd knocked it over. I'd already decided to let the whole thing go, but now I changed my mind. There were too many unknowns nagging me. I turned back toward her. "Actually, Bridget?"

"Yeah."

"I've been meaning to ask you about something." I scratched my elbow. Lily raced past me, giggling as she ran laps up and down the long hallway. "I saw something in your apartment a week or so ago. I accidentally knocked over a box when you were in the bedroom and some photos spilled out. They were of Alex."

Bridget closed her eyes, dropping her head in dramatic fashion. "Oh, boy. This is embarrassing." She glanced toward the box and then refocused on me, her ivory cheeks flushing. "I took those photos a long time ago, when Alex first moved into the building. But it's nothing like whatever you're imagining."

"Why did you take them?"

"I'd moved in right around the same time as Alex and I was eager to meet people. I scoped out his running group and started snapping some pictures because I thought he was good-looking. Like I told you, I had a little crush on him, but he didn't feel the same." She waved a dismissive hand in the air. "I quickly moved on, of course. But I couldn't get rid of the photos. Alex made such a good subject. There's just so much hidden emotion behind his eyes, something almost mysterious about the way he stares ahead, like he's chasing down a dream or running from something terrifying."

I recalled a few of the photos I'd seen and knew the passion and sentiments she described were correct. Alex made an eye-catching subject, his raw emotion surfacing through the black-and-white ink. I nodded. "Your photos were really stunning."

"Thanks. I've been meaning to show them to him, to ask him if I can use them in an exhibit I've been thinking about putting together for the open show at the art museum. But I'm just so afraid of what he'll think of me. I swear I'm not a creeper."

"I know." I rubbed my forehead. "You know what? I bet he'd be flattered. He might even want a copy of one or two of them."

"You think?"

"Yeah. They're really good."

Bridget smiled and I could see the relief on her face. We said good night, and I heard Bridget's locks click behind her door after she closed it.

I followed Lily down one flight of steps. Listening to Bridget's explanation of the photos had capped my overactive imagination. Her intentions hadn't been anything sinister, but I was glad to have cleared the air. She'd been more thrown off by the news of Ben Brickman's non-arrest than I'd expected, but she was a single woman living alone in the same building. Just like me, she probably worried about being at risk herself, now that she knew the predator was still at large.

Back inside our apartment, I set Lily up with her watercolors and got myself a large glass of water, gulping it down. After showering and changing into fresh clothes, I sat next to her, admiring the painting. I texted Alex: *Can we talk? It's important.* Movement thumped from his apartment, and I knew he was home. He didn't respond to my message. Tilting my head toward Lily, I said, "I have to go talk to Alex about something. Can you come with me?"

Lily frowned. "Can I stay here?"

"I think it's better if we stick together." I hoped Lily wouldn't argue, that she wouldn't make me tell her our apartment was unsafe, a crime scene like Liz Meyer-Barnes had described it as yesterday. To my relief, Lily set down her paintbrush and slid off the chair.

A minute later, we knocked on Alex's door. He'd been so angry yesterday when he'd thought Brickman was getting away with murder. Now I had to tell him that neither Brickman nor his wife was responsible for whatever had happened to Annie. It was better if Alex knew that truth as soon as possible so that he could come up with a plan to keep his job at Shorewood.

And, as uncomfortable as it would be, I had to ask him about Peggy Neuman.

Alex swung the door open, a gust of air whooshing past my face. His arm jerked like he wanted to slam the door closed, but he stopped himself. "Hi, Lily." A smile twitched on his lips as he spotted her next to me.

"Hey." I inched forward, forcing him to make eye contact. "Sorry to bother you, but can I talk to you for a minute?"

Alex exhaled but waved us forward.

"Lily, you sit on the couch." I handed her my phone. "You can play the maze game. We're going to talk about grown-up stuff in the bedroom."

"Okay." She sat on the couch, swinging her feet and angling the screen toward her face.

Alex and I went into his bedroom and closed the door. I lowered myself onto a tangle of sheets and blankets at the edge of the bed, waiting for him to sit next to me. He remained standing, arms crossed.

"Alex, we'll figure out a way for you to keep your job. We've got dirt on Brickman, right? We can use it to our advantage."

"Did they arrest him yet?"

I struggled to speak, my tongue thick in my mouth. "That's the thing. The detective called me this morning. The police cleared Brickman. And his wife." I repeated their iron-clad alibi to Alex as his hands dropped to his sides.

"Toronto?" He tipped his head toward the ceiling, closing his eyes. "He didn't do it?"

"No. It would have been impossible. Annie was still alive on the date they left."

"Well, isn't that convenient?" Alex slammed his fist into the palm of his other hand.

I flinched. "Let's not panic. You'll be able to explain your way out of any involvement in this."

He paced the room, hugging his elbows. "Rachel, you need

to schedule a meeting with Brickman and tell him that you were the one who reported the information to the police. Say Annie's sister was the one who told you about the affair. And then when you saw the blood, you had no choice but to report it. You have to say that I wasn't even there."

I nodded. "Okay. Yeah. I can do that."

Alex slumped next to me on the bed, the mattress creaking. "I don't know. Maybe Brickman will buy that and decide not to fire me." He placed his hand on top of mine.

I cleared my throat, gathering the courage to bring up the next topic, which was sure to be difficult. "You know, I went out to that riding stable this morning."

Alex raised his shoulders, looking a little confused by the change of subject. "How was it?"

"Fine, I guess. It turns out the stable was in Morton Grove, which was where you grew up, right?"

Alex's eyes widened. "Oh. Yeah. I think I remember those stables."

"The woman who gave me the lesson—her name was Heather. She went to your high school." I squeezed his hand and waited for him to meet my eye. "She told me about the accident. About Peggy Neuman."

Alex dropped his head, eyelids blinking. "I wasn't trying to hide anything from you. There's not a day that goes by that I don't think of Peggy and what she could have become."

"I'm sorry. It must be so difficult for you to carry that burden. I wish you had told me. I'm always here to listen if you want to talk."

Alex hesitated, sniffling with his eyes focused on the floor. "The reason I love running so much is that it's one of the only times I don't think about the accident. I can focus on my breathing, my footsteps, my stride. There's no room for the past or future. Only the present."

"Yeah. That makes sense." I rubbed his shoulder, remembering how Bridget had noticed the intensity in Alex's face as he ran.

"I didn't go to Peggy's funeral." Alex's voice cracked as his chest heaved. "I couldn't face the family. That's something I'll always regret." Tears leaked down Alex's face, and he did not attempt to wipe them away. "I'm a horrible person."

"No. That's not true. We've all made bad mistakes, especially when we were teenagers. It doesn't mean we're bad people."

"Losing Peggy is the reason all my relationships fail. I've never dated anyone longer than a year." Alex faced me, his lips contorting into a grimace. "You should just leave me now. Save yourself the heartache."

"But I don't want to leave you. We can keep taking things slow, but I still want to be with you."

"Trust me on this, Rachel. We need to break up. You'll figure out soon enough that you shouldn't be around me."

My stomach contracted as if he'd punched me. I steadied myself on the edge of the bed. "We can take some time and space if that's what you want. But I'm not giving up on us." I could feel the heat building behind my face, the emotion rising in my throat. I gritted my teeth, refusing to believe this was the end. I'd waited my whole life to meet someone like Alex, and now I'd found him. I wouldn't walk away so easily. "Can we talk in a few days?"

"Yeah." His voice was flat though, and I couldn't tell if he meant it. "I'm really sorry, Rachel. I'm sorry I'm not the person you thought I was."

Legs shaky, I stood and staggered out of the room, finding Lily on the couch where I'd left her. I bit back tears and led her back to our apartment, where I locked the door.

"Mommy needs to use the bathroom." Lily nodded at me as I bolted into the tiny bathroom, the room where I was sure someone had murdered the last woman who'd rented this apartment. I closed myself inside, turning on the vent. Averting my eyes from the invisible blood spatter on the wall and the square of drywall the detective had removed, I tried to banish Mom's chiding voice from my head: *The higher you climb, the harder you fall.* I crumpled into a heap on the tiled floor and sobbed.

THIRTY-FOUR

On Sunday afternoon, Julia perched on my living room couch, drinking a cup of tea. I'd worried about how she was holding up after the authorities cleared the Brickmans, so I'd invited her over. Having another person with me also helped to keep my mind off Alex. True to his word, we'd had no further contact since yesterday.

Julia set her mug on a coaster. Her face was haggard and concern clouded her eyes. "Who else would have done something to Annie?"

"I don't know." I glanced toward Lily's bedroom, where she played inside with her dollhouse. The truth was, I'd started suspecting several people in the building. Drake with his suspicious lurking, his fascination with serial killers, and his fear at the idea of having his apartment searched. The Levys with their long history in the building and probing stares. Even the owner of 4B, Oliver Daniels, who was supposedly in California but surely held a key to the apartment. "You said Annie saw something in the basement that scared her?"

Julia dipped her chin. "Yes. Something inside of a box. That's all I know."

I thought of the cavernous, cage-filled storage room. Many of the storage lockers were stacked floor to ceiling with boxes. "There must be hundreds of boxes down there."

"I'd like to go down to the basement and take a look."

"Honestly, I don't think it will get us anywhere. Everyone's belongings are locked inside separate cages." A memory flickered through me. The day I retrieved Lily's bike, Leo helped Bridget carry up a box. *What had been inside it? Why did she invite an ex-con into her home?* Then there was the other box in Bridget's apartment, the one I'd accidentally bumped into, spilling photos on the floor. I'd accepted her explanation for having them, but there was a part of me that wondered if Bridget had been more infatuated with Alex than I'd realized. Had she been jealous of what she thought was a relationship between Alex and Annie? Maybe Annie had discovered the box of photos, the obsession. Was it possible Bridget had snapped and beaten Annie to death, that Leo—no stranger to criminal activity—had somehow helped her dispose of the body?

"Can I borrow your key?"

Julia's voice snapped me from my wild thoughts. "Yes," I said, noticing the desperation on her face, the way her mouth pulled down. I stood up and swiped my keys off the counter. "I'm going to stay here with Lily. Take the elevator down to the lower level. The storage room is on the right. Maybe take an extra look at the storage locker marked 5B."

"Why?"

"Nothing. Bridget is my friend. I just get weird vibes from her sometimes. Still, she has a good heart, and I can't imagine her doing anything like that." My eyes darted toward the bathroom. "She said she didn't even know Annie."

Julia stared at me, blank-faced.

"Also, 4D. That's Drake, across the hall. And 10ABC. That's the Levys' unit. I don't know." I tipped my head back, realizing I was sending Julia on a fool's errand. "It's probably nothing to do with any of these people."

Julia tightened her grip on the keychain. "I have to try. I'll check those first. I'll be back in a few minutes."

I tidied up the apartment while Julia was gone, checking in on Lily, who'd lost herself in an imaginary dollhouse world, where two happy parents lived with a boy, a girl, a baby, and a dog. Twenty minutes passed before Julia knocked on my door. I peered through the peephole, making sure it was her, then let her inside.

"Well?"

Julia hung her head, shaking it. "All of the cages were locked like you said. I couldn't see anything."

"I'm sorry."

"I poked my head into the boiler room, staff room, and janitor's closet. I got reprimanded by Henry, who was in there on his break. He knew I didn't live in the building and started asking why I was down there. I made up an excuse about getting something from your locker for you and got out of there."

"He's big on security. Sorry about that."

"It's okay. It was stupid of me to think I could find the answer so easily." She slumped on the couch, cradling her head in her hands. "I only have a few days left, and I haven't gotten any closer to finding my sister."

I stepped closer. "The police are still working on it."

Julia lowered her eyelids, shifting her weight away from me. "You mentioned that this furniture was here when you moved in?"

"Yes. The apartment came partially furnished."

"Do you mind if I look through some drawers and cupboards? I know it's a long shot, but Annie could have left something behind."

The last thing I wanted was this woman, who I barely knew, rummaging through my things, to see that I'd opened her letters to Annie, but the desperation on Julia's face pulled at my heart-strings. "I checked everything when we moved in. The drawers were empty. So were the cupboards. I'm sorry." Julia's eyes followed mine as I surveyed the contents of my apartment.

Lily's bedroom door swung open, and she marched toward us with a devious smile. She held up Daisy, her raggedy stuffed elephant. "Look at Daisy's new necklace. It was broken, but I fixed it."

A silver chain encircled the animal's floppy neck. Lily had tied two ends of the fine metal chain into a knot to secure it. A tiny turquoise flower hung at the center, sparkling.

Julia leaned closer, gasping. "Where did you get this?" She took Daisy from Lily and held the toy up close.

Lily shirked away, clearly worried she was in trouble. "I found it under the couch yesterday."

Something grim passed over Julia's face. "This necklace belonged to Annie." She gasped, "Look. The chain is broken."

Now I was the one stunned, my heart practically lurching into my throat as I stared at the silver chain I'd never seen before. "Are you sure?"

Julia shook her head. "Yes. I gave it to my sister for her twenty-first birthday. I picked out this turquoise flower myself."

I turned toward Lily, resting my hand on the couch frame. "You found it under this couch?"

She shook her head. "No. I found it yesterday when I dropped your phone. It was under Alex's couch."

I nearly toppled forward. "Alex's couch?"

Lily nodded.

"Oh my God."

"I should take this to the police. It might be a clue." Julia's eyes traveled in the direction of Alex's apartment. "Maybe he ripped this from her neck. What if he—?"

I raised my palm in the air. "Stop. That can't be right. Alex and Annie were friends. He's a good guy." I could feel the panic creeping into my voice, and I took a breath. "You can keep the necklace, of course. But it isn't evidence of anything."

"But the chain is broken."

"It probably got caught on something and fell off. You can't accuse Alex of murdering your sister over this. He's a teacher. An accusation like that will ruin his life."

Julia dropped her arm to her side, lowering her chin.

I turned away, a strange mixture of defensiveness and horror flowing through me. *What had Annie's broken necklace been doing under Alex's couch?* He'd told me Annie had never been inside his apartment. He must have lied about that, at a minimum. *What if he and Annie had been dating?*

"Maybe the baby was his," Julia said, reading my thoughts as an image of the sheer red panties flashed in my head.

You make such horrible decisions with men, Rachel. Mom's gloating voice echoed in my ears.

"I don't think... They weren't even dating." My mouth had gone dry, my voice barely above a whisper. I realized I didn't know anything for sure.

"I need to talk to him right now. I want to know how this got under his couch. And why it's broken." Julia's sharp voice cut through the air. She had removed the necklace from Daisy's neck. Her eyes watered as she stared at the silver chain coiled in her hand.

I shook my head. "He's not home. He has marathon training on Sundays. Let me take a picture of it." Julia held up the necklace, and I snapped a photo. "I'll talk to Alex about it as soon as he gets home. Then I'll call you and tell you everything he said." I stood in front of Julia, blocking her path. "Can you please hold off turning this over to the police until I hear his side of the story?"

Julia jutted out her chin, turning away. "I don't know."

"Just for an hour or two? You'll have the necklace with you. It won't make a difference in the end."

"I guess. But I'm taking it to the police today. You have an hour."

"Okay. Thank you."

Julia edged around me toward the door but stopped. "Do you feel safe living here?"

I lowered my gaze, remembering the noises during the night, the paper square on the floor. I'd burned all my bridges in Addison. There was nowhere else for me to go. Although I didn't want to admit it, lately I'd felt as trapped as that hopeless monkey in the enclosure at the zoo. Still, I lifted my chin and hardened my voice. "As safe as anyone can, living alone in the city, I guess."

Julia locked eyes with me. "Annie never felt safe in this apartment. That's one thing I know for sure."

THIRTY-FIVE

I pulled my knees into my chest, wedged into a corner of the couch. A cartoon movie played on our TV. The animated characters competed in a singing competition, entrancing Lily. But I could only stare at the locks on the door, aware of the way my skin clung to my bones.

Something Alex had said yesterday now scraped at my nerves: *All my relationships end badly... I'm sorry I'm not the person you thought I was.* Had he been lying to me about Annie this entire time? I wondered again if Alex had been romantically involved with her. Both Drake and Bridget had suggested as much. I clutched my phone in my hand, palms clammy. What if Alex had been responsible for Annie's unwanted pregnancy? What if *his* reaction to the news—not Brickman's—had been angry and violent? I raked through my mind, remembering the cursive lettering I'd seen on the inside band of the crimson lingerie: *Maidenly.* I'd assumed the skimpy underwear had belonged to Alex's ex-girlfriend, Sarah, but I could have gotten it wrong. On a whim, I typed *Maidenly* into the search engine and held my breath, not really expecting it to lead anywhere. A moment later, the results appeared. The third one down caused me to sit up.

Maidenly — A boutique lingerie store located in Melbourne, Australia.

The room seemed to spin around me as I sank into the couch cushions. The odds of Alex's ex-girlfriend—a Chicago native—wearing lingerie purchased from a boutique in the same city where Annie had lived seemed exceptionally slim.

I recalled the tragic fate of Alex's high school girlfriend, Peggy Neuman. She was another person who'd been new to her town that Alex had befriended and dated, and who'd ended up dead. Annie Turner had also been a woman in an unfamiliar city looking for a fresh start. And so was I. Was it a pattern like Drake had suggested? Maybe that car accident hadn't been an accident at all. I remembered the article about Alex slamming the student into the locker. Then there was the incident on the first night in my new bedroom when Alex had punched the drywall so hard it left a dent. I'd been so quick to accept his account of things, to see in him only what I'd wanted to believe, and to ignore red flags, the same red flags I'd ignored with Keith. Mom had been right about one thing. I was too trusting.

I studied the necklace photo on my phone, wondering if I should send it to Alex, give him a chance to respond. On the other hand, I wasn't sure I could believe anything he said. Maybe calling Julia and telling her to turn it over immediately to the detective was the best thing to do. It would provide a new lead for them to follow. And if some unforgivable darkness or murderous compulsion hid inside Alex, it was better to find out now. Lily giggled at something in the movie, swiveling around to look at me. I forced a smile but felt sick inside.

Something thumped from Alex's apartment. My spine straightened, pressing into the cushion as I wondered what he was doing now. How had my radar been so off? I'd fallen in love with someone who might be a murderer. Maybe even a serial killer. How terrifying to think that Drake had spotted the warning signs, but I hadn't. I squeezed my eyelids closed. "Stop it. Stop it," recognizing my imagination was spiraling. I didn't even know for sure what the broken necklace meant or if it held any significance at all. And even if Alex and Annie had been having sex, it didn't mean Alex had killed her.

A fist pounded at our door, bangs echoing in rapid succession. Lily looked at me, scared, and I paused the movie.

"Rachel. It's Alex. I have to tell you something. Please, let me in."

I widened my eyes at Lily and held my finger to my lips. I needed more time to digest the latest findings and recalibrate my feelings. It was better if he thought we weren't home.

"I heard your TV a second ago. Please, open up."

Lily stared at me, but I shook my head. I wasn't going to open the door to someone who could be violent. My fingers typed a message into my phone: *If you have something to tell me, then call me.* I sent him the text.

I heard footsteps outside, then a door opening and closing. A second later, my phone buzzed.

"Hello."

"Hi. We need to talk in private. It's urgent."

"I don't think that's a good idea."

"Listen to me. The police were right. Brickman didn't kill Annie."

"Who was it?" I gripped the phone, afraid to hear the answer.

"I can't say any more." He breathed heavily. "I need to tell you in person, somewhere outside of this building."

A warning traveled over my scalp. *What was Alex going to tell me, and why couldn't he tell me over the phone?*

"I'm sending you a text telling you what to do next. Make sure you follow the instructions. Promise me."

"Okay." I tapped my toe, unsure.

A minute later, a message appeared on my screen: *Take the stairs and leave out the emergency exit in the basement. I'll meet you at the north entrance to the zoo at 2 p.m. Bring Lily with you!*

I looked at the time, 1:40 p.m. Alex's panic felt real, but part of me wondered if this was another act in an elaborate play, a trap to ambush us in a vacant alley. I stared at my hands, paralyzed with indecision. I was standing on the precipice of something dangerous. No matter which way I stepped, I felt I might tumble off the side of a tall building and free fall to my death.

Another text from Alex popped through: *Say you'll go!*

I knew Alex. Despite my doubts, my gut told me he was good. He'd been nothing but kind to us. He must have an explanation for the broken necklace and the lingerie from the boutique in Melbourne. He seemed frantic to get us out of here.

Yes. We'll meet you at the zoo.

"Lily, go put your socks and shoes on. We might need to leave in a minute."

"Why? What about the movie?"

"We'll finish it later."

"Why didn't we answer the door for Alex?"

"Because..." I bit my tongue, realizing there was no good way to explain what was happening to a six-year-old. "I don't know. Mommy's not sure if he's a good friend anymore."

Lily stuck out her lower lip. "But he's nice. I like him."

"I know. Just get your shoes. Okay?"

Lily nodded and trudged into her bedroom. I paced to the window, looking down at the people streaming along the sidewalk, the cars gridlocked at the intersection. It was best to get outside where people could see us.

I held Lily's hand as we raced down five flights of stairs and out the emergency exit in the basement. We popped out in the alley, next to three dumpsters filled with rotting garbage. "It smells bad," Lily said as we skittered through the alley toward the sidewalk. I glanced over my shoulder every two seconds, feeling like someone was watching us, and not sure if it was Alex.

"Why are we running, Mommy?"

"Because we're meeting Alex at the zoo and we don't want to be late." My half-truth seemed to satisfy her as she jogged along next to me. Once we'd reached Fullerton Avenue, I slowed our pace so as not to draw attention to ourselves. We reached the entrance to the zoo five minutes before the scheduled meeting time. Lily asked all sorts of questions about what we were doing and whether we would buy popcorn as I gave her vague answers and scanned the people and cars moving in all directions. I wasn't sure if I'd made us sitting ducks by following Alex's directions.

Five minutes passed, then ten. The afternoon sun seared my face as parents and kids paraded in and out of the zoo. No one approached us. By 2:15 p.m., Alex had still not arrived. I texted him a single question mark, but received no response. I felt like a fool and I couldn't help wondering if he'd tricked me, if there'd been a more harrowing reason he'd needed us to leave the apartment, if he'd encouraged us to leave so that he could let himself inside.

I told Lily we were going home because Alex wasn't here. She whined, saying she wanted to see the zoo animals.

"We'll go home and watch the rest of that movie, okay?"

Lily reluctantly agreed and trudged back to Roslyn Place beside me. This time, we entered through the front door. No one else was in the lobby, except for a woman I vaguely recognized from the laundry room exiting as we entered. We let ourselves through the glass barrier and rode the elevator up to our floor.

Once Lily and I were inside our apartment, I locked our door and checked all the rooms and closets for anything suspicious, but found nothing. As Lily flopped onto the couch, I wondered if I should call Alex and see why he hadn't met us. He hadn't responded to my texts. Just then, something crashed from beyond the shared wall to Alex's apartment. The noise jolted me upright.

"Lily, wait here. I'm going to check next door for a second." I clutched my phone in my hand and peered through the peephole, finding an empty hallway. I slipped outside, closing Lily inside the apartment and pinching Alex's spare key in my fingers. My feet inched closer to Alex's door, where a muffled grunt echoed from within 4A. My body went rigid, the tiny hairs on my neck standing on end. *He was in there.* "Alex?" I spoke toward the door. I had no idea what was happening, but I knew it wasn't good.

I unlocked the door to his apartment and slipped inside. Alex lay on the hardwood floor in front of his coffee table, his arms splayed out at unnatural angles and a milky liquid dripping from the corner of his mouth.

"Oh my God!" I closed the door behind me and hurried toward him. The rise and fall of his chest provided a speck of hope. He was unconscious, not dead. An empty bottle of pills lay on the floor next to him, and I grabbed it, finding they were painkillers. That's when I saw the note pinned under his other arm.

I edged closer and lifted the paper, my eyes reluctant to read the words scrawled in Alex's handwriting.

I can't live with myself. I killed Annie Turner. She cheated on me and got pregnant with Brickman's baby. I wanted to tell you in person, but I couldn't do it. I'm sorry, Rachel.

"Oh no. Oh no. Oh no." Alex had left a suicide note, confessing the ugly truth. He must have sent me and Lily to the zoo so we wouldn't interfere with the horrible thing he had planned. The floor seemed to fall away beneath me as I dropped to my knees.

THIRTY-SIX

I clutched Alex's shoulders, shaking him. Even with his handwritten confession, I didn't want to believe it, couldn't believe it. "Alex. Why?" Nausea overtook me along with the realization. I'd been dating a violent killer. I'd let a murderer into my life, left him in charge of my daughter. There'd been so many warning signs and I'd discounted them all. I thought I was going to be sick. My limbs had gone numb, but I managed to lift my phone to dial 911. But before I could press the numbers, a noise thumped from the bathroom.

I gasped, suddenly aware that another person was in the apartment. I whipped around, crouching as I approached the bathroom door. I couldn't imagine why someone else would be lurking nearby as Alex overdosed on pills. I hoped the bumping noise was only the thin walls and creaky floors of the old building, playing tricks on me again. Holding my breath, I pulled the door open. The last person I expected to see faced me. I froze, stunned. "Henry? What are you doing here?"

The doorman lunged toward me, grabbing my arm and placing a cold object to my neck. His face glistened with sweat. Behind his glasses, his dark eyes glittered with something dangerous. He barely resembled the friendly man who greeted me in the lobby several times a day.

Lily's face flashed in my mind. A scream gathered in the back of my throat, but I swallowed it as Henry put more pressure on the metal object, which I now realized was a handgun. I squeaked, finding my voice. "What are you doing, Henry?"

He shifted me to the side, glaring toward Alex. "Your knight in shining armor here killed my daughter."

I struggled for breath, attempting to register his words. "Lisa?"

"Her name was Peggy."

I turned the name over in my head. "The little girl in the picture you showed me? She's dead?"

He grunted. "We'd only been in Morton Grove a year when it happened."

It took me a second to absorb the information, for my mind to connect the car accident in Morton Grove so many years earlier to what was happening now. *Peggy.* Was Henry Peggy Neuman's father?

Henry stepped away from me, still pointing the gun at my face. The barrel was too long for a handgun, and I realized he'd attached a silencer to it. "Stand against the wall. Put your arms up."

I did as he said, my eyes traveling back to the floor, to my dying boyfriend.

Henry blinked several times, face twitching. "Peggy was at the top of her class and could have gone to any college she wanted, would have been successful at anything she did. She wanted to become an architect, but she never had the chance. She was only seventeen when this dirtbag killed her." He gestured toward Alex.

I held a breath of air in my lungs, realizing Henry's story about having a grown daughter, Lisa, was merely a cover, a coping mechanism he'd created. Henry must have confronted Alex, stopping him from meeting us at the zoo by holding a gun to his head. He must have forced Alex to swallow pills and write a suicide note. I'd arrived back too early and messed up his plan.

"Henry, I'm so sorry about your daughter. But you don't have to do this."

"My life fell apart after Peggy died. I'm too far down this road. There's nothing left to lose."

I swallowed, keeping my palms up. "That must have been terrible. But please—"

"As if losing my daughter wasn't bad enough, my wife left me, and then the bank fired me."

"I'm sorry," I said, hoping he'd lower the gun. "I had no idea."

"Of course you didn't."

"But your daughter died years ago. Why are you doing this now?"

The sneer on Henry's face softened. "Tragedy can destroy a person. Things went downhill for years after I lost Peggy. I turned to alcohol. Drugs, too." Henry paused, clearing his throat. "I got caught selling pills and had to spend a year at Cook County."

My muscles tensed. "The prison?"

"Yes. Twelve months in Division Six." Henry's chest rose and fell with his labored breath. "All because this idiot killed my daughter." He followed my gaze toward Alex. "It was okay, though. Turned out my time behind bars was a blessing in disguise. Sometimes volunteers came to talk to me and offer advice or classes. I saw things clearly then and began to deal with the demons. *Take control.* That's what they always told us, to take control over our lives. Face the pain head-on. I did what they said, and I even got clean."

"That's great, Henry. I know that's not easy." I hoped a little encouragement would cool him down, make him realize he was making a mistake. We still had time to save Alex.

But the man continued speaking as if I hadn't said anything. "I thought about Peggy's death all the time, for months and years. I pictured Michael Ballard's face every night before I went to bed and first thing when I woke up. I imagined him living his perfect life, teaching kids, running marathons, taking pretty women out to dinner, while my daughter rotted beneath the earth. I realized revenge was the best way to take control, the only way to get over my loss. An eye for an eye, as they say."

I gasped. Henry had convinced himself that what he'd done to Alex was justified. I struggled to remain still so he wouldn't accidentally pull the trigger.

He waved the gun in the air. "You should have minded your own business! Just like Annie!" The force of his voice caused me to jump.

"I'm sorry." I closed my eyes, struggling to make sense of everything. This must have been the true crime Annie had uncovered, a crime that hadn't happened yet. "So you followed Alex here?"

"I knew he lived here when I applied for the doorman position last year."

Last year? I didn't know why, but I'd assumed Henry had been working in the building for years. "Didn't Alex recognize you?"

"No. Because he'd never had the courtesy to meet me in person. He didn't even bother to come to the funeral after he'd killed my daughter."

"I'm sure he regrets that," I said, my voice weak. "He was only a kid himself."

"Shut up!" Henry lunged toward me, a spray of his saliva landing on my cheek. "Don't make excuses."

I squirmed at his reprimand but gave up, biting my tongue as I listened.

Henry shook his head. "Even if he'd seen my photo, he never would have made the connection. I look so different now."

"Do you know what happened to Annie Turner?" I forced the question out, something inside me understanding that everything happening was somehow connected to the missing woman, the woman who'd likely been murdered in the bathroom next door.

Henry's breath heaved. "I never meant to hurt Annie."

I gasped, closing my eyes. It had been Henry all along, the man who'd been so welcoming and kind, the man who'd offered out pieces of fatherly advice like candy. It had all been an act. But now Henry was in a manic state, a man ready to spill his secrets if he didn't kill me first. I had to keep nudging him, hoping he'd keep talking and reveal whatever horrible things he'd done if only to buy myself a little more time to escape.

"What happened to Annie, Henry? Was there an accident?"

His frown deepened.

"Annie was always nosing around where she didn't belong, looking for material for her book." Henry swapped the gun to his other hand and aimed it at my chest.

I shut my eyes again, the blood spatter on the bathroom wall staining my thoughts. "What did Annie do that was so bad? Please, I have to know."

A grunt came from Henry's throat, his face turning red. "She walked in on me in the staff room in the basement one day. I was holding a newspaper clipping about my daughter's car accident, and I was emotional at the time. Annie kept asking me what was wrong and if that was one of my relatives who died. I shoved everything back in the box and told her not to worry about it, but I could see she wasn't going to let it go."

"The box?" I squeezed my eyes shut, afraid to hear whatever was coming next.

"I kept a box with papers about Alex in my desk in the break room. There were photos of me and my daughter inside, a newspaper clipping about the car accident, a copy of the court order for community service against Michael Alex Ballard. There was a printout of his address, the address of the school where he worked. I already knew his middle name was Alex, so his name change didn't fool me. Everything I'd looked up about him after getting out of prison and before applying for the job as a doorman here at 420 Roslyn Place was in that box."

"Oh." My throat was parched, and I still didn't fully comprehend what he was saying.

Henry was too close to me now, his breath sour against my skin. "That first time Annie caught me down there, I didn't think she had time to read much more than the headline, and the article didn't mention Alex by name. But I saw the curiosity in her eyes, and I kept a close watch on her after that. She and Alex were friends. I monitored her every move."

"Monitored?"

"I may as well tell you now—there's a hidden camera in your apartment. A microphone in here too."

I let out another gasp, stomach turning.

"Did you ever notice how one of the bulbs in the ceiling fan looks a little different than the others?"

A sense of betrayal surged through me, but I forced myself to remain still.

"Annie would have ruined everything if she told him."

I squeezed my eyes shut. "But Annie was leaving. Why did you have to kill her?"

"She gave me no choice. If she had just left that night back in March, everything would have been fine. But she had to mess everything up."

"What did she do?"

Henry drew in a long breath as if gathering his strength. "I was at my post in the lobby before she left for the airport, and I saw her coming up with her luggage. She stopped at the mail-boxes, then went to the elevator. I had a bad feeling, so I rushed down to the staff room and realized she'd been poking around again. My box was gone. I knew she would show Alex what she'd discovered. Or worse, she could have written about what she'd found in her stupid book."

I steadied my feet, remembering how Julia and Drake had both mentioned Annie's book, had suspected her research had something to do with her disappearance.

Henry's jagged breathing continued as he held the gun level in my direction. "I took a few minutes to gather my courage. Then I went to 4B and let myself inside. The building keeps duplicate keys for every apartment in case of emergencies. I wore a tool belt to pretend I was doing a repair for the owner. I found Annie huddled in the bathroom. She said she knew what happened to my daughter and asked if I'd followed Alex to the building. I could feel my plan slipping away." Henry's words were frantic, tumbling over each other as if he felt some strange allegiance to me, desperate to confess what had really tran-spired. "I begged her to return the box. I told her to give it to me and pretend she never saw anything. Then she could leave town and never come back just as she'd been planning to do anyway." Henry made a pained face. "But she leaped up and grabbed my wrench. She tried to whack me on the head with it. Before I knew what I was doing, I wrestled it back and hit her instead."

A whimper sounded from my mouth as I tried not to envi-sion the horrific scene.

"I couldn't believe what I'd done," Henry said, voice crack-ing. "But I figured if I cleaned up the scene and disposed of the body and her belongings, everyone would think Annie had just left for Europe. Her other bags were already packed and ready to go. When you moved in a short time later, I was nervous about you finding evidence of her death, especially after I saw how interested you were in the letter from Australia."

A shiver crawled over my scalp as I remembered the noises I heard in my apartment at night, the footsteps, the open bedroom door that I was sure I'd closed. Henry had been watching me, entering my apartment.

My body wavered. "It was you I heard at night, inside my apartment."

Henry stared at me, stone-faced. "I realized I forgot to check the drawers in the living room table for Annie's belongings. I didn't want you finding anything of hers. But she hadn't left anything in there. A week or two later, the camera went on the fritz, and I had to replace it."

I felt exposed, violated. Tears leaked from my eyes. "Please, let me go. I won't tell anyone what you've done. I'll move out tonight." I had the feeling my time was running out, that I'd never see Lily again.

Henry grunted. "I knew you found the blood spatter and called the police. I thought that the principal from Shorewood would take the fall, and I could continue with my plan to end Alex's life. But even before they cleared Ben Brickman, I thought of a better idea to make Alex pay for my daughter's murder, something to prolong his suffering so he had to spend the rest of his life in prison."

"You tried to frame him." The realization popped out of my mouth. "*You* put Annie's necklace under the couch."

"And her underwear in the bathroom cupboard."

I couldn't speak.

"Also a pair of Annie's earrings in his kitchen drawer, but no one found those." Henry chuckled, but it sounded sad. "I had you fooled. Didn't I?"

My breath was hot and jagged. I couldn't respond.

"And when you found that square of paper on the floor, you

thought it was Alex who'd entered your space because you didn't trust him."

I hardened my voice, angry this man's tricks had caused me to doubt my instincts. "Alex is a good man. I knew he didn't do it."

"It doesn't matter now. You know all my secrets. I was happy to kill this loser, but now I have to silence you too. I'm sorry, Rachel. There's no other way out for me."

I stretched my neck away from him, back arching as I pictured Lily next door. "You can't do this. There are people everywhere."

"Not true. I know exactly how to do this. Two oversized suitcases with wheels. A rental car. A short drive to the swamp in the nature preserve several miles west of here. Plenty of cleaning supplies downstairs in the janitor's closet. A call to your ex-husband to let him know you ran away and abandoned your daughter after your lover killed himself. There are no cameras in the hallways or in the freight elevator. But you know that already." He paused, glancing toward Alex. "Or maybe I should make it look like Alex shot you before taking his own life."

"Don't do this, Henry. Everyone in the building will hear the gunshot."

"There's a silencer. Don't worry." The pressure on my neck increased.

"Please, don't. You're only going to hurt Lily by killing me."

I tried to squirm from his grip, but I couldn't catch my breath as Henry's finger tightened on the trigger.

THIRTY-SEVEN

A line burned across my neck as I flailed my arms and kicked my leg, my body brimming with fear as I awaited death. But a loud bang behind us caused Henry to look over his shoulder. The moment he lost his focus, I lunged forward, my elbow connecting with his face. He doubled over, the gun falling to the floor.

Drake sprinted inside, his long trench coat floating behind him like a cape. He tackled Henry, pinning him to the ground as I secured the gun. "Call 911." Drake's voice was louder than I'd ever heard it. "Now."

Henry struggled. But without his weapon, he was no match for Drake, who kneeled on the older man's chest and held his arms down.

I found my phone on the floor and dialed the numbers, detailing the attack at 420 Roslyn Place, apartment 4A, by Henry Neuman, the doorman. "We need police and an ambulance right away. My boyfriend is unconscious and has been drugged. He needs his stomach pumped." The operator assured me that help was on the way.

"Are you okay?" Drake angled his head at me as I ended the

call. I struggled to nod as I opened Alex's closet to retrieve the roll of duct tape I'd spotted while cleaning days earlier. I tore off a length of it and wrapped it around Henry's wrists. Drake kneeled on the man's chest and held his arms together.

Drake peered toward me. "I saw Lily wandering the hallway. I knew something was wrong. Then I heard Henry's voice through the door."

"Where's Lily?" I asked, sheer panic tearing through my core.

"She's with that girl Bridget, who lives upstairs. At least, that's where I told her to go."

"Thank you." I dropped my head, tears flowing freely. Lily was safe. I'd never been so close to death. For the first time, I was thankful for Drake lurking in the shadows. I crawled over to Alex on hands and knees, sobbing and placing a hand on his cold cheek. "Help is coming," I said, my voice no more than a whisper. I watched him lying there, clinging to life, and I couldn't believe I'd ever doubted him.

A few minutes later, sirens whirred in the distance, getting louder.

THIRTY-EIGHT

Three weeks later

I unlocked my mailbox and reached inside, fingers closing around a single envelope resting on the bottom. I pulled it out, immediately recognizing the sky-blue color of the paper, the neat handwriting, the return address in Melbourne. This time, the envelope was addressed to me. My heart pumped faster as I ripped it open, thankful no one else was around.

Dear Rachel,

Thank you for all you've done to help us with Annie. Her death has left us heartbroken, of course, but we learned the truth in the end, and I am grateful for that. I'm relieved that you and Alex have recovered from the attack and that Henry is behind bars, awaiting trial. Hopefully, justice will be done. We are holding a memorial service for Annie soon. Please know

*that you helped give our family the gift of closure during this
very difficult time.*

Best wishes to you and Lily,

Julia xx

I reread the letter, grateful for the kind message. I'd share it with
Alex later. I tucked it into my bag and proceeded through the
lobby, nodding at the new doorman. His name was Zach, and he
kept to himself, which I didn't mind at all.

The toes of my shoes brushed the cement as I continued
along the sidewalk toward the parking garage where Bridget
kept her car. I'd decided to give riding lessons another shot. The
first time hadn't been a fair trial. A bag hung from my forearm,
containing a used pair of paddock boots, a full water bottle, and
a couple of carrots for Chester.

Car brakes squealed nearby, and I flinched. My head ached
from the get-together at Bridget's last night, which had lasted at
least an hour longer and involved one more glass of wine than I'd
anticipated. Last week, Bridget had finally cornered Alex in the
hallway and made a sheepish confession about the secretive
photos she'd taken of him running, holding up a few of them for
him to see. He'd reacted to Bridget's admission with surprise and
then laughter. He'd even seemed a bit flattered as he gave her
permission to use them in her exhibit and admired a couple of the
candid shots she'd taken. It had been fun to gather in her apartment last night with Lily, Alex, Marie and Sheldon, Drake, and
Bridget's newest flame, a quiet guy named Pete. We cheered as
Bridget pulled the sheet off the easel, unveiling her completed art
exhibit, entitled "Marathon." The piece was a collage of dramatic
black-and-white photos featuring runners striding along the lakefront or in front of skyscrapers, the urban backdrop accentuating

the razor-sharp determination on the athletes' faces. We'd all clinked our glasses and agreed that Bridget had an artistic eye and a talent for photography. Then Alex had returned to the apartment with me, our relationship on a clear path forward.

Now I entered the parking garage, smiling at the other good news we'd heard a few days before. A teacher had come forward, accusing Ben Brickman of sexual harassment. According to an email Alex received, the school was working with the police to uncover the facts. I had an appointment to speak to the person in charge of the investigation on Monday and share my personal account of my experiences with the predatory principal. The upcoming meeting felt like another weight lifted off my shoulders.

Lily's last day of school had been a week ago. To my surprise, Liz Meyer-Barnes had sought me out near the fountain as I waited for Lily to exit the school. Liz lowered her gaze and admitted she owed me an apology. After having spent more time with Keith, she'd realized how manipulative he was. Not at all like the guy she'd remembered from high school. I kept my face still as I told her I appreciated the apology, but inside I was cheering. Although Keith still had his once-a-month supervised visits with Lily, another door had just slammed in his face. He wasn't going to ruin our lives.

I lifted the key fob, unlocking the back of Bridget's SUV with a beep. I'd throw my supplies back here and retrieve them when I arrived at the riding stable. Bridget had been correct about the benefits of doing something for myself. I'd been looking forward to this outing all week, happy to know Lily was enjoying a morning playdate at Marnie's house. My bag tipped to the side as I set it down, a panel beneath it sitting slightly ajar. I placed my fingers through the cutout to adjust the floor of the trunk, but my fingertip brushed against something in the storage area beneath. My skin stung with a paper cut, and I yanked my hand away. A sliver of blood formed on my finger.

Sucking my fingertip, I pulled the panel back with my other hand, where an accordion file lay in the shadows of the hidden compartment. A small label on the front read WINDY CITY JUSTICE PROJECT. These were the files for Bridget's volunteer work.

I pictured all the weeks Leo had been hanging around Bridget's apartment and wondered what he'd really done to wind up in prison and to get arrested a second time. For Lily's sake—and after what we'd all just been through—I wanted to make sure Leo wasn't a dangerous person. Curiosity got the better of me, and I flipped through the tabs. But before I found Leo's name, something else caught my eye.

COOK COUNTY, DIV. VI

It was the heading on one of the files toward the front. *Division Six.* Those were the words Henry had said to me as he'd held a gun to my head three weeks ago. He'd served a year in Cook County, Division Six. He said a volunteer had helped him to get his life on track, to see things clearly, and take action.

A darkness descended on me, like hands holding my head beneath the water. Although Henry's arrest had been a relief, I'd also been wondering how the sixty-two-year-old man had pulled off Annie's murder and disappearance by himself, how he'd been able to rent a car, dispose of Annie's body, and clean out the apartment in a matter of hours with no one seeing. Things Bridget had said flew through my mind: *Revenge is the best medicine... Sometimes justice needs a little push in the right direction.* Bridget had an explosive sense of justice; strong ideas about what should happen to the people who'd wronged her. Suddenly, her story about being fired from her previous law firm, her former boss overdosing before she could take him to court, took on a new and dire meaning. A suicide by overdose was the same way Henry had attempted to frame Alex's death. Where had he gotten that idea?

My legs wavered beneath me, my heavy gut expecting the

worst. I opened the file, spotting a flurry of Bridget's notes written in blue ink and flowery handwriting. She'd helped someone in Division Six. I flipped past the notes, finding two glossy black-and-white photos; they were close-ups of Alex's face as he ran. Behind that, a printout of a job listing: *Seeking Part-time Doorman at 420 Roslyn Place.* My hand flew to my mouth, air clogging my throat. The last name in the world I wanted to see stared back at me from the top tab of the file: *Case #28 — Henry Neuman.*

I blinked at the name, dark spots floating before my eyes. Bridget, my friendly neighbor, generous friend, and trusted babysitter, had been helping Henry execute his plan for revenge all along. Whether she was actively involved or merely coaching him, I didn't know. But either way, she'd crossed the line. I clutched the file to my side and ducked into the driver's seat, finding my breath. Again, I cycled through my interactions with Bridget over the last three months. Bridget's photos of Alex had clearly been more than an innocent infatuation turned art project; she'd been stalking him. I recalled her sly smiles toward Henry as we entered the building, the conversation I'd overheard between her and Leo in the basement, her tale of the suicide of the partner at her former law firm, and the way she'd run from the man at the diner. I'd sensed something wasn't quite right with her, but I'd never been able to put my finger on it. I hadn't listened to my gut. Alex had sensed it too. He'd almost been killed because of Henry—and Bridget.

It pained me that one of Mom's theories of human behavior had been correct, that sometimes people were only friendly because they wanted something in return. I'd been too trusting. Bridget's betrayal sliced through my core, and I could feel the reality of city life hardening around me, sharpening my edges.

I lifted my head, a breath expanding in my chest, along with a powerful resolve. I refused to play the victim anymore. I would do whatever was necessary to protect my daughter and the new life we were building. It turned out that Bridget shouldn't have trusted me either.

In the front seat of her SUV, I laid out each page of Bridget's file on Henry Neuman, snapping photos one by one, and texting the images to Detective Monroe. Then I pressed his number. When he answered on the first ring, I told him everything.

A LETTER FROM LAURA

Dear reader,

I want to say a huge thank you for choosing to read *The Girl Before Me*. If you enjoyed it and want to keep up to date with all my latest releases, just sign up at the following link. Your email address will never be shared and you can unsubscribe at any time.

www.bookouture.com/laura-wolfe

I enjoyed the many months I spent writing and revising *The Girl Before Me*, in part because of the downtown Chicago setting. For ten years—from my early twenties to early thirties—I lived in and around Chicago's Lincoln Park neighborhood. Revisiting this location brought back so many emotions and milestones, allowing me to take daily trips down memory lane. When writing about Rachel's long-awaited move-in day on Roslyn Place, I relived my own experiences of what it had felt like to move to the big city as a single young woman living alone. The energy of the city was exciting, life was full of possibilities, and I was sometimes too quick to trust people. It was the first time I'd lived without roommates, and I'd initially enjoyed the freedom of living by myself. Of course, nothing nearly as traumatic as the events in this book happened to me while living in my apartment. But I do recall how difficult it was to fall asleep those first nights when my ears weren't used to the frequent sirens and boisterous late-night conversations from people outside. Even then, the constant noises made me think that it would be difficult to know if someone else was inside my apartment. Now, years later, that unsettling idea made an ideal premise for a psychological thriller. To make it creepier, what if the woman who'd lived in the apartment before me had mysteriously disappeared? And, what if I had reason to believe that I—or my young daughter—would be the next victim? That is how the seed for *The Girl Before Me* was planted.

I hope you loved *The Girl Before Me,* and if you did, I would be very grateful if you could write a review. Reviews make such a difference in helping new readers discover one of my books for the first time.

I love hearing from my readers – you can get in touch on my Instagram, Facebook page, Goodreads, or my website. To receive my monthly book recommendations in the mystery/suspense/thriller genre, please follow me on Bookbub.

Thanks,

Laura Wolfe

www.LauraWolfeBooks.com

 facebook.com/LauraWolfeBooks

instagram.com/lwolfe.writes

 bookbub.com/profile/laura-wolfe

ACKNOWLEDGMENTS

So many people have supported and assisted me in various ways along the journey of writing and publishing this book. First, I'd like to thank the entire team at Bookouture. I was lucky enough to have two sets of editorial eyes on my story this time around. Many thanks to editors Isobel Akenhead and Catherine Cobain for their comments and suggestions, particularly during the structural editing phase. Their insights into my story's structure, pacing, and characters made the final version so much better. Additional gratitude goes to copyeditor, Lucy Cowie, and proofreader, Shirley Khan, for their keen eyes, and to Bookouture's top-notch publicity team led by Noelle Holten and Kim Nash. Thank you to those who continuously support my writing and provide inspiration and encouragement, especially Lisa Richey and Karina Board, along with many others. A special thanks to Meredith Lovelace for talking me through the nuances of Chicago's western suburbs. Thank you to the many book bloggers and bookstagrammers who have helped spread the word about my books. I'm so thankful for the authors in the Bookouture Authors' Lounge Facebook group, who are always there to prop me up, offer laughs, and answer questions. It's a joy to be a part of such a supportive group of talented writers from around the world. Thank you to my parents, Robert and Susan Peterson, for supporting my books. I dedicated this book to them because they instilled a love of reading in me from an early age, which is part of the reason I was able to become a published author. Thank you to my brother, sister, mother-in-law, and other extended family for supporting my books. I appreciate everyone who has taken the time to tell me that they enjoyed reading my stories or has left a positive review. Thank you to my "writing partner," Milo, who inspires all the canine characters in my books (in this case, Bingo), even as he sleeps. Most of all, I'd like to thank my wonderful children, Brian and Kate, for always cheering for me, and my husband, JP, for reading my crappy first drafts and supporting my writing. As always, I wouldn't have made it to the end without his encouragement.